T0254912

Cloud Reliability Engineering

Cloud Reliability Engineering

Technologies and Tools

Edited by Rathnakar Achary and Pethuru Raj

CRC Press
Taylor & Francis Group
Boca Raton London New York

CRC Press is an imprint of the
Taylor & Francis Group, an **informa** business

First edition published 2021
by CRC Press
6000 Broken Sound Parkway NW, Suite 300, Boca Raton, FL 33487-2742
and by CRC Press
2 Park Square, Milton Park, Abingdon, Oxon, OX14 4RN

© 2021 Taylor & Francis Group, LLC
CRC Press is an imprint of Taylor & Francis Group, an Informa business

No claim to original U.S. Government works

The right of Rathnakar Achary and Pethuru Raj to be identified as the authors of the editorial material, and of the authors for their individual chapters, has been asserted in accordance with sections 77 and 78 of the Copyright, Designs and Patents Act 1988.

Reasonable efforts have been made to publish reliable data and information, but the author and publisher cannot assume responsibility for the validity of all materials or the consequences of their use. The authors and publishers have attempted to trace the copyright holders of all material reproduced in this publication and apologize to copyright holders if permission to publish in this form has not been obtained. If any copyright material has not been acknowledged please write and let us know so we may rectify in any future reprint.

Except as permitted under U.S. Copyright Law, no part of this book may be reprinted, reproduced, transmitted, or utilized in any form by any electronic, mechanical, or other means, now known or hereafter invented, including photocopying, microfilming, and recording, or in any information storage or retrieval system, without written permission from the publishers.

For permission to photocopy or use material electronically from this work, access www.copyright.com or contact the Copyright Clearance Center, Inc. (CCC), 222 Rosewood Drive, Danvers, MA 01923, 978-750-8400. For works that are not available on CCC please contact mpkbookspermissions@tandf.co.uk

Trademark notice: Product or corporate names may be trademarks or registered trademarks and are used only for identification and explanation without intent to infringe.

Visit the Taylor & Francis Web site at
http://www.taylorandfrancis.com

and the CRC Press Web site at
http://www.crcpress.com

ISBN: 978-0-367-71373-7 (hbk)
ISBN: 978-0-367-46775-3 (pbk)
ISBN: 978-1-003-03097-3 (ebk)

Typeset in Adobe Garamond Pro
by KnowledgeWorks Global Ltd.

Contents

Preface

Cloud reliability engineering is one of the buzzwords in cloud services. Various cloud service providers guarantee computation, storage and applications and provide inclusion in several continuous offering service-level agreement (SLA)-backed performances and uptime guarantees for their services.

This book represents these issues by presenting the readers with the cloud reliability paradigm. The chapter authors provide case studies of various types of existing cloud services and their challenges, demonstrating the capabilities of the reliability mechanism adopted by cloud service providers. This lets the readers realize the techniques needed to harness cloud reliability and availability requirements in their own particular endeavors. At last many open research challenges that have emerged from the quick update of cloud reliability, load balancing and cloud security are explained.

Organization of the Book

This book contains chapters authored by numerous leading specialists in the field of cloud computing and reliability engineering. It is introduced in an organized and integrated manner beginning with the basics followed by the technologies that deploy them. The content of the book is structured into three sections: cloud reliability and availability, load balancing and cloud security.

The cost of providing reliability is increasing exponentially. On a functional level, it is straightforward that 100% availability is unlikely when you factor in all the pieces that a service provider emphasizes on a reliability of 99.999%, even then the downtime will be several hours per year. That is, the service error budget and the product team can utilize the availability for experimentation and development.

Cloud Reliability Engineering: Technologies and Tools contains several real-life examples and best practices that bring the subject to life. The editors offer several chapters about the hard assignments of cloud reliability management. Reliability and high availability, load balancing and cloud security are the primary line of defense. The chapters describe reliability theory and the best practices adopted by the cloud service that provide companies with high availability.

The chapters cover a comprehensive study of cloud reliability and availability issues and analyze the solutions provided by the researchers and the proposed methods to address these issues. Various reliability class distributions and their effects on cloud reliability are briefly discussed. An important aspect of the reliability block diagram is used to categorize the poor reliability of a cloud infrastructure and where enhancements can be made to lower the failure rate of the system. This technique can be used in the design and functional stages to determine poor reliability of a system and provide target improvements.

Reliability of quantum information is also achieved by two level error correcting codes; in the first level, error-detection or syndrome diagnosis is performed that measures the error syndrome on the quantum state, if it occurred.

The contributions related to load balancing in pursuance of reliability are made by migrating processes or by using virtual machines in the system. The approach employed to identify the lightly loaded destination node to which the processes/virtual machines migrate can be optimized by employing a genetic algorithm (GA).

To analyze the security risk and reliability, a novel technique for minimizing the number of keys and security systems is presented. The authors also contributed a comprehensive overview of the various types of testing methods and how these conventional methodologies can be moved to the cloud along with their pros and cons. Feasibility of cloud testing in terms of quality parameters like reliability, installability, security, and so forth are discussed with a suitable use case.

Various authors composed this book and the chapters are currently filled with research identified with cloud reliability engineering. These chapters are similar to their research activities or case studies, and some of the chapters depend on the analysis of recently published articles. Despite this format, which makes the book somewhat less homogeneous and more permissive than ideal, the editors – *Rathnakar Achary* and *Pethuru Raj* – excellently meshed this wealth of knowledge together. You can read the complete book from start to finish and it will feel cohesive. But reading the principle chapters and then concentrating on the particular practices you are most interested in is the best way to appreciate this book.

Rathnakar Achary
Alliance University, India

Pethuru Raj
Reliance Jio Platforms Ltd., India
September 2020

Acknowledgments

This book is a result of over a hundred enthusiastic and generous contributors, including authors and reviewers. Every chapter has a byline for the individual authors. We would like to take a moment to thank everybody not recorded there.

We want to thank all the reviewers for their valuable feedback. Although the authors are explicitly acknowledged in each chapter, we would like to recognize those that contributed to each chapter by providing thoughtful contribution, discussions and review. In chapter order they are:

- Chapter 1, Reliability Theory: To Analyze Cloud Datacenter Reliability: Rathnakar Achary.
- Chapter 2, Reliability and High Availability Analysis for Cloud Datacenter: Rathnakar Achary.
- Chapter 3, Engineering Resilient Microservices toward System Reliability: The Technologies and Tools: Pethuru Raj and G. Sobers Smiles David.
- Chapter 4, Service Resiliency in Cloud and Network Function Virtualization: Rathnakar Achary.
- Chapter 5, Achieving Reliability of Quantum State in Cloud Infrastructure: Chetan Shelke, I. Diana Jeba Jingle, and P. Mano Paul.
- Chapter 6, Reliability and Authenticity of Cloud-based Technologies in Mobile Grid Environment Using Parameter-based Malicious Node Detection Method: T. Sasikala, S. Vimala, S. Vigneshwari, and G. Nagarajan.
- Chapter 7, Datacenter Reliability Pursuance with Optimized Load Balancers: K. S. Resma and G. S. Sharvani.
- Chapter 8, Dynamic Load Balancing by Employing Genetic Algorithm: S. Sandhya and N. K. Cauvery.
- Chapter 9, Predicting Reliability and Risk: S. Sharanya, S. Karthikeyan, and E. Sasikala.
- Chapter 10, Experimental Analysis and Performance Enhancement of Security in Cloud Databases: T. Sasikala and R. Ramya.
- Chapter 11, Cloud Execution Model to Attain Quality for Non-functional Testing: D. Sudaroli Vijayakumar and D. Monica Sneha.
- Chapter 12, Fault Tolerance Algorithms for Distributed Computing: P. Beaulah Soundarabai and Pethuru Raj.

About the Editors

Rathnakar Achary, PhD, is an associate professor in the Department of Information Technology, Alliance College of Engineering and Design, Alliance University, Bangalore, India. He holds a doctoral degree in Computer Science and Engineering from SASTRA University, Thanjavur, Tamil Nadu, India. He is an alumnus of Mysore University. Dr. Achary is certified in mobile computing from the Indian Institute of Science Bangalore, National Accreditation Board for Testing & Calibration Laboratories (NABL; ISO-IEC: 17025) certified from the Federation of Indian Chambers of Commerce & Industry (FICCI) and is a certified Microsoft professional. The focus of his research is on mobile computing and wireless networks, cryptography and network security, the Internet of Things, cloud computing, edge/fog computing and cloud security. Dr. Achary has published more than 15 research papers in peer-reviewed journals for publishers such as Springer, Institute of Electrical and Electronics and Engineers (IEEE) and Association for Computing Machinery (ACM). He has authored a book titled *Cryptography and Network Security*. He is a member of the Institute of Engineering and Technology (IET), Indian Society for Technical Education (ISTE) and Computer Society of India (CSI).

Pethuru Raj, PhD, works as the chief architect and vice president at the Site Reliability Engineering (SRE) division of Reliance Jio Platforms Ltd., Bangalore, India. His previous stints were at the IBM Global Cloud Centre of Excellence (CoE), Wipro consulting services (WCS) and Robert Bosch Corporate Research (CR). In total, he has more than 19 years of information technology (IT) industry experience and 8 years of research experience.

Dr. Raj finished the Council of Scientific & Industrial Research (CSIR)-sponsored PhD degree at Anna University, Chennai, India, and continued with the University Grants Commission (UGC)-sponsored postdoctoral research in the Department of Computer Science and Automation, Indian Institute of Science (IISc), Bangalore, India. Thereafter, Dr. Raj was granted a number of international research fellowships (Japan Society for the Promotion of Science [JSPS] and Japan Science and Technology Agency [JST]) to work as a research scientist for three and a half years in two leading Japanese universities. He has published more than 30 research papers in peer-reviewed journals for publishers such as the Institute of Electrical and Electronics and Engineers (IEEE), Association for Computing Machinery (ACM), Springer-Verlag, Interscience and so forth. He has authored and edited 20 books and contributed to 35 book chapters for various technology books edited by highly acclaimed and accomplished professors and professionals. His work focuses on some of the emerging technologies such as the Internet of Things (IoT), artificial intelligence (AI), Big and Fast Data Analytics, blockchains, digital twins, cloud-native computing, edge/fog clouds, reliability engineering, microservices architecture (MSA), event-driven architecture (EDA) and so forth. His personal website is https://sweetypeterdarren.wixsite.com/pethuru-raj-books.

Contributors

Rathnakar Achary
Alliance College of Engineering
and Design
Alliance University
Bengaluru, Karnataka, India

N. K. Cauvery
Information Science and Engineering
R.V. College of Engineering
Bengaluru, Karnataka, India

G. Sobers Smiles David
PG Department of Computer Science
Bishop Heber College (Autonomous)
Tiruchirappalli, Tamil Nadu, India

I. Diana Jeba Jingle
Department of Computer Science
School of Engineering
CHRIST (Deemed to be University)
Bengaluru, Karnataka, India

S. Karthikeyan
BSACIST
Chennai, Tamil Nadu, India

G. Nagarajan
Sathyabama Institute of Science and
Technology
Chennai, Tamil Nadu, India

P. Mano Paul
Department of Information
Technology
Alliance University
Bengaluru, Karnataka, India

Pethuru Raj
Site Reliability Engineering (SRE)
Division
Reliance Jio Platforms Ltd. (JPL)
Bengaluru, Karnataka, India

R. Ramya
SRM Institute of Science and
Technology
Kattankulathur, Tamil Nadu, India

K. S. Resma
Department of Computer Science and
Engineering
PES University
and
R.V. College of Engineering
Bengaluru, Karnataka, India

S. Sandhya
Department of Computer Science and
Engineering
R.V. College of Engineering
Bengaluru, Karnataka, India

E. Sasikala
SRM Institute of Science and
    Technology
Kattankulathur, Tamil Nadu, India

T. Sasikala
School of Computing
Sathyabama Institute of Science and
    Technology
Chennai, Tamil Nadu, India

S. Sharanya
SRM Institute of Science and
    Technology
Kattankulathur, Tamil Nadu, India

G. S. Sharvani
Department of Computer Science and
    Engineering
R.V. College of Engineering
Bengaluru, Karnataka, India

Chetan Shelke
Department of Information
    Technology
Alliance University
Bengaluru, Karnataka, India

D. Monica Sneha
Department of Computer Science
PES University
Bengaluru, Karnataka, India

P. Beaulah Soundarabai
Department of Computer Science
CHRIST (Deemed to be University)
Bengaluru, Karnataka, India

S. Vigneshwari
Sathyabama Institute of Science and
    Technology
Chennai, Tamil Nadu, India

D. Sudaroli Vijayakumar
Department of Computer Science
PES University
Bengaluru, Karnataka, India

S. Vimala
Anna University
Chennai, Tamil Nadu, India

Chapter 1

Reliability Theory: To Analyze Cloud Datacenter Reliability

Rathnakar Achary

Alliance University

Contents

1.1 Introduction

In this chapter we discuss reliability and consider four goals for the cloud service provider. These are very important requirements used to keep clients happier with their dependencies on remote service and databases, network connection and hardware services. In such an environment, it is easy to search what is important to keep current customers and track new ones. This is possible only by creating a reliable cloud service and making it available to clients. What is it that makes the service provider a reliable service? According to the Institute of Electrical and Electronics Engineers (IEEE), software reliability is defined as "the probability that software will work as expected for a specified period of time in the environment in which it was designed to run". From the customer's perspective this means the service "just works". The four goals to keep the cloud service on track are as follows:

1. ***Maximize service availability:*** Regardless of the time/day or location, as long as the customer is connected to the Internet, it should work the way it is supposed to.
2. ***Minimize impact of failure:*** Sometimes things go wrong no matter how effectively we maintain the cloud infrastructure. This may be possible even during service expansion. Consider the following recommendations to maintain service availability and to keep customers happy:
   – Minimize impact on average for any given customer. If a remote service goes down the customer should still be able to use the service.
   – Minimize the number of customers impacted. Design the service to isolate the failed systems so that the other services continue to work as expected.
   – Minimize the amount of time customers can use the service by connected redundant units to provide the service without disruption with a minimum downtime.
3. ***Maximize performance and capacity:*** When there is an unexpected spike and traffic occurs, reduce its impact on performance, which is running for the intended customers. Prioritize customers that are using the services.
4. ***Maximize business continuity:*** Respond to average outages when they occur and make sure you can handle them when there is a large-scale outage. Automatically and quickly recover and protect the integrity of the customer's data as needed. If there is an automated recovery, create a disaster recovery plan and store the services.

As the adoption of cloud computing continues to rise, and clients request 24/7 access to their service and applications, reliability becomes a challenge for cloud service providers [1, 2]. It is a complex process to make design and delivery of cloud service more reliable. The contributions of researchers and the way they think about reliability concepts and reliability theory and analysis, and how they might be useful for organizations and analysts in designing a reliable cloud service are described in this chapter.

Cloud service providers and the service consumers have varying degrees of responsibility depending on the cloud service model (Figure 1.1). In some services (such as Infrastructure as a service [IaaS]) both the service providers and customers have shared responsibility. The service providers are responsible for reliability of the infrastructure [central processing unit (CPU), memory, storage and network] components, whereas the customers are responsible for ensuring that the solutions they build on the provided cloud infrastructure run in a reliable manner. Where customers are provided software as a service (SaaS), the cloud service providers hold primary responsibility for ensuring reliability of the service (for example, using SaaS to run an email inbox). Platform as a service (PaaS) models occupy the middle of this responsibility spectrum with providers being responsible for the infrastructure and public control layers.

Better understanding of failure, improved manufacturing techniques, careful planning and designing of new systems and proper selection of components are some of the approaches that can be tried to reduce the level of unreliability of the systems.

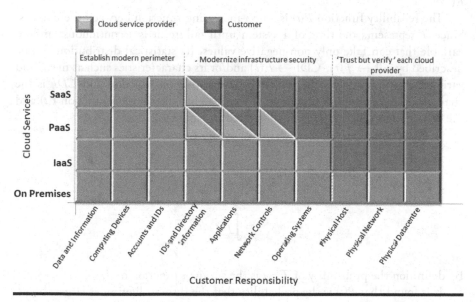

Figure 1.1   Cloud service providers and cloud customers responsibilities.

Let R be the unreliability of an unrepairable system. To assess the reliability, the system status needs to be analyzed to find the chances of system failure under a given condition during the time interval $[0, t]$.

Reliability is defined as the probability that a component or a system will perform a required function for a given period of time when used under stated operating conditions. It is the probability of non-failure of a system over a particular time. Failure should be defined relative to the function being performed by the system. The reliability definition highlights four key components: probability, intended function, time and operating condition.

For a given system if T is the time until failure occurrence (a random variable), then the probability that it will not fail in a given environment before the time t is the reliability function $R(t)$. It is represented as $R(t) = P\{T > t\}$.

It also indicates the probability of the system failure for the first time or, in other words, the system survival for a period of t.

1.2 Reliability Engineering Theory

Let T be the time until failure of the unit occurs, which is a random variable. The probability that it will not fail in a given environment before t is

$$R(t) = P\{T > t\}\dots\dots\dots \tag{1.1}$$

where reliability is always a function of time, referring to Eq. (1.1) if $R(0) = 1$ and $R(\infty) = 0$.

The reliability function $R(t)$ is a non-increasing function between these limits. Since T represents the time of a system until failure, it is a continuous random variable that can take only non-negative values. Its statistical distribution can be described by pdf $\rightarrow f(t)$, CDF $\rightarrow F(t)$ and/or its characteristics such as mean and variance [3], where *pdf* is the probabilistic distribution function and *CDF* is the characteristic distribution function. The probability distribution function $f(t)$ and the distribution function $F(t)$ are illustrated in Figure 1.2.

It is observed that

$$R(t) = P\{T > t\}$$
$$= 1 - F(t)$$
$$= \int_{t}^{\infty} f(t)dt$$

By definition the probability of $T > t$ is the survivor function of T.

It is found that $R(t)$ is the probability that the systems lifetime is larger than t, and the probability that the system will survive beyond time t or probability that

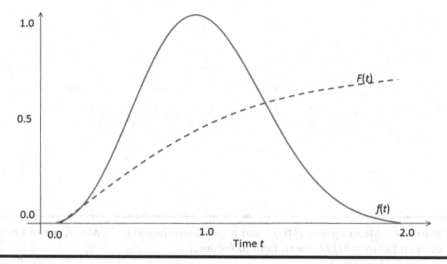

Figure 1.2   Probability distribution function $f(t)$ and distribution function $F(t)$.

the device will fail before time t (Figure 1.3). $R(t)$ is also called the survivor function and *CDF* of T is called the unreliability function. The expected value of the system or mean of the lifetime T is also called the mean time to failure (*MTTF*). It is primarily utilized for the characterization of non-repairable or non-replaceable systems in a datacenter. *MTTF* is a basic measure of reliability. It will be preferably measured over a long period of time and with a large number of units. The mean downtime (*MDT*) and mean uptime (*MUT*) are shown in (Figure 1.4).

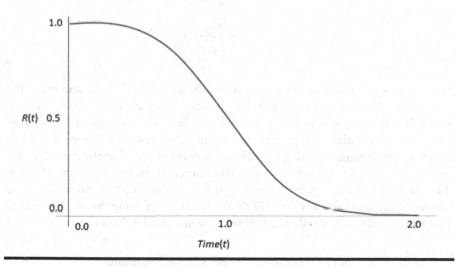

Figure 1.3   Reliability function $R(t)$.

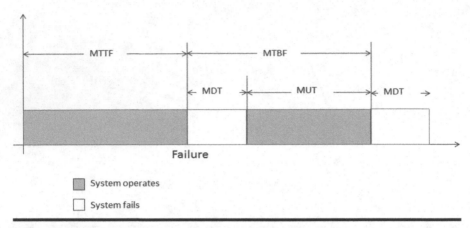

Figure 1.4   Mean uptime (*MUT*) and mean downtime (*MDT*). *MTBF*, mean time between failures; *MTTF*, mean time to failure.

MDT is the duration, during which a unit of datacenter is in the down state and cannot perform any task.

MUT is the continuous up or operation time of the datacenter without any downtime.

In mathematical representation [4, 5], the expected life of the system is given as

$$MTTF = E(T)$$

$$= \int_0^\infty t f(t)dt$$

$$= \int_0^\infty R(t)dt$$

Parts of the system may go through several failures before they are scrapped. The systems are said to be repairable. For these devices the mean time to the first failure is *MTTF*. Once the system is repaired and put into operation again, the average time to the next failure is represented as mean time between failures (*MTBF*). It represents the average operating time from the point of time that the operation was restored to the point of time that was needed to repair the failed system. *MTBF* is also considered as the expected operating time duration between two consecutive failures of the repairable system. *MTBF* is calculated by using the total operating lifetime divided by the number of failures. It is measured in hours or years.

$$MTBF\,(\text{hours}) = \frac{1}{\lambda} \text{ where } \lambda \text{ is the failure rate}$$

$$MTBF(\text{years}) = \frac{MTBF(\text{hours})}{24.365} = \frac{1}{0.8760\lambda}$$

When there is a perfect repair, it reduces a unit failure, and it is functional as a new system, such a repair is called a *perfect repair*. If there is a perfect repair then $MTBF = MTTF$.

Repairs of the system also are known as *corrective maintenance*. In the case of a perfect repair, the $MTBF$ is equal to $MTTF$. This is an indication that the aging of most systems decreases $MTBF$, and as a result more failures are experienced by the system. Due to this the system experiences more failures. The average amount of time required to repair a failed system is called mean time to repair ($MTTR$). Another important requirement of reliability is availability. For a repairable system availability is often used as a measure of its performance.

The $MTTR$ is also known as *mean time to recovery*, during which a unit of the datacenter is down due to failure and is under repair. It represents the average time required to repair a failed component of a system. If the time taken for recovery is longer, it is said that the system will have a low availability. To achieve high availability, $MTBF$ is larger compared with $MTTR$ ($MTBF \gg MTTR$).

The lead time for the datacenter modules not readily available or other administrative and logistic downtime are not included for the calculation of $MTTR$. In general, availability is defined as the probability that the system is available whenever required.

$$\text{Availability} = P\{\text{the system is available whenever needed}\}$$

For a system with a perfect repair on any failure its availability is

$$\text{Availability}(A) = \frac{MTBF}{MTBF + MTTR}$$

$$A = \frac{\text{Mean uptime}}{\text{Mean uptime} + \text{Mean downtime}}$$

where the uptime representing the operational time of the system and the downtime indicate the system is non-functional. If MUT is approximated with $MTBF$ and MDT with $MTTR$, the system availability is represented as

$$\text{Availability}(A) = \frac{MUT}{MUT + MDT}$$

1.2.1 Reliability Block Diagram (RBD)

The reliability block diagram (RBD) is a graphical representation used to depict how the components of a system are reliably connected. Sometimes within a system independence can be assumed across the components, which means that the failure of a component does not influence the functioning of other components. The RBD shall not be equivalent to the physical or logical block diagram of a cloud system.

1.2.2 Unavailability (U)

Unavailability (*U*) is the complement of availability, and it is defined as the probability that a unit of the cloud system cannot perform its function even though the required resources and the operational conditions are satisfied. Unavailability is represented by *U*.

$$\text{Unavailability} = 1 - \text{Availability}$$

$$U = 1 - A$$

$$U = 1 - \frac{MUT}{MUT + MDT} = \frac{MDT}{MUT + MDT}$$

$$U \cong 1 - \frac{MTBF}{MTBF + MTTR} = \frac{MTTR}{MTBF + MTTR}$$

Another important measure, which is often used in reliability, is conditional reliability. Conditional reliability is defined as the probability of a system to function satisfactorily for an additional duration of τ given that it has worked properly for a duration of time t.

It is represented as

$$R(\tau \mid t) = P\{T > t + \tau \mid T > t\}$$
$$= \frac{R(t + \tau)}{R(t)}$$

The conditional reliability represents that the system was functional for a t unit of time. It means that the probability of availability of a system with a lifetime T survivor is more than the τ unit of time. The total operating time of the system without failure is $T > t + \tau$ and total unit of survival of the system without failure is $t + \tau$.

1.3 Failure Rate Function

The failure rate function is also called *hazard function* $h(t)$ and is defined as the probability that a device will fail in the next time unit given that it has been working properly up to time t. It is also a conditional probability represented as

$$h(t) = {\lim_{\Delta t}}^{it} P\{t < T \le t + \Delta t | T > t\}$$

.... (1.2)

$$= \frac{f(t)}{R(t)}$$

Eq. (1.2) represents that the system has survived for t unit of time, and the probability that it will fail in the next time unit Δt. Where Δt is very small for a given probability $T > t$, the lifetime of the system lies between t and $(t + \Delta t)$.

When $\Delta t \to 0$

$$h(t) = \frac{f(t)}{R(t)}$$

where $f(t)$ is failure rate function and $R(t)$ is survivor function.

Function $h(t)$ represents the system's susceptibility to failure depending on the failure rate function $f(t)$ or the hazard rate function $h(t)$.

1.3.1 Cumulative Hazard Rate

The cumulative hazard rate function or cumulative failure rate function is represented as $H(t)$.

$$H(t) = \int_0^t h(x)dx$$

The random variable T representing the lifetime of a system is a continuous random, variable that takes only non-negative values. The average failure rate of a system over an interval of time (t_1, t_2) is given as

$$\overline{h}(t_1, t_2) = \frac{1}{t_2 - t_1} \int_{t_1}^{t_2} h(t)dt$$

where t_2 to t_1 is the length of the interval, which is used to evaluate the average failure rate of the system. The cumulative hazard rate is

$$\overline{h}(t_1, t_2) = \frac{H(t_2) - H(t_1)}{t_2 - t_1}$$

The significance of the failure rate function represents the health condition of a working system. A high failure rate indicates a depraved health condition, because the probability for the system to fail in the next instant of time is high.

Among the different functions, such as $f(t)$, $F(t)R(t)$, $H(t)$ and $h(t)$, one of them is adequate to completely specify the lifetime distribution of the system. Having data related to any one of these functions is sufficient to represent the lifetime of a system. The relationship between these different functions is

$$h(t) = \frac{-d}{dt} \log R(t) \text{ and } R(t) = e^{-H(t)}$$

1.4 Bathtub Curve

When studying about reliability engineering theories, a bathtub curve is widely used. According to this theory, when a cloud system is implemented, there is a substantial rate of early failures, which commonly results from an error with installation and management [5]. As the system life approaches an end, the rate of failure increases due to the final wave of ware-out failure. The failure rate function of a cloud system is represented by means of a bathtub curve (Figure 1.5).

1. The first part of the bathtub curve is known as the *early failure* or infant mortality period. It is characterized by a decreasing failure rate (DFR). During this period the weak or marginally functioning components of the datacenters may fail. The best practice is to screen out obviously defective components.

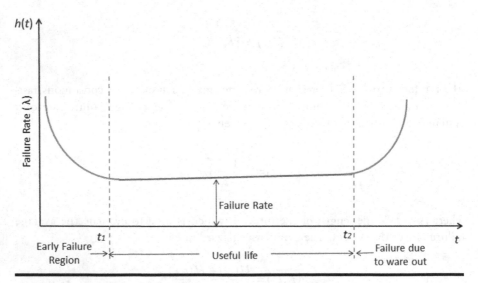

Figure 1.5   Bathtub curve.

In the curve between $(0, t_1)$, there is a DFR. Generally, the failures are due to the defects in the cloud infrastructure (CPU, memory, storage and network connectivity), which are also due the manufacturing defects.

2. The longer and roughly flat portion of the curve is called the *intrinsic failure period* or useful period. Failure occurs randomly in this region and failure rate is approximately constant. Due to the useful life of the datacenter components, they are spent here so that a great deal of reliability is conducted to determine $h(t)$ in this region. Between (t_1, t_2) is the failure rate function, which is constant; hence, it is also called *useful life*. The failure during this interval is also known as chance failure or random failure. The reasons for these failures are a sudden spike in the end-user's load, accidents, physical failure of the system and so forth.

3. This region also is known as the *ware-out failure regime*. Due to component degradation at an accelerated pace, the failure rate also increases in this section. Many devices of the datacenters do not readily fail, but become absolute as a result of design changes and introduction of new technologies. Between (t_2, ∞) intervals are known as the *increased failure rate* (IFR). These failures are due to ware out, aging or serious deterioration of the cloud systems. The life of the cloud system is entering into an end unless a preventive mechanism is not adopted, which may lead to a failure of the cloud system and loss of data.

1.5 Class of Life Distribution

The main class of life distributions are in Figure 1.6.

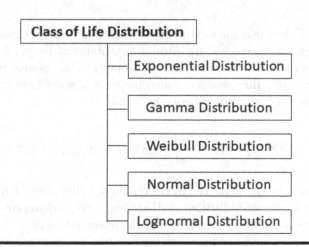

Figure 1.6   Classification of class of life distribution.

1.5.1 Exponential Distribution

Exponential distribution is the most widely used distribution in reliability analysis. It is defined as the measuring unit of the parameters λ in the probability per unit of time. The failure function indicates the probability of failure in the next instant of time, no matter how old the system is. The memoryless property of exponential distribution represents that a system that has an age t is as good as a new system with the age of zero. In case of discrete distribution, the geometric distribution adores this lack of memory property. The probability function of an exponential random variable is mathematically represented [4, 6] as

$$\text{If } f(x) = \lambda e^{-\lambda x} \text{ for } x > 0; \ \lambda > 0$$

The conditional probability [7] of failure of the system for age t is

$$R(x|t) = P\{T > x + t | T > t\}$$
$$\quad\quad\quad\quad\quad\quad\quad \cdots\cdots \quad\quad\quad (1.3)$$
$$= \frac{P\{T > x + t\}}{P\{T > t\}}$$

where x indicates that the system will survive for a additional amount of time.

Both the numerator and denominator of Eq. (1.3) indicate the survival function of random variable x. For exponential distribution

$$R(x|t) = \frac{e^{-\lambda(x+t)}}{e^{-\lambda t}} = e^{-\lambda(x)} = R(X)$$

Here X is the failure that the total number of systems will experience during the interval of time $(0, t)$, which is the survival probability of the system. Normally the probability of $T > X$. $R(X)$ indicates the property of lack of memory adored by the random variable. The exponential distribution is closely related to the Poisson distribution, and the relationship between them is

$$P\{R(x|t) = n\} = \frac{e^{-\lambda t}(\lambda t)^n}{n!} \text{ where } n = 0,1,2,\ldots t \geq 0$$

The number of failures experienced by the system in a time period 0 to t, the inter-arrival rate, is exponentially distributed. These inter-arrival failures are $X_1, X_2, \ldots$, and the process of counting these failures in the interval 0, t is $X(t)$. The probability distribution function $f(t)$ and the reliability function for the exponential distribution [8] is illustrated in Figure 1.7.

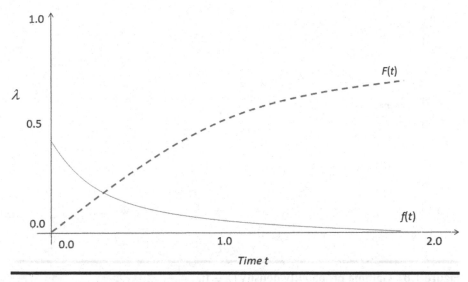

Figure 1.7   Exponential distribution $(\lambda = 1)$.

1.5.2 Gamma Distribution

Let T be the time to failure of a system. The random variable T is the sum of n and the other random variable as

$$T = X_1 + X_2 + \ldots + X_n$$

Each of these X_i exponentially distribute the random variable with parameter λ.

$$X_i \approx \exp(\lambda) \qquad \lambda > 0 \quad \text{where } i = 1, 2, \ldots n$$

The *pdf* of the gamma random variable is

$$f_T(t) = \frac{e^{-\lambda t}(\lambda t)^{n-1}}{\Gamma n}\lambda, \ n > 0, \ t \geq 0, \ \lambda > 0 \text{ where } T \approx (n, \lambda)$$

where $t = t_1, t_2, \ldots, t_n$ is the length of the interval, t_1 is the first failure, t_2 is the second failure and so on.

The gamma random variable represents the failure of the system, and t_n is, respectively, the instant at which the nth failure occurs. Also, the representation of the gamma distribution is

$$f_T(t) = \frac{e^{-\lambda t}(\lambda t)^{n-1}}{\Gamma n}\lambda, \ n > 0, \ t \geq 0, \ \lambda > 0$$

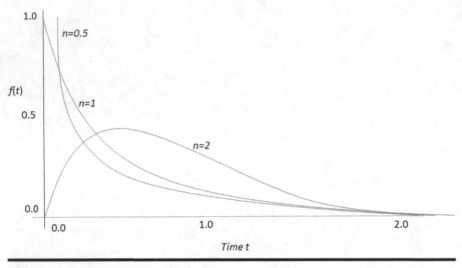

Figure 1.8 Gamma probability density $(\lambda = 1)$.

The reliability function $R(t)$ is

$$R(t) = \overline{F_T}(t) = \int_t^\infty f_T(u)\,du = P\{T > t\}$$

The probability distribution function $f(t)$ drawn for different values of n is shown in Figure 1.8.

This is also the definition of survival probability

$$R(t) = \frac{\int_t^\infty e^{-\lambda u}(\lambda u)^{n-1}}{\Gamma n}\lambda\,du = e^{-(\lambda t)^n} \quad t \geq 0$$

The plot of reliability function $R(t)$ for different values of n is shown in Figure 1.9.

$$F_T(t) = 1 - R(t)$$

The failure rate, $h(t) = \dfrac{f(t)}{R(t)} = \dfrac{n}{\lambda}(\lambda t)^{n-1} \quad t \geq 0\ldots\ldots$ \hfill (1.4)

In Eq. (1.4) λ – considered as the scale parameter, and its value ranges between $0 < \lambda < 1$,

$h(t)$ is a DFR distribution, when $\lambda = 1$,

$h(t) = \text{constant}\ \lambda > 1$,

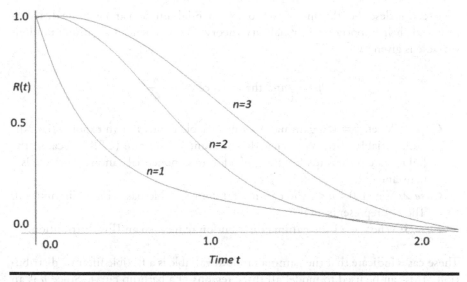

Figure 1.9   Reliability function $R(t)$ for the gamma distribution ($\lambda = 1$).

$h(t)$ = IFR distribution and
$n-$ shape parameter $n > 0$

$$n = 1, f_T(t) = \frac{e^{-\lambda t}(\lambda t)^{1-1}}{\Gamma 1}\lambda, \quad \lambda > 0, \quad t \geq 0$$

The above expression represents that we can get an exponential distribution from the gamma distribution when $n = 1$.

$$R(t) = \int_t^\infty u\,du = \frac{\int_t^\infty e^{-\lambda u}(\lambda u)^{n-1}}{\Gamma n}\lambda\,du = P\{T > t\}$$

which is the survival probability of random variable under consideration.

$$\text{CDF } F(t) = \int_0^t f_T u\,du = \frac{\int_t^\infty e^{-\lambda u}(\lambda u)^{n-1}}{\Gamma n - 1}\lambda\,du = P\{T \leq t\}$$

$$\text{The } MTTF = \int_t^\infty R(t)\,dt$$

This section describes the importance of exponential function and gamma distribution and their importance in reliability theory. The moment of a gamma random variable is given by

$$\mu = \frac{n}{\lambda} \text{ and the variance } \sigma^2 = \frac{n}{\lambda^2}$$

> ***Case 1:*** When $n = 1$, a gamma random variable reduces to an exponential random variable. This represents the constant failure rate (CFR), because the failure rate or hazards function $h(t)$ for an exponential random variable is a constant (λ).
>
> ***Case 2:*** When $0 < n < 1$ the gamma random variable has a DFR distribution. The $h(t)$ represents a DFR.
>
> ***Case 3:*** When $n > 1$ the gamma distribution reduces to an IFR distribution.

These cases indicate that the gamma random variable is a flexible lifetime distribution. This can be used to model all three regions of a bathtub curve. Since n is an integer, the gamma distribution is represented as an Erlang distribution.

1.5.3 Weibull Distribution

The *pdf* of a Weibull random variable T is given as $f_T(t) = \dfrac{e^{-\left(\frac{t}{\eta}\right)^\beta} \beta_t \beta^{-1}}{\eta^\beta}$, $t \geq 0$

where the η – scale parameter and β – shape parameter. The probability distribution function $f(t)$ for selected values of the shape parameter β is shown in Figure 1.10.

For the Weibull distribution, the reliability function $R(t)$, cumulative distribution function $F(t)$ and hazards rate function (failure rate function) $h(t)$ are given as

$$R(t) = e^{-\left(\frac{t}{\eta}\right)^\beta}, \ t \geq 0$$

$$F(t) = (1 - R(t)) = 1 - e^{-\left(\frac{t}{\eta}\right)^\beta}, \ t \geq 0$$

$$h(t) = f_T(t).R(t) = \frac{\beta}{\eta}\left(\frac{t}{\eta}\right)^{\beta-1}, \ t \geq 0$$

The moments of Weibull distribution are represented as

$$\text{Mean } \mu = \eta\Gamma\left(1 + \frac{1}{\beta}\right) = E(X)$$

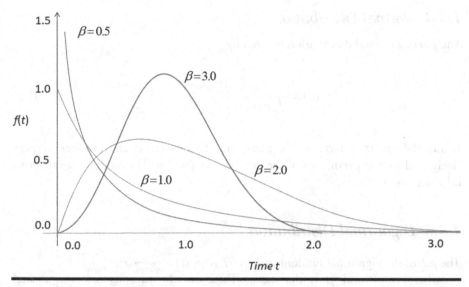

Figure 1.10 Probability distribution function of the Weibull distribution for selected values of β, $(\lambda = 1)$.

$$\text{Variance} = E(X^2) - E(X)^2$$

$$= \eta^2 \left\{ \Gamma\left(\frac{2+\beta}{\beta}\right) - \left[1 + \frac{1}{\beta}\right]^2 \right\}$$

Referring to the above parameters, the failure rate distributions are when

Case 1: $0 < \beta < 1$ It is a DFR distribution.
Case 2: $\beta = 1$, It is a CFR.

$$f_T(t) = \frac{e^{-\left(\frac{t}{\eta}\right)}}{\eta} = \frac{1}{\eta} . e^{-\left(\frac{t}{\eta}\right)}$$

$$= \lambda e^{-\lambda t}, \quad t \geq 0 \quad \text{where } \lambda = \frac{1}{\eta}$$

When $\beta = 1$ the Weibull distribution reduces to an exponential distribution. **Case 3:** When $\beta > 1$ the Weibull random variable represents an IFR distribution.

From the above observations it is clear that the Weibull random variable is a flexible distribution, and all three regions of a bathtub curve can be modeled for any system suitably.

.

1.5.4 Normal Distribution

The *pdf* of a normal distribution is given by

$$f_T(x) = \frac{1}{\sqrt{2\pi}\sigma} e^{-\frac{(x-\mu)^2}{2\sigma^2}}, \quad -\infty < x < \infty \quad \ldots\ldots \tag{1.5}$$

In Eq. (1.5) μ, σ and σ^2 are the mean, standard deviation and variance, respectively, and are the parameters of the normal distribution. The random variable can take negative value.

1.5.5 Lognormal Distribution

The *pdf* of the lognormal random variable T is $f_T(t) = \frac{1}{\sqrt{2\pi}\sigma t} \cdot e^{-\frac{1}{2\sigma^2}(\ln t - \mu)^2}$

where $\sigma > 0$ and μ is the mean. These are the parameters of lognormal distribution.

Also σ – share parameter and μ – scale parameter.

$$\text{Let } X = \log T \sim N(\mu, \sigma^2)$$

$X \sim N(\mu, \sigma^2)$ if and only if $T = e^X \sim$ lognormal distribution.

For a lognormal distribution

$$R(t) = 1 - \varphi\left(\frac{\ln t - \mu}{\sigma}\right), \quad t > 0$$

$$F(t) = \varphi\left(\frac{\ln t - \mu}{\sigma}\right), \quad t > 0$$

$$h(t) = \frac{f(t)}{R(t)} = \frac{f(t)}{1 - \varphi\left(\frac{\ln t - \mu}{\sigma}\right)}, \quad t > 0$$

$$E[T] = e^{\mu + \sigma^2/2}$$

The variance of T is $var = e^{2\mu + \sigma^2}\left(e^{\sigma^2} - 1\right)$.

For a lognormal distribution the failure rate function in Figure 1.11 initially increases and then it reaches to its peak and decreases when $t \to \infty$.

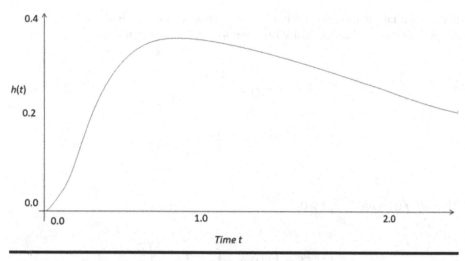

Figure 1.11 Failure rate function of the lognormal distribution.

1.6 Constant Hazard Rate of the Weibull Distribution

The hazard rate is constant, linear and nonlinear. These characteristics are exhibited by the component of a cloud infrastructure. For an exponential distribution *pdf*

$$f(t) = \lambda e^{-\lambda(t)}$$

$$R(t) = e^{-\lambda(t)}$$

$$F(t) = 1 - e^{-\lambda(t)}$$

where λ is the parameter of the exponential random variable.

The $MTTF = \int_0^\infty R(t)dt = \int_0^\infty e^{-\lambda t}dt = \frac{1}{\lambda}$,

the variance of the random variable is $\sigma^2 = \frac{1}{\lambda^2}$ and

the failure rate $h(t) = \frac{f(t)}{R(t)} = \frac{\lambda e^{-\lambda t}}{e^{-\lambda t}} = \lambda$,

i.e., for an exponential random variable $h(t) = \lambda$ is a constant. Such distributions are referred to as CFR distributions, where $\sigma^2 = \frac{1}{\lambda^2}$ represents the variability of the failure time. This value increases as the reliability increases.

Linear hazard rate: $h(t) : h(t) = bt, t > 0$ where b is a constant.

Many components are subjected to mechanical stress (for example, power-generating units used in datacenters) and they fail due to wear out or deterioration. The hazard rate of such a component increases with time. For such components the hazard rate is modeled with a linear hazard rate, which is the simplest time-dependent model. The reliability function for such components is

$$R(t) = e^{-\int_0^t h(u)\,du}$$

$$= e^{-\int_0^t b(u)\,du} = e^{-bu^2}\bigg|_0^t = e^{-bt^2/2}$$

The *pdf* $f(t) = bte^{-bt^2/2}$, $t > 0$

$$MTTF = \int_0^\infty R(t)\,dt = \int_0^\infty e^{-bt^2/2}\,dt = \sqrt{\frac{\pi}{2b}}$$

This is a representation of Raleigh's distribution.

1.7 Simple Configuration

The main requirement of reliability for engineers is to understand the system configurations. These systems are classified into two types as simple systems and complex systems. As the name indicates, a simple system is comprised of a fewer number of components, whereas a complex system has many components. The approaches used to analyze the complex system includes decomposing them into subsystems of convenient size. These subsystems comprise many subcomponents associated with a specific system function and size. Reliabilities of these subsystems are computed and then combined to determine the reliability of the entire system using probability laws. To consider the physical configuration, the physical structure of the system must be in focus. The physical selection of the system and nature of its functions is known to determine the behavior of the system in the event of failure of a subsystem. The combination of these subsystems also depends on the system's reliability. A subsystem may consist of one or more components. The failure of a subsystem may be due to the failure of a component or a greater number of components. To estimate the reliability, the system configuration is represented by an RBD, which is used to depict the relationship between the functioning of a system and its components.

The fundamental structure of a system in reliability theory is classified as *series* and *parallel*. These classes of systems are used to understand the classical reliability theory.

1.7.1 Series Configuration

In a series configuration a number of subcomponents are connected in series as seen in Figure 1.12. The failure of the system depends on the failure of each component. A series system works if and only if every component works. If any one of the components fails, then the system fails. The lifetime of a series system is equal to the smallest lifetime among the lifetime of all the components. Also, the series systems can only last as long as the weakest component in the system. This indicates that the reliability of a series system is no more than the reliability of the worst component or the weakest component. The lifetime of the component that fails first determines the lifetime of the series system. For a reliable system the optimal design is to reduce the number of components that are connected in series.

For serial mode with n components connected in a series its reliability function is $R(t)$,

$$R_S(t) = R_1, R_2, \ldots R_n$$

$$R_S(t) = \prod_{i=1}^{n} R_i(t)$$

The lifetime of the system is $T = \min(T_1, T_2, \ldots T_n > t)$. Assuming $T_1, T_2, \ldots T_n$ are independent, the reliability of the series system is

$$R_S(t) = P\{\min(T_1, T_2, \ldots T_n) > t\}$$

$$= P\{T_1 > t, T_2 > t, \ldots T_n > t\}$$

$$= \prod_{i=1}^{n} P\{T_i > t\}$$

$$= \prod_{i=1}^{n} R_i(t)$$

The mean life of the system is $MTTF = \int_0^{\infty} R_S(t)dt$.

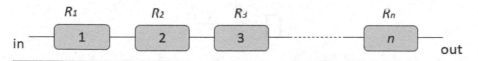

Figure 1.12   System with series connection of components.

Since reliability R_S is a probability of a system reliability and is determined from the component reliability in the following ways, E_1 is the event that component C_1 does not fail and E_2 is the event that component C_2 does not fail.

$$P\left(E_{C_1}\right) = R_1$$

$$P\left(E_{C_2}\right) = R_2$$

where R_1 is the reliability of component C_1 and R_2 is the reliability of component C_2. Hence the function of these two components does not depend on each other. A series system is based on all of the components working. Also, failure or non-failure of one component does not change. The system reliability is

$$R_S = P\left(C_1 \ C_2\right)$$

$$= P(C_1) \cdot P(C_2)$$

$$R_S = \left(R_1 \ R_2\right)$$

If a system with n mutually independent components are connected in a series, then the system reliability is

$$R_S(t) = R_1(t).R_2(t).R_3(t). \dots R_n(t) \le \min\left\{R_1(t), R_2(t) \dots R_n(t)\right\}$$

$$0 < R_i(t) < 1, \ i = 1, 2, \dots n$$

Here $R_i(t)$ is the probability of survival, and its value lies between 0 and 1. The system reliability can therefore be no greater than the smallest component reliability. It is important for all components to have a high reliability, especially if the system contains a large number of components.

Exponential distribution: In a system connected with series components, each component has a CFR of λ_i, so the system reliability is represented by

$$R_S(t) = \prod_{i=1}^{n} R_i(t)$$

$$= \prod_{i=1}^{n} e^{-\lambda_i t} = e^{-\sum_{i=1}^{n} \lambda_i t}$$

$$R_S(t) = e^{-\lambda_S t}$$

where λ_S is the failure rate of the system and $\lambda_S = \sum_{i=1}^{n} \lambda_i$, λ_i represents the CFR.

Weibull failure distribution: The component failure is governed by the Weibull failure rate

$$R_S(t) = \prod_{i=1}^{n} R_i(t) = \prod_{i=1}^{n} e^{-\left(\frac{t}{\theta_i}\right)^{\beta_i}} = e^{-\sum_{i=1}^{n}\left(\frac{t}{\theta_i}\right)^{\beta_i}},$$

The failure rate is $\lambda(t) = \dfrac{e^{-\sum_{i=1}^{n}\left(\frac{t}{\theta_i}\right)^{\beta_i}} \cdot \left[\sum_{i=1}^{n}\left(\frac{\beta_i}{\theta_i}\right)\left(\frac{t}{\theta_i}\right)^{\beta_i-1}\right]}{e^{-\sum_{i=1}^{n}\left(\frac{t}{\theta_i}\right)^{\beta_i}}} = \dfrac{f(t)}{F(t)},$

which is also the hazard rate function $h(t) = \frac{f(t)}{F(t)}$.

$$\lambda(t) = \sum_{i=1}^{n}\left(\frac{\beta_i}{\theta_i}\right)\left(\frac{t}{\theta_i}\right)^{\beta_i-1}$$

This indicates that the system does not exhibit the Weibull failure and every component has a Weibull failure distribution. Generally, for a series connected components, the CFR of component is

$$MTTF = \frac{1}{\sum_{i=1}^{n}\lambda_i} = \frac{1}{\sum_{i=1}^{n}\frac{1}{MTTF_i}} \text{ where } MTTF = \frac{1}{\lambda}$$

1.7.2 Parallel Systems

A parallel system works if and only if at least one component works, and it fails if all components fail. The representation of a parallel system is illustrated in Figure 1.13.

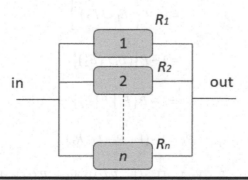

Figure 1.13   System parallel connected components.

Having n components connected in parallel, the system reliability is high due to redundancy. The other $(n-1)$ components are called redundant components and increase the probability that there is at least one working component.

Parallel model: Consider a system consists of n unit elements connected in a parallel way, in which only when all n elements are failed, the whole system fails. The lifetime of the ith component is T_i, its operational reliability is $R_i(t)$ and the lifetime distribution function is $F_i(t)$.

$$F_i(t) = i = 1, 2, \ldots n$$

Then the lifetime of the system is

$$T = \max(T_1, T_2, \ldots T_n > t)$$

assuming $T_1, T_2, \ldots T_n$ are independent to each other. The reliability of the parallel system is

$$R_P(t) = P\left\{\max(T_1, T_2, \ldots T_n) > t\right\}$$

$$= 1 - P\left\{T_1 \leq t,\ T_2 \leq t, \ldots T_n \leq t\right\}$$

$$= 1 - \prod_{i=1}^{n}\left(1 - R_i(t)\right)$$

Reliability of the system is $R_P(t) = 1 - \prod_{i=1}^{n}\left(1 - R_i(t)\right)$.

For a system with its components connected in parallel, the probability that at least one component does not fail is

$$P\left\{\text{at least one component does not fail}\right\} = R_P = P\left\{E_1 \cup E_2\right\}$$

$$= 1 - P\left\{\left(E_1 \cup E_2\right)'\right\}$$

$$= 1 - P\left\{\left(E_1' \cap E_2'\right)\right\}$$

$$= 1 - P\left\{E_1'\right\} P\left\{E_2'\right\}$$

$$R_P = 1 - \left(1 - R_1\right)\left(1 - R_2\right)$$

The system reliability $R_P(t) = 1 - \prod_{i=1}^{n}\left(1 - R_i(t)\right)$ where $R_i(t)$ is the reliability of the ith component.

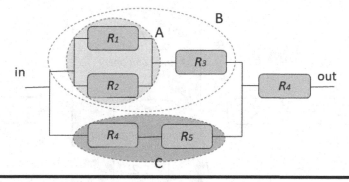

Figure 1.14   Combined series-parallel system.

$$R_P(t) \geq \max\{R_1(t), R_2(t), \dots R_n(t)\}$$

$\Pi_{i=1}^{n}(1 - R_i(t)) <$ the failure probability of most reliable component.
Generally for a redundant system with a CFR

$$R_S(t) = 1 - \prod_{i=1}^{n}\left(1 - e^{-\lambda t}\right)$$

where λ_i is the failure rate of the ith component.

1.7.2.1 Combined Series-Parallel Systems

A series-parallel combination system (Figure 1.14) with individual segments are A, B and C.
Reliability of the individual segment is

$$R_A = 1 - (1 - R_1)(1 - R_2) \quad R_B = R_3.R_4 \quad R_C = R_4.R_5$$

The reliability of the entire system is

$$R_S(t) = R_6\left(1 - (1 - R_B)(1 - R_C)\right)$$

1.7.3 Standby Systems

A parallel system of n components is the redundant components, and they are the inactive components of a standby system as seen in Figure 1.15. These components are available whenever they are called into service, in case of failure of an active component. In standby redundancy only one component is active and one or more additional components may be placed in the system, but in the standby mode. In

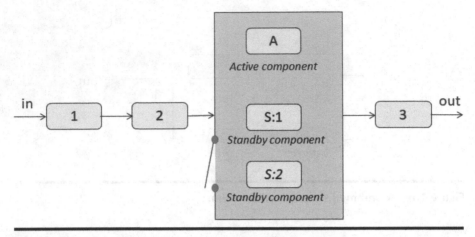

Figure 1.15 Block diagram of a standby system.

a standby system a sensing and switching mechanism is used to monitor the status of the active components. In case of failure the standby component is immediately switched into the active state. There are three types of standby systems

1. *Host standby:* An active redundant component with the failure rate the same as the active component.
2. *Warm standby:* An inactive component with a failure rate between 0 and the failure rate of active components.
3. *Cold standby:* It has a zero failure rate. These systems do not fail while in standby mode.

System redundancy may be classified in two ways:

1. *Low-level redundancy:* Each component comprising a system may have one or more parallel components.
2. *High-level redundancy:* The entire system may be placed in parallel with one or more identical systems.

Consider two systems, A and B; their combinations for low-level redundancy and high-level redundancy is seen in Figure 1.16, and its system reliability on component failure is illustrated in Figure 1.17. The reliability of these two redundant connections are

$$R_{\text{low}} = (1 - (1-R)^2)^2 \quad R_{\text{high}} = (1 - (1-R^2)^2$$

$$R_{\text{low}} - R_{\text{high}} = 2R^2\left(1 - R^2\right) \geq 0$$

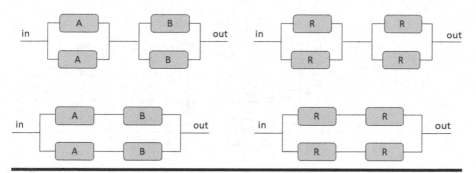

Figure 1.16   Components in low redundancy and high redundancy.

In the redundancy model, if any one of the components (e.g., A) fails then the system is functional. If both A and B fail then the system is functional, whereas in the other connection if both A and B fail then the system is not functional. This shows that lower level redundancy has higher reliability R_{low} than higher level redundancy R_{high}.

1.7.4 k-out-of-n Redundancy

Let a system consist of n redundant components, out of which "k" components are functional as seen in Figure 1.18.

> *Case 1:* If $k = 1$, there is complete redundancy.
> *Case 2:* If $k = n$, there is no redundancy

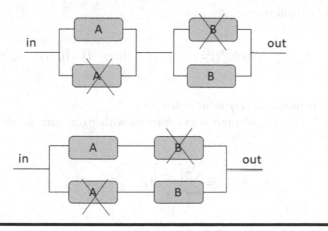

Figure 1.17   System reliability on component failure.

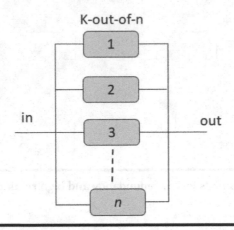

Figure 1.18 The *k*-out-of-*n* redundancy.

If the reliability of a component t is R, then the reliability of the system at time t in *k*-out-of-*n* redundancy mode is [9]

$$R_{sys} = \begin{bmatrix} n \\ k \end{bmatrix} R^k (1-R)^{n-k}$$

$$\text{Or} = \sum_{i=k}^{n} \begin{bmatrix} n \\ k \end{bmatrix} R^i (1-R)^{n-i} \text{ where } i = 1,2....k$$

For example, if $n = 4$ and $k = 3$, then each component has a reliability of 0.97 and the system reliability is

$$R_{sys} = \begin{bmatrix} 4 \\ 3 \end{bmatrix} 0.97^3 (1-0.97)^1 + \begin{bmatrix} 4 \\ 4 \end{bmatrix} 0.97^4 (1-0.97)^0 = 0.994$$

k-out-of-*n* redundancy: *exponential failure*

If the failure distribution is exponential with parameter λ, then the system reliability is

$$R_{sys}(t) = \sum_{x=k}^{n} \begin{bmatrix} n \\ x \end{bmatrix} \left(e^{-\lambda t}\right)^x \left(1 - e^{-\lambda t}\right)^{n-x}$$

The expectation is $E(T) = \int_0^\infty R_S(t)dt = \frac{1}{\lambda}\sum_{x=k}^{n} \frac{1}{x}$.

1.8 Conclusion

A precise definition of reliability and some associated concepts are explained in this chapter. Various failure models or life distributions are elaborated based on these models. Throughout this chapter we systematically analyzed essential reliability and failure models and calculated their reliability functions, which led to proving some interesting characteristics regarding the systems and their components. From this it is clear that the reliability of a system is equal to the product of the reliability of the individual components, which make up the systems. If the system comprises a large number of subsystems or components, the system reliability may be rather low, even though each component has high reliability. A detailed discussion related to exponential distribution is of great importance in the field of reliability engineering. This chapter ultimately brings clarity to just some of the key concepts in reliability theory related to cloud computing.

References

1. Ardagna Danilo. Cloud and Multi-Cloud Computing: Current Challenges and Future Applications. In: 7th International Workshop on Principles of Engineering Service-Oriented and Cloud Systems (PESOS) 2015. Piscataway, NJ: IEEE/ACM, pp. 1–2, 2015.
2. Puthal Deepak, BPS Sahoo, Sambit Mishra, Satyabrata Swain. Cloud Computing Features, Issues, and Challenges: A Big Picture. In: International Conference on Computational Intelligence and Networks (CINE). Piscataway, NJ: IEEE, pp. 116–123, 2015.
3. Nelson, Wayne. Accelerated Testing: Statistical Models, Test Plans, and Data Analysis. Edited by SS Wilks Samuel. Wiley Series in Probability and Mathematical Statistics. New York: John Wiley & Sons, 1990.
4. Barlow, Richard E, Frank Proschan. Mathematical Theory of Reliability. New York: John Wiley & Son, Inc., 1965.
5. Bauer, Eric, Randee Adams, Reliability and Availability of Cloud Computing, Hoboken, NJ: John Wiley & Sons, Inc., 2012.
6. Ireson, William Grant, Clyde F Coombs, Richard Y Moss. Handbook of Reliability Engineering and Management. *2nd edition*. New York: McGraw Hill, 1996.
7. Smith CO. Introduction to Reliability in Design. London: McGraw-Hill, 1976.
8. Ravindran, A Ravi. Operation Research and Management Science Handbook. Boca Raton, FL: CRC Press, 2008.
9. Ross, Sheldon M. Introduction to Probability Models. Amsterdam: Academic Press, 2010.
10. Cluzeau, T, T Keller, W Scheneewiss. Consecutive-K-out-of-n-F systems, IEEE Transactions on Reliability 2008, vol. 57(1), pp. 84–87.

Further Readings

Osaki, S. Stochastic Models in Reliability and Maintenance. Springer publisher, Nanzan University, Aichi, Japan, 2002.

Billinton, R, R Allan. Reliability Evaluation of Engineering Systems Concepts and Techniques. Springer publication, 1992.

O'Connor, Patrick DT, Andre Kleyner. Practical Reliability Engineering. Chichester: Wiley, 2012.

Gupta, PP, A Kumar, SK Mittal. Stochastic behaviour of three state complex repairable systems with three types of failure, Microelectronics Reliability 1985, vol. 25, pp. 853–858.

Billington, R, R Allan. Reliability Evaluation of Engineering Systems. Springer, 2007.

Ebeling, Charles E. An Introduction to Reliability and Maintainability Engineering. TMH, 2004.

Grant, Eugene Lodewick, Richard S Leavenworth. Statistical Quality Control. *6th edition*. McGraw-Hill Series in Industrial Engineering and Management Science. New York: McGraw-Hill, 1987.

Chapter 2

Reliability and High Availability Analysis for Cloud Datacenter

Rathnakar Achary

Alliance University

Contents

2.1 Introduction

2.1.1 Cloud Reliability Engineering: Failure Management

Cloud computing basically refers to a shared computing process. It is a digital disruption that moves more processes online. The three standard models associated with cloud computing are infrastructure as a service (IaaS), software as a service (SaaS) and platform as a service (PaaS). A major portion of these services is provided by the tech giants in the market including Amazon, Google and Microsoft. This shifted the application deployment from a local server to a remote server hosted via the Internet to store and manage large amounts of data. The service provider manages thousands of high-performance servers, with a large number of processing elements, storage devices, memory segments and network interface cards, with the provision of hot swapping. This removes the troubles of legacy computer infrastructure; however, the growing adaptation of cloud datacenters are rapidly expanding the size and increasing the complexity of the systems. This leads to increased resource failure. Any such failure could have major ramifications on the future of the cloud service to deliver services to millions of customers. The increased reason of failure can be service-level agreement (SLA) violation, data loss and degradation of cloud service performance.

Cloud service providers also enhanced their cloud resources with architectures, technologies, organization designs, processes and workflows to guarantee that the service providers are less vulnerable to attacks and to help to protect against human errors. Also, another potential source of failure is the interaction between applications and the cloud infrastructure.

2.2 Reliability Issues Related to Critical Infrastructure

Reliability is defined as the continuity of service or the probability that a system or service remains operable for a specific period of time. It is also the ability of a system to perform its required function under stated conditions for a specific period of time. High availability (HA) and reliability are the paramount requirements in cloud services [1], and they are independent entities. Researchers have defined the availability of a system in different ways. Availability is the probability that a system is operational and functional correctly at the instant of time *t*, and reliability is the probability that the system is operational in the said time interval without failure.

Availability of a cloud service is an essential requirement to minimize business loss, to maintain customer confidence and to prevent penalties due to the violation of the SLA. The popularity of cloud-enabled services has received critical consideration from worldwide business and government organizations. However, for the expected customers' acceptance, availability becomes a major issue. The service outage in cloud computing can seriously impact the entire value chain, which includes corporate customers managing their enterprises' systems containing customer data and applications. Some of the researchers defined HA of the cloud as being accessible 99.999% of the time. To offer HA, the cloud service providers have adopted many services and techniques such as failure detection, monitoring and replications, as illustrated in Figure 2.1. The various HA services are defined in Table 2.1.

Several technologies and mechanisms are proposed by the researchers and cloud service providers for reliability and HA services (HASs). As in [2], the two

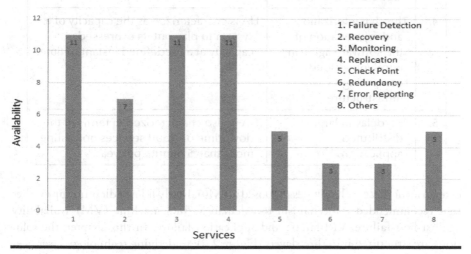

Figure 2.1 High availability implemented in the services.

Table 2.1 High Availability Services

	Services	Definition
1.	High availability (HA) at application level	The cloud services provided by the service provider are considered as profoundly accessible 99.999% of the time. This is also referred to as five-nine's of cloud service.
2.	Managing application-level elasticity and availability	The HA is not just providing a high level of uptime on a day-to-day basis; rather, it indicates the ability of the cloud service provider to provide a high level of cloud reliability, which is capable of ■ Scheduling and managing maintenance operations to avoid disruption. ■ Handling disaster situations without allowing for significant downtime. ■ Offering storage redundancies to ensure there are no single points of failure that could cause extended outage. ■ For HA cloud services the outage is less than 5–25 minutes per year.
3.	Scheduling HA applications on the cloud environment	HA systems are categorized by reduced failure and faster uptime.
4.	The characterization and rejuvenation of the software aging in eucalyptus cloud computing infrastructure	HA is characterized as the capacity of a system to play out its expressed capacity at a predefined instant of time.
5.	The delay in large distributed applications	HA is also characterized in terms of the downtime of cloud services not lasting more than 5 minute per year.

categories of these technologies proposed are visualized and middleware approaches that recommended a mechanism to calculate virtual machine (VM) availability against host failure, VM failure and application failure. In this chapter, the solutions are structured into three layers (Figure 2.2); underlying technologies, services and middleware.

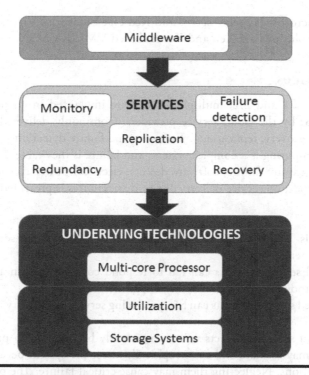

Figure 2.2   Classification of HA solutions (three layers).

2.2.1 *Underlying Technologies*

Virtualization is the bottommost layer with the objective to provide HA using commodity systems. The idea of virtualization inside cloud computing empowers the adaptability with respect to re-allocation of outstanding tasks across the physical infrastructure offered by virtualization [3]. This flexibility allows continuity of the cloud instances without stopping the end-user applications. As a result, there is improved resource utilization through migration of VMs. Another benefit of this flexibility is delivering new VMs using designs, which enables the service providers to offer adaptable services. Another advantage is to provide new VMs through the use of templates, which enables providers to offer elasticity services for applications developers. Virtualization can also be used for different cloud-related entities, such as server virtualization, operating system virtualization, hardware virtualization, process virtualization, memory virtualization, storage virtualization and network virtualization, with the same objectives of failure and attack isolation, checkpoint and rollback as recovery mechanisms. At the network level, redundancy is for the virtualization of network functions. Implementation of virtualization is done by both proprietary solutions and open source connectivity. The proprietary solutions include

VMware, Microsoft Hyper-V server and Red Hat Enterprise Virtualization; the open source solutions are Xen and Kernel-based VMs (KVM).

2.2.2 Services

As in Figures 2.1 and 2.2, multiple services are implanted in conjunction with offering HASs by the cloud service providers. Commonly delivered services are redundancy, recovery, replication, monitoring and failure detection.

Cloud computing is a complex system, and failure is inevitable. Failure occurs because of hardware failure, software defects, electrical power disruption and so forth. The impact on service delivery due to these failures is presented in three different ways:

1. There is a degraded service response time, producing service latency impairments.
2. Isolated service requests can fail to respond correctly within an acceptable time, producing service reliability impairments.
3. Repeated service requests can fail, producing service availability impairments.

Hardware and software defects will intermittently be initiated to produce error. These errors may escalate and catastrophically affect the system performance and disrupt operations. Neglecting them may cause critical failure. The primary characteristic of the service impact of a failure is the duration of service disruption. A prolonged service disruption is likely to cause service to degrade and violation of the SLA.

The researchers at Bell Labs developed an 8i framework to consider all key systems vulnerabilities. The ingredients of this framework are shown in Figure 2.3. The first two ingredients are considered internal and the remaining six as external.

i. **Hardware:** Hardware failure means the failure of physical objects, which is a well-known physical failure. Hardware reliability depends on the quality of the hardware system with an acceptable low failure rate. Optionally, the system must rapidly detect hardware failures and isolate them to the appropriate file replaceable unit (FRU).
ii. **Software:** Software enables the system's hardware to deliver service to the users. Software errors are mainly due to the programming defects, design and integration issues. This causes an incorrect system behavior.
iii. **Power:** This type of failure is due to the surge or spikes in the electricity power sources or battery banks.
iv. **Environments:** Computer hardware systems are very sensitive to the ambient environmental conditions including the variations of temperature, humidity, dust and corrosive fumes.

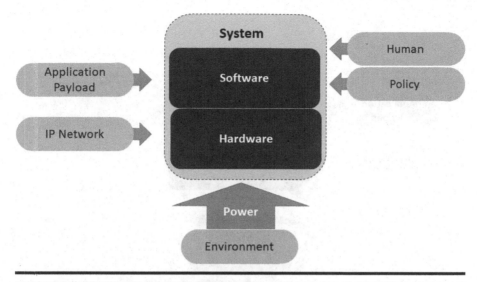

Figure 2.3   8i, eight-ingredient framework.

v. ***Networks:*** Network errors or failures are due to errors in the network devices, such as routers, switches or gateways due to the impairment of communication links, thus, disrupting prompt and reliable delivery of the applications payload to the intended nodes.

vi. ***Payloads:*** These errors are due to the properties of an Internet Protocol (IP) network, wherein the different IP network facilities and infrastructures performance may likely be different for handling messages or data.

vii. ***Users:*** The users or the operators responsible for the routine maintenance of the system must productively anticipate the emergency maintenance required. The negligence or wrong action by the users or operators may catastrophically impact the availability of the systems.

viii. ***Policy:*** For HA of the cloud system, it is essential to have a policy and process that organize workflow and governance operations and behavior. The operational policy often includes the industry standards, regulatory compliance, SLA, maintenance and repair strategies. Several policies will help to minimize the failure rate. Some of these policies impact the cloud services failure and others may impact service on service outages and recovery time.

Policies that impact the failure rate:

■ Policies for software updates and deploying critical software packages
■ Policies for engineering and staff training
■ Policies for the security of the network and system against cyber attacks

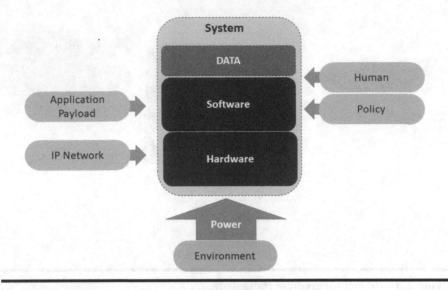

Figure 2.4   8i plus data and disaster event (8i + 2d) model.

Policies that impact service outage recovery time:

- Policy for emergency outage recovery time
- Outage escalation policy
- Agreement with software and hardware suppliers for technical support

The 8i reference model is overlaid with two more ingredients, data and disaster event risk. The data or user data is an independent or co-equal ingredient with the hardware and software. Another important ingredient is the disaster event, which is typically mitigated via disaster recovery and business continuity plan. With these two added ingredients, the 8i model is recreated as the 8i + 2d model, as illustrated in Figure 2.4.

2.2.3 Cloud Service Availability Metric

In this section, the availability of the system is specified concerning the availability of the various ingredients mentioned in the previous section. The logical relationship between the various individual ingredients is considered to estimate the system-level availability. Consider the cloud service provisioning system (CSP) by referring to the previously mentioned eight ingredients $C = \{C_i = 1, 2.....8\}$. The success of CSP depends on the success of every ingredient C_i. The HA of CSP is represented as $A_{CSP} = \Pi_{i=1}^{8} A_i$, where A_i denotes the availability of subsystem i.

2.3 Redundancy

Redundancy means multiple resources can perform the same task. It will help to overcome the problem of single point failure. The redundancy model denotes a wide range of ways the HA system can merge dynamic and standby replicas of facilitated applications. The redundancy model refers to many different ways HA systems can combine active and standby replicas of hosted applications. The availability management framework (AMF) manages the HA of applications by organizing their redundant entities [4], which specifies the characteristics of the entities comprising the system, their types and the way they are organized.

The main objective of redundancy is zero downtime with multiple processing facilities in a datacenter such as $2N$ and $N + 1$ redundancy. Where N equals the amount of capacity required by the datacenter infrastructure at full information technology (IT) load as illustrated in Figure 2.5. If N is equal to the amount of capacity needed to run the cloud datacenter, then $N + 1$ indicates an additional component added to support a single failure or required maintenance on a component; $2N$ refers to a full redundant, mirrored system with two independent facilities.

AMF defines five redundancy models including the number redundancy and the $2N$ redundancy. The $N + M$ model represents an extension of the $2N$ redundancy. This model guarantees a backup copy of each dynamic application. An extension of the $2N$ model is the $N + M$ model [5]. This model guarantees beyond what two system units can deal with by taking dynamic or standby tasks from

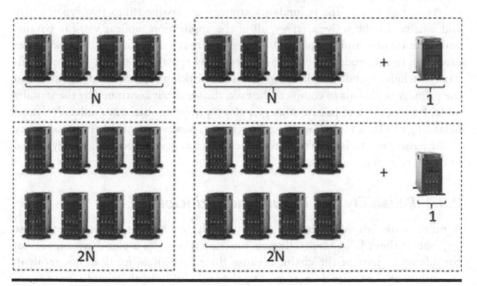

Figure 2.5 $2N$ and $N + 1$ redundancy.

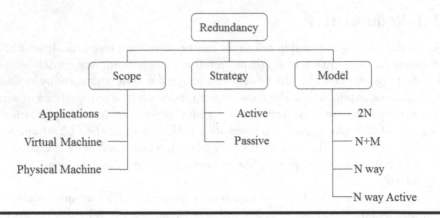

Figure 2.6 Classification of redundancy.

an application. In the $N + M$ model, N represents the number of dynamic tasks handled and M represents standby tasks. Another high-priority redundancy is the N-way redundant service, which utilizes two servers communicating in real time over a dedicated network connection to the remote server and provides the benefits of load splitting. The $N + M$ and N-way models look identical. The main distinction is that the N-way model unit deals with both dynamic and standby tasks from various application instances. The N-way dynamic model recognizes only the dynamic task from unit applications. It does not permit standby tasks; however, it allows an application instance to be assigned as dynamic tasks into different units. Usually the $2-N$ model is implemented due to its simplicity.

As in Figure 2.6, the redundancy strategy is classified into two types: active and passive. In the active strategy, all of the application replicas work in parallel and there are no standby replicas. Whenever there is a node failure, the tasks under execution in this node can be restarted from any remaining nodes. Passive redundancy includes standby replicas along with a working replica. At the point when the primary node fails to complete the task, the service is continued by the standby node. Both active and passive strategies play an important role in availability. Load balancing can be achieved by the active strategy; however, maintaining consistency in the passive model is simpler. Due to these advantages, the passive strategy is used in different applications.

2.3.1 Reliability and Redundancy Principle

A number of redundant system units in a chain becomes unavailable in case any one of them fails. Generally non-functional units of a cloud system are not considered as part of the chain, because their unavailability does not result in the failure of the entire datacenter, and the availability of the cloud service is not affected.

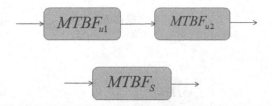

Figure 2.7 System mean time between failures (*MTBF*) of two units chained.

The estimation of system availability, unavailability, system failure rate λ_S and $MTBF_S$ of two units in a chained system (Figure 2.7) is written as

$$A_S = A_{u1} \cdot A_{u2}$$

$$= (1 - U_{u1}) \cdot (1 - U_{u2})$$

$$U_S = U_{u1} + U_{u2} - U_{u1} \cdot U_{u2}$$

$$\lambda_S = \lambda_{u1} + \lambda_{u2}$$

$$MTBF_S = \frac{1}{\lambda_S} = \frac{1}{\lambda_{u1} + \lambda_{u2}}$$

$$MTBF_S = \frac{MTBF_{u1} \cdot MTBF_{u2}}{MTBF_{u1} + MTBF_{u2}}$$

In case of using redundant units in a chain, the availability A_S, unavailability U_S, failure rate λ_S and $MTBF_S$ are represented as

$$A_S = A_{u1} \cdot A_{u2} \Big|_{\text{for } u1 = u2} = A_u^2$$

$$U_S = U_{u1} + U_{u2} - U_{u1} \cdot U_{u2} \cdot \Big|_{\text{for } u1 = u2} = 2U_u - U_u^2$$

$$\lambda_S = \lambda_{u1} + \lambda_{u2} \Big|_{\text{for } u1 = u2} = 2\lambda_u \tag{2.1}$$

$$MTBF_S = \frac{1}{\lambda_S} = \frac{1}{2\lambda_u} = \frac{MTBF_u}{2} \tag{2.2}$$

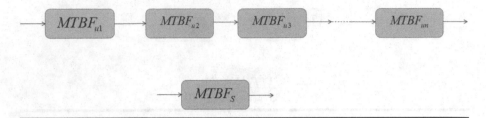

Figure 2.8   Cloud system with *n* redundant units.

If a cloud system composed of several redundant units in a chain becomes unavailable due to the failure of single or multiple units fails. The representation of such *n* chained redundant system is illustrated in Figure 2.8.

The system failure rate λ_S in Eq. (1) and system $MTBF_S$ from Eq. (2) for *n* chained units is represented as

$$\lambda_S = \lambda_{u1} + \lambda_{u2} + \lambda_{u3} + \ldots + \lambda_{un}$$

$$= \sum_{i=1}^{n} \lambda_{ui}$$

$$MTBF_S = \frac{1}{\lambda_S} = \frac{1}{\displaystyle\sum_{i=1}^{n} \lambda_{ui}}$$

If these connected *n* redundant units have identical characteristics, then the system failure rate λ_S and system $MTBF_S$ results in

$$\lambda_{u1} = \lambda_{u2} = \lambda_{u3} = \ldots = \lambda_{un} = \lambda_u$$

$$\lambda_S = n\lambda_u$$

$$MTBF_S = \frac{1}{\lambda_S} = \frac{1}{n.\lambda_u} = \frac{MTBF_u}{n} \qquad (2.3)$$

Equation (2.3) represents that the longer the chain with more redundant units is, then the smaller the system $MTBF_S$.

The cloud system availability

$$A_S = A_{u1}.A_{u2}.A_{u3}\ldots A_{un} \qquad (2.4)$$

Equation (2.4) indicates that less available units within the chain determine the overall system availability. If there are *n* identical units, then Eq. (2.4) simplifies to

$$A_S = A_{u1}.A_{u2}.A_{u3}\ldots A_{un} \bigg|_{u1 = u2 = \ldots = un} \qquad (2.5)$$

Referring to Eq. (2.5), the system unavailability is

$$U_S = 1 - A_S = 1 - A_u^S$$

In the case of HA, the units working in a chain is $A = 99.9\%$ and the percentage of unavailability is negligible. The product of very small unavailability figures result in negligible magnitude.

$$U_S = U_{u1} + U_{u2} + \dots + U_{un} - U_{u1} \cdot U_{u2} - \dots \leq \sum_{i=1}^{n} U_{ui}$$

Adopting parallel units for redundancy significantly increases the availability of the system. It is unlikely that both the units fail at the same time. In case of system failure, the failed systems are repaired or replaced as early as possible to restore the backup.

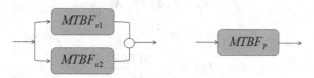

For such a system, the parameters such as availability A_P, unavailability U_P, failure rate λ_P and $MTBF_P$ for two redundant unit is $A_P = A_{u1} + A_{u2} - A_{u1}.A_{u2}$

$$U_P = U_{u1}.U_{u2} \Big|_{u1 = u2} = U_u^2$$

$$\lambda_P = \lambda_{u1}.\lambda_{u2}.(MTTR_{u1} + MTTR_{u2})$$

$$MTBF_P = \frac{1}{\lambda_p} = \frac{MTBF_{u1}.MTBF_{u2}}{MTTR_{u1} + MTTR_{u2}}$$

For two parallel units, the availability in terms of unavailability is

$$A_P = 1 - U_u^2$$

$$= 1 - (1 - A_u)^2$$

$$A_P = A_u (2 - A_u) \tag{2.6}$$

When

$$A_u < 1 \rightarrow 2 - A_u > 1 \rightarrow A_P > A_u \tag{2.7}$$

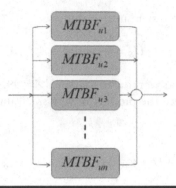

Figure 2.9   The *n* parallel units.

The system failure rate for two identical parallel units is

$$\lambda_P = 2.MTTR_u.\lambda_u^2$$

and

$$MTBF_P = \frac{MTBF_u^2}{2.MTTR_u}$$

A redundant system may also be built with *n* units operating in parallel as shown in Figure 2.9.

If N is the number of working units and x is the space units, supporting working units in the redundancy method are $N + x$. Let n be the total number of units, where $n = (N + x)$ and m be the number of simultaneous failed units; m/n is used for the representation of failure.

For *n* parallel units the overall $MTBF_P$ is calculated as

$$MTBF_{P,m/n} = \frac{MTBF^m}{\frac{n!}{(n-m)!(m-1)!} \times MTTR^{(m-1)}}$$

If $m = n = 2$ gives back

$$MTBF_P = \frac{MTBF_u^2}{2.MTTR_u}$$

2.3.2 System Representation and Assumptions

Based on the cloud computing reference architecture from the National Institute of Standards and Technology (NIST), consider the following two implementation scenarios that are used by the cloud service provider. In the first scenario a cloud service provider may implement a high-level service model SaaS, which

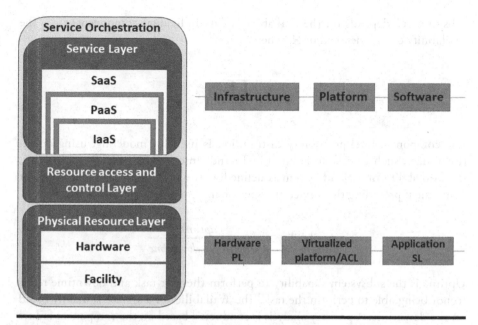

Figure 2.10 Cloud computing reference architecture – NIST orchestration model.

built on PaaS, where PaaS is built on IaaS (for example, consider the Google cloud services). The Google high-level services SaaS include Gmail, Google Search, Google Docs, Google Apps, Google Maps and so forth. The PaaS offers Google App Engine services [6, 7] and IaaS includes the Google Cloud Platform. Based on NIST architecture, the dependency among SaaS, PaaS and IaaS components is shown in Figure 2.10. In the second scenario, the service orchestration, the components are arranged in three layers: hardware physical layer (PL), virtualized platform/ access control list (ACL) and application service layer (SL). Among these services, the cloud service provider may choose to provide an application SL without the support of lower-layer interface points, i.e., SaaS application can be provided directly on top of cloud resources rather than using an IaaS. For example, Salesforce.com provides both SaaS and PaaS. The SaaS layer is built using the well-defined interface components from the PaaS. The SaaS runs directly on the resource abstraction with no explicit IaaS components.

Referring to the three ordered layers PL, ACL and SL, each subsystem C_i consists of a set of components

$$C_i = \left\{ C_{ij}, i = 1, 2, 3, \ j = 1, \ldots n_i \right\}$$

where $C_{i,j}$ represents the jth component of the ith subsystem and n_i denotes the total number of components in subsystem i. From this, it is clear that the availability of subsystem C_i depends on the availability of its individual components $C_{i,j}$. The availability of C_i is denoted by A_i where

$$A_i = \prod_{j=1}^{n_i} A_{i,j}$$

The component-level probability distribution is used for modeling, using operational data, such as time to failure (TFT) and time to repair (TTR). Using this, the availability of a cloud system is defined as the probability of a subsystem or component providing the service at a specific instant of time [8] as

$$\text{Availability } A = \frac{uptime}{uptime + downtime}$$

Uptime is the subsystem capability to perform the user task and downtime refers to not being able to perform the task. The availability of a system is mainly based on the downtime. A primary analysis is conducted based on the component failure data [9, 10]. These data include characteristic failure rate, mean time to failure (*MTTF*), mean time to repair (*MTTR*) and related quantities.

For the *i*th subsystem, $MTTF_{i,j}$ is the *MTTF* of the *j*th component; where $i = 123$ and $j = 1, \ldots n_i$. The TTF is represented by a random variable $x_{i,j}$ and the probability density function of the component failure as $f_{i,j}(t)$. The $MTTF_{i,j}$ is defined as the expected value of the $x_{i,j}$ as

$$MTTF_{i,j} = E[x_{i,j}]$$

$$= \int_0^{\infty} tf_{i,j}(t)dt \tag{2.8}$$

Let *MTTR* be the amount of time taken to run the failed component after failure. The random variable $Y_{i,j}$ represents the TTR of a *j*th component of an *i*th subsystem where $i = 123$ and $j = 1, \ldots n_i$.

The probability function of the components repair time is $g_{i,j}(t)$. Using this, the $MTTR_{i,j}$ is represented as

$$MTTR_{i,j} = E[Y_{i,j}]$$

$$= \int_0^{\infty} tg_{i,j}(t)dt \tag{2.9}$$

Considering Eqns. (2.8) and (2.9), the availability of a component $C_{i,j}$ is denoted as [11, 12]

$$A_{i,j} = \frac{MTTF_{i,j}}{MTTF_{i,j} + MTTR_{i,j}}$$

The cloud system availability can be enhanced by means of redundant components as mentioned in the previous section. The redundancy is achieved by combining two components of a subsystem to function in parallel. These redundant components may be server, storage and VMs. The system failure may occur only if both components fail [13].

Let us consider n_i components at the ith subsystem with parallel composition, the subsystem availability A_i is given by

$$A_i = 1 - \prod_{j=1}^{n_i} \left(1 - A_{i,j}\right) \tag{2.10}$$

In Eq. (2.10), $A_{i,j}$ represents the availability of the jth individual component within the subsystem i.

Promising a significant level of business continuity in a cloud datacenter demands the activity in a system design stage to work in the HA method and to distinguish accessibility in the sixth decimal place. In this manner the evaluation of a system plan to perform a configuration trade-off requires a genuine point-by-point advancement of stochastic methods. Ongoing research has demonstrated various methodologies to create analytical stochastic methods for reliability and availability enumeration of various systems. The classification of analytical stochastic methods for the quantification of reliability metrics, which are typically utilized in practice, is explained as follows,

2.3.2.1 Non-State-Space Model

These models are also known as combinational models. They include models such as fault trees (FTs), reliability graphs (RGs) and reliability block diagrams (RBDs). These models permit the quick quantification of system reliability and availability with the assumptions of statistical independence [14]. FTs give an organized methodology utilizing a graphical representation of basic events causing a system failure. In any case, the FT just catches a single event of system failure as a top occasion. In this way if an alternative kind of system in a network, or all the more by and large an arrangement of systems, is involved in the modeling, extra FTs must be built. The FT is typically useful in demonstrating an individual system failure cause due to the system architecture. The RG has been widely utilized for network reliability quantification [15, 16], which is an acyclic graph with two distinct nodes marked: a source node(s), which has no incoming edge, and a sink (D), which has no outgoing edges. The edge in an RG indicates the component of the system to be modeled. The system, which is modeled by an RG, is viewed as reliable if at least (at any cost) one path with no failed edge between the source and the sink is found with an instinctive graphical representation. RG is beneficial in quantifying the reliability or availability of networks. Since an RG can be nested if other nodes are incorporated into the edges, the modeling by means of an RG can catch scalability from easy profound complex systems. RBDs give an alternative graphical modeling approach when accessibility-related system dependencies are thought about. In contrast with other combinational models, RG has a decent modeling power for complex networks over the other modeling tools. RG models were utilized to assess the reliability of various networks, for example, the dodecahedron network and 1973 ARPANET systems [17].

2.3.2.2 State-Space Models

State-space models are normally used to demonstrate complex interactions and properties within a system under proper assumptions. The state-space models are also useful in modeling large-scale systems when considering explicit properties with repetition throughout the large system; a variety of such state-space modeling techniques were used in modeling systems. Markov chain is one system among them that is often used to represent the state transition for quantifying different consistency metrics for availability and performance measurement. A Markov chain comprising all transitions named with rates is called a continuous time Markov chain (CTMC). In the event that its change is named, the model is called the discrete time Markov chain (DTMC). When a dispersion work is utilized for progress transition names, the model is a semi-Markov process (SMP) or Markov regenerative stochastic process (MRGP).

In [11], the research was stretched out with the consolidation of programming restorations alongside programming utilization, which were all modeled utilizing CTMC. In [18], the researchers utilized CTMC to show the VM subsystem and performed a point-by-point affectability investigation of accessibility and operational expenses for a double visualized server system (VSS). An SMP was utilized to quantify availability of a group of systems with disaster recovery in [19]. The other number of state-space models that are utilized for modeling complex systems are the Petri net–based model, such as the stochastic Petri net (SPN), stochastic reward nets (SRNs) and fluid stochastic Petri net (FSPN). A Petri net is a directed bipartite graph with two principle components including place and transitions. In the event that tokens are related with places, the PN is marked. The transition and allocation of tokens over the PN catch dynamic properties of the system to be modeled. In the event that all transitions are related with an exponential distribution of the firing time, the PN is an SPN. A generalized stochastic Petri net (GSPN) has an instantaneous transition and a planned transition. Some of the researchers also analyzed an SRN. When a rate is associated with each marking of the net in this way, numerous parts of a system would be represented by Boolean expression and arithmetic involving reward rates. The SRN has a modeling capacity to catch complex practices of a system in an exhaustive way while the model's size and intricacy are minimized altogether.

2.3.2.3 Hierarchical Models (Multi-Level Models)

There is a great deal of research on reliability and availability quantification of sophisticated systems in datacenters using hierarchical models. Hierarchical models are inherent in modeling large-sized and complex systems. The upper layers of an analytical hierarchical model are typically non–state-space model types, whereas in the lower level state-space models such as CTMC or SRN are used to capture complex operational behaviors or subsystems or individual components. There are a number of examples of the implementation of hierarchical models in datacenters. In [20], a hierarchical model consisting of an FT at the upper level and the different subsystems (hardware and software), a number of CTMC models are at the lower level. A two-level hierarchical model consisting of an FT and a CTMC was also developed to quantify a system of blade servers, with the FT as the overall system of multiple blade servers, whereas the CTMC corresponds to the physical subsystems [21]. In [22], the researchers proposed a three-level hierarchical model for a system with a higher level of complexity. The approach mixed RBDs and Markov chains to develop an availability model for a higher availability platform in the telecommunication industry.

2.3.3 Simulation of Availability

To illustrate the availability modeling and analysis, numerically consider the RBD of the IaaS provisioning systems (IPS) as shown in Figure 2.11. It demonstrates the average availability of a cloud system after 8760 hours of operation. Let A_{IPS} be the availability of IPS.

If a_1, a_2 and a_3 are its subsystems, the $A_{\text{IPS}} = a_1 \times a_2 \times a_3$, where a_1, a_2 and a_3 represent the availability of the subsystems, such as hardware, virtualized platform and applications, respectively.

If a_1 is the availability of the hardware subsystem, then it is determined by its constituent components, such as processor, memory, storage, network and power systems. The availability of the subsystem is the product of its constituent components, which are represented as

$$a_1 = a_{1,1} \times a_{1,2} \times a_{1,3} \times a_{1,4} \times a_{1,5}$$

Similarly, the availability of virtualized platform a_2 is $a_2 = a_{2,1} \times a_{2,2} \times a_{2,3} \times a_{21,4}$.

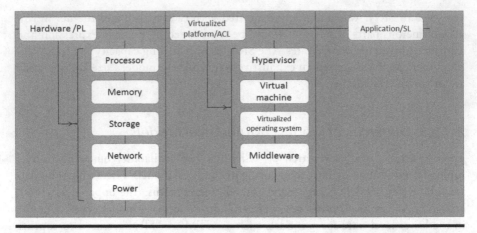

Figure 2.11   IPS in RBD.

The constituent components of the virtualized platform a_2 — $a_{2,1}$, $a_{2,2}$, $a_{2,3}$ and $a_{2,4}$ — represent the VM, hypervisor, virtualized operating systems and middleware. The mean time between failures (*MTBF*) and *MTTF* are estimated by using the probability distribution model of failure. The availability of these components is determined by substituting the *MTBF* and *MTTF* values. As a result, the availability at the subsystem level is analyzed based on the system RBDs as below. Substituting the values of the constituent's available components, the hardware availability a_1 [23] is represented as

$$a_1 = \left[MTTBF_{1,1} / \left(MTBF_{1,1} + MTTR_{1,1} \right) \right]$$
$$\times \left[MTTBF_{1,2} / \left(MTBF_{1,2} + MTTR_{1,2} \right) \right]$$
$$\times \left[MTTBF_{1,3} / \left(MTBF_{1,3} + MTTR_{1,3} \right) \right]$$
$$\times \left[MTTBF_{1,4} / \left(MTBF_{1,4} + MTTR_{1,5} \right) \right]$$
$$\times \left[MTTBF_{1,5} / \left(MTBF_{1,5} + MTTR_{1,5} \right) \right]$$

Considering their numerical values as illustrated in Figure 2.12, the availability is

$$a_1 = \left[296 / (296 + 1.5) \right] \times \left[494 / (494 + 2.5) \right]$$
$$\times \left[692 / (692 + 3.5) \right] \times \left[98 / (98 + 0.5) \right]$$
$$\times \left[395 / (395 + 2) \right]$$
$$= 0.975$$

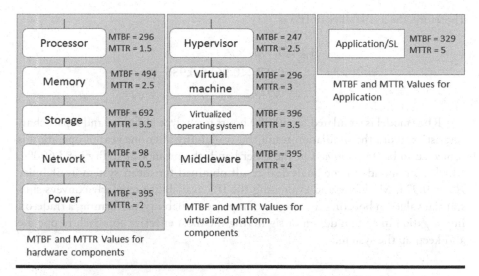

Figure 2.12 IPS components and their constituents' availability value.

Similarly, substituting the values of components available in a virtualized platform availability a_2

$$a_2 = \left[MTTBF_{2,1} / (MTBF_{2,1} + MTTR_{2,1}) \right]$$
$$\times \left[MTTBF_{2,2} / (MTBF_{2,2} + MTTR_{2,2}) \right]$$
$$\times \left[MTTBF_{2,3} / (MTBF_{2,3} + MTTR_{2,3}) \right]$$
$$\times \left[MTTBF_{2,4} / (MTBF_{124} + MTTR_{2,5}) \right]$$

$$a_2 = \left[247 / (247 + 1.5) \right] \times \left[296 / (296 + 3) \right]$$
$$\times \left[396 / (296 + 3.5) \right] \times \left[395 / (98 + 4) \right]$$
$$= 0.961$$

Also let us assume the numerical value of *MTBF* and *MTTR* for an application as $MTBF = 329$ and $MTTR = 5$

The application availability a_3 is

$$a_3 = \left[MTTBF / (MTBF + MTTR) \right]$$
$$= 329 / (329 + 5)$$
$$= 0.986$$

Therefore, the availability of IPS is

$$A_{IPS} = a_1 \times a_2 \times a_3$$
$$= 0.975 \times 0.961 \times 0.986$$
$$= 0.924$$

The RBD model is simulated for 30,000 hours to analyze its failure and repair characteristics. From the simulation result the availability after one year of operation is projected to be 93.6000%. On the other hand, the mean availability is 93.600%, which corresponds to the analytical result obtained for mean system availability $A_{IPS} = 0.924$. Modeling and evaluating the IPS availability regularly conveys substantial values in boosting the efforts to improve availability, performing a trade-off investigation in system design or signifying the most effective approach to operate and keep up the system.

2.4 Recovery Services

The recovery mechanism is accountable for guaranteeing failure mitigation performance through the most common techniques like redundancy [24]. This method provides HA during the crash at the physical machine, VM and application levels. The recovery mechanism includes simple and smart techniques as illustrated in Figure 2.13. The smart recovery mechanism uses monitoring and checkpoint services. This provides an efficient repair with minimum damage to the running applications, whereas in the simple recovery mechanism the faulty application can be recovered by rebooting it in a healthy node to provide service continuity, but all state data are lost. A smart recovery technique suggested in [25] guarantees and maintains an application backup synchronized with active applications but

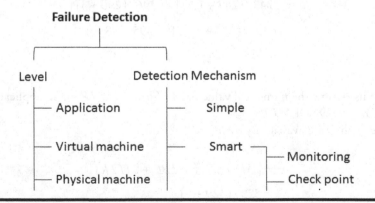

Figure 2.13   Recovery classification.

deployed in different VMs through a fault tolerance mechanism. In [26], Imran et al. proposed the recovery process by adopting an active replication technique with a controller, which maintains a priority list through backup ID from resources. Whenever a failure occurs, the message is communicated to the other nodes in the list for service continuation.

2.4.1 Information Replication

Information replication is utilized to keep up state consistency between copies. The principle issues related to this mechanism are to manage the trade-off among uniformity and the resource utilization. In cloud services this is accomplished either by having a redundant state of the system (checkpoint) or by replaying input to all replicas. Classification of information replication is shown in Figure 2.14. Information replication methodology is mainly divided into two types: look-step and checkpoint based.

The look-step methodology is also known as "state machine replication". Its main objectives are to assign identical tasks to be executed by all copies of an application in an organized way, then ensuring message request and state. These methodologies are common in the Tcloud platform [27], which is applied to the state maintenance of application copies. It also maintains consistency among the objects stored in a group of cloud storage services. A similar methodology is applied in the cloud-Niagara middleware [19] to offer a service to check resources used and to prepare failure notices with insignificant delay. Referring to this, an identical methodology is proposed by Pereez-Sorrosal et al. [28], that uses a multi-version database reserve structure to help elastic replications of multi-tier stateless and stateful applications. This implements a replica of applications and database by introducing

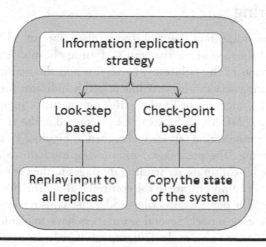

Figure 2.14   Classification of information replications.

a multicast protocol, which maintains data consistency between replicas. The objectives of this approach are to maintain elasticity and failure management. Checkpoint-based replication provides continuous updates of a dynamic application to its standby replicas. To enhance the reliability, it is desirable that application with fewer checkpoint replicas distributed over various components guard against failure. A centralized checkpoint method assigns all checkpoint replicas in a distributed mode. Many researchers proposed various replication strategies. Some of the replication mechanisms result in an unacceptable resource usage overhead due to tracking a large number of communications between applications propagated to all replicas. In contrast, the checkpointing occurs periodically between the active and standby replicas at a time interval of milliseconds. This provides a better trade-off between resource usage overhead and updates. Another cost-effective approach is proposed by Chan and Chieu [12], which is an HA mechanism in a virtualized environment by utilizing VM snapshots coupled with a smart on-demand snapshot collection mechanism. Its objective is to extend the snapshot service to include the checkpoint data of a VM.

Kanso and Lemieux [6] agreed that in a PaaS cloud service, the checkpoint service must be performed at the application level to manage the inside application failure. These application failures might be unnoticed in a VM-based HAS. Research proposes a mechanism of sending its state details to the HAS through a well-defined checkpoint interface. Manno [8] proposed a checkpoint mechanism with a direct approach for both application and process checkpoint levels through a distributed checkpoint repository. In [29], An et al. proposed a middleware technique converging on HA for real-time applications. The authors derived this mechanism from technologies such as Remus, Xen and Open Nebula.

2.5 Monitoring

Monitoring is an important control mechanism for an HA cloud service. Monitoring will help to observe the status of an application continuously. This enables the detection of the failure of the replica and the malfunctioning of the replica. A monitoring service also acts like a health indicator for the central processing unit (CPU), memory utilization, disk and network input-output time to respond to requests [24]. All of these can be performed at the virtual and physical machine level. The monitoring service is classified in Figure 2.15 as push- and polling-based monitoring. The push-based monitoring mechanism is an application that is responsible for continuously sending messages to the controller, whenever it is required. This will communicate to the controller about the changes in the monitored applications. The publish-subscribe model mechanism is implemented in the push-based monitoring model. Several researchers have implemented push-based monitoring for different services. In [30], a push-based monitoring mechanism is adopted in web service workflow to deliver fault tolerance. The fault monitoring is

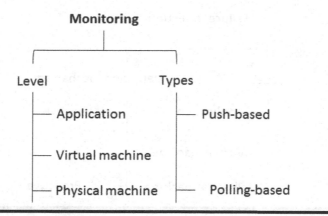

Figure 2.15   Classification of monitoring.

implemented through Zookeeper's watches to check if a ZooKeeper's ephemeral node is active. The controller also notifies in case of failure. Push-based monitoring with a publish-subscribe model is employable in a profoundly unique condition of cloud computing for timely decision-making in which the monitoring controllers are subscribers and monitoring agents are publishers.

The most common type of monitoring technique is polling-based monitoring, which functions by periodically sending an echo signal to the hosted applications. These details are communicated to the operating system of the host by using the standard communication protocols such as Internet Control Message Protocol (ICMP) or Simple Network Management Protocol (SNMP), in the case of a web-based application using the Hyper Text Transfer Protocol (HTTP) [24]. The polling-based monitoring can also be sent from a backup replica to an active mechanism. The polling-based agent can be implemented directly in the application by using a standard application programming interface (API), which handles the memory sent by the cloud or outside application. Using this type of intrusive mechanism, the internal status of an application can be monitored. This enables the earlier detection of the adverse conditions and offers a service such as checkpointing. Both of these monitoring approaches contribute to the HA cloud services [12]. Among this polling, the host failure is periodically monitored by an agent and the host notifies the monitoring controller. Global-level monitoring using the publish-subscribe model combined with local-level monitoring by polling is implemented as a hierarchical monitoring mechanism in [10].

2.6 Failure Detection

Failure detection is a process of cloud system for fault identification that provides the required information for service to ratify the issues to maintain service continuity. There are many failure detection techniques proposed by researchers. In [24],

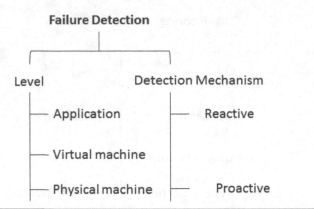

Figure 2.16 Classification of failure detection.

the researchers used the mechanism to detect faults such as ping, heartbeat and exceptions. Based on the detection mechanisms, the failure detection can be classified into two types, reactive and proactive [26], as illustrated in Figure 2.16. The former one waits for a KEEP ALIVE message and recognizes the failure after being held up for some time. The latter method is tougher and more capable of finding the anomalous behavior in the cloud environment, checking the detection mechanism understanding the data gathered to validate whether the failure has occurred.

Among these two methods, the reactive method is simpler and implemented more often. In [12], the researchers proposed a heartbeat technique for failure detection, where Chan and Chieu considered the failure detection by implementing the heartbeat hosted in each node of the datacenter. An absence of heartbeat is an indication of failure; hence, the intended recovery process begins. Alexandrov and Dimov [26] proposed a proactive mechanism of failure detection, which is an intelligent system for monitoring and notification of failure, and proposed a mathematical model for the early detection of failure. In [29], the researchers proposed an architecture with the entity called local fault manager (LFM), which gathers resource information of these nodes, such as CPU, memory usage, connectivity and input-output communication, communicating it to the next layer for processing and decision-making. LFM also runs a HAS, which establishes synchronization between primary and backup VMs. Whenever there is a failure, the primary VM becomes active.

There are several reasons for cloud service failure, such as failures due to human error, extreme spike in customer demand, cloud service provider downtime and failure due to a third-party service provider. Effective steps are taken to mitigate these failures. The cloud failure may lead to unavailability of the cloud resources. Due to the dynamic nature of the changing workload in datacenters, it is extremely difficult to collect the real-time data to predict the failure. On the other hand, the

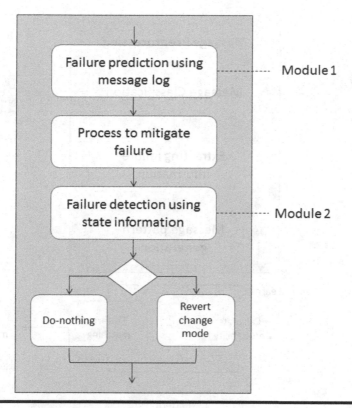

Figure 2.17   Failure detection and prediction.

cloud datacenter's hardware and software components are constantly replaced or updated. Hence, an accurate failure detection mechanism is necessary to distinguish between the normal variations in datacenter characteristics and real-time failures. Also, if the cloud service providers are able to proactively predict the failure, then the effect of failure across the cloud system resolves before it leads to a catastrophe. A simple flowchart depicting the detection and prediction of failure is given in Figure 2.17. This model includes four steps: failure prediction, mitigation of the effect of failure, failure detection using state information and in step four if failure is not detected we revert back to the processes when the failure was predicted.

2.6.1 Failure Prediction

In this stage, the failure prediction module will predict the failure in the datacenters by fetching and analyzing the real-time information. Forecasting effectively is challenging due to the message format and dynamically changing configuration settings. Failure prediction architecture to fulfill the above requirement is depicted in Figure 2.18.

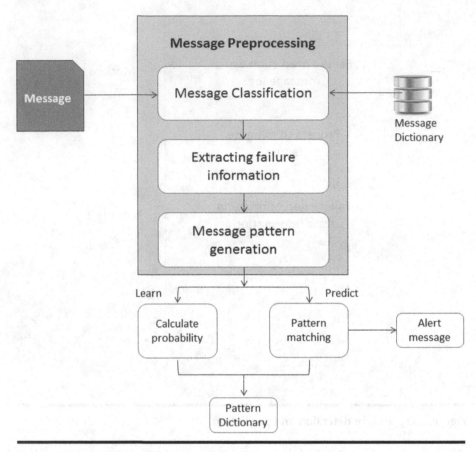

Figure 2.18   Failure prediction architecture.

The message preprocessor stage classifies the message input and derives the pattern for it. The probability of the message pattern coexisting with the failure is assessed by the learning phase. In the third stage, a comparison between the real-time messages with the learned message is predicted. This stage forecasts the possibility of failure. The message preprocessor stage gathers the message recorded in the message log to analyze the message pattern. The preprocessor involves message classification, separating the failure information from the message and message pattern generation. A sample of the message gathered is shown in Figure 2.19, which includes four fields such as message text, time stamp, source and priority. Using this message sample and using the message dictionary, the message will be classified based on their similarity index.

Let D_i be a set of words to the ith message type. The words corresponding to this message are di_1, di_2, di_3....

For a given message m_j, which needs to be classified, it is split into set of words as $w_j = \{w_{j1}, w_{j2}, \ldots w_{jn}\}$, where n represents the number of words in w_j.

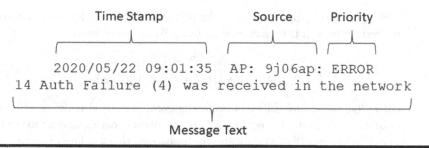

Figure 2.19 Message sample gathered.

The degree of similarity between D_i and w_j is S_{ij} is represented as

$$S_{ij} = \sum_{k=1}^{n} S_{ik}$$

$$\text{where} \quad S_{ik} = 1 \text{ if } w_{jk} \in D_i$$
$$S_{ik} = 0 \text{ if } w_{jk} \notin D_i$$

Once the similarity score for all i is calculated, the candidate message type c for a set of words D_c with a maximum score as S_{ij} is obtained. The similarity score S is compared with the threshold value t_{classify} to decide whether the given message is in the same class or a newly created one. If $S > t_{\text{classify}}$, the given message m_j is classified as class type c; otherwise, it is treated as a new word not in D_c and added to message dictionary.

From the message input sample the failure information is extracted. The cloud administration uses the priority information in the message to decide about the severity of the failure. If the priority field contains ERROR, ALERT, CRITICAL or EMERGENCY, it is an indication of the occurrence of failure. Details obtained from this failure information are extracted as depicted in Table 2.2 and used later for the learning process.

Message pattern generation: Message pattern is expressed as the sequence of messages in the message window. The message pattern is stated by using a set of binary message types in the window instead of using event vectors.

Table 2.2 Sample Failure Information Extracted

ID	Time Stamp		Failure Type
75	2020/05/22	09:01:35	CODE 10 FAULT IN AVAILABILITY OF PORCESS
76	2020/05/22	09:02:23	CODE 20 INSUFFICIENT MEMORY

Message patterns help to estimate the probability that a failure has occurred in a certain period. It is estimated by using Bayes' theorem as

$$P\left(G_i \mid mp_k\right) = \frac{P(G_i)P(m(mp_k)) \mid G_i}{P(G_i)P(m(mp_k)) \mid G_i + P(\neg G_i)P(m(mp_k) \mid \neg G_i)} \quad (2.11)$$

where $P(x)$ is the probability of occurring event x, $P(x \mid y)$ is the conditional probability of x given y has occurred, G_i is a set of event corresponding to the ith type of failure and $P(x \mid y)$ indicates the probability that a failure Fi occurs in a predictive period after using the frequency of the time stamp of mp_k.

Equation (2.11) is simplified into Eq. (2.12) by using the number of each event

$$P(G_i \mid mp_k) = \frac{n(m(mp_k)) \cap G_i}{n(m(mp_k))} \quad (2.12)$$

$$n(m(mp_k)) \cap G_i = \sum_{i=1}^{k} n\left(mp_1, mp_k, F_i\right)$$

$$n(mp_1, mp_k, F_i) = \begin{cases} 1 \text{ if } m(mp_k) = m(mp_l) \text{ and } (t(F_i) - d) \leq t(mp_l) < t(F_i) \\ 0 \text{ otherwise} \end{cases}$$

$$n(mp_i, mp_k, F_i) = \begin{cases} 1 \text{ if } m(mp_k) = m(mp_i) \text{ and } (t(F_i) - d) \leq t(mp_l) < t(F_i) \\ 0 \text{ otherwise} \end{cases}$$

where $t(F_i)$ is the time stamp of F_i and d is the predictive period length

$$n(m(mp_k)) = \sum_{l=1}^{k} g(mp_l, mp_k)$$

where

$$g(mp_l, mp_k) = \begin{cases} 1 \text{ if } m(mp_s) = m(mp_l) \\ 0 \text{ otherwise} \end{cases}$$

The above equations help to estimate the co-occurrence probability of an observed message pattern and the failure occurrence using the message pattern dictionary.

As explained in the previous section, failure can be estimated utilizing the message pattern and probability from the pattern dictionary. For a given message pattern (mp_k), the pattern dictionary is referred to and the column matching the message pattern is selected. Using this probability for each type of message, failure is assessed. If its value is higher than the threshold, it is considered as a failure, and steps are taken to rectify it.

2.6.2 Failure Detection Using State Information

The objective of the failure detection and prediction model is to develop a probabilistic model, based on the runtime state information like CPU utilization, memory usage, CPU idle time, number of input-output operations per unit time, temperature of the cloud server and so forth. These parameters provide two types of information, one in which the cloud system is behaving normally and the other situation represents the occurrence of failure. The information gathered is divided into two classes, class 1 and class 2, and saved in this module. If the module fails, due to the failure of other modules, there is no provision for getting the state information for further analysis, through which we can calculate probabilities related to class 2 for each of the runtime state parameters. The data gathered may not be sufficient for a supervised learning algorithm to estimate probabilities related to class 2. To solve this problem, a semi-supervised method can be adopted, which helps to build a model based on the major class. An unbalanced data set of the state information may be used to calculate the probabilities relating to class 1, which contributes major data. State information-related data are gathered from the datacenters. To maintain their uniform format, a common transformation technique is also used. These data sets contain many features. Using dimensionality reduction will help to obtain x_a new data set with only a relevant set of features. The dimension reduction technique used here is a relevance deduction.

> ***Relevance deduction:*** Let a data set with many features be represented as $x_1, x_2, x_3 \ldots x_n$.
> Now consider a set of these features as x_a and x_b. To calculate the mutual information that indicates the covariance between the two features as

$$\text{Mutual Info}_{(x_a, x_b)} = \sum_{x_a} \sum_{x_b} P(x_a, x_b) \log \frac{P(x_a, x_b)}{P(x_a)P(x_b)} \qquad (2.13)$$

In Eq. (2.13), if mutual information between two features x_a and x_b are minimum, then we can consider that they are completely independent; on the other hand, if they are maximum, the features are identical. The purpose of using this mutual information is to minimize the significance of a selected subset of features. If a feature has a high mutual information with other features, it should be excluded from the subset. The index for calculating the relevance is defined as

$$\text{Index}(x_a) = \sum_{b=1}^{a-1} I(x_a, x_b) + \sum_{b=a+1}^{n} I(x_a, x_b)$$

A high relevance between the features is indicated as two features with a linear relation. The unnecessary features are excluded by calculating their index values as

$$\text{Index}(x_a) = \sum_{b=1}^{a-n} (\text{Mutual Info}(x_a, x_b))$$

Redundancy deduction: For feature selection, it has been realized that a mix of independent features does not really lead to a good performance of grouping and probabilistic analysis. The presence of a redundant dimension can cause issues. Principle component analysis (PCA) has been broadly utilized and demonstrated to be powerful in excluding redundancy of a subset of features. To detect the failure, let us consider a statistical model *m* with reduced dimensionality, which takes a data point as input, and provide its probability. An unsupervised model is used to learn the parameters related to the model. When the output of the model is $m(d) < t$, a data point *d* is detected. Where *t* is the threshold value, it is determined based on assumptions and historical knowledge. An input data point *d* can be classified as normal behavior or abnormal behavior, but a majority of classes are treated as normal behavior, based on their probability of its occurrence.

To develop the probabilistic model and ensure high detection accuracy, a group of Bayesian submodels is selected, which represents a multi-model probability distribution. This submodel is a non-parametric data model in which no single simple parameterized probability density is assumed. Its probability distribution is determined from the frequency counts of training data. Each submodel has an estimated prior probability $P(m)$, where *m* is the submodel index. For a data point *d*, the probability estimate assigned is

$$P(d) = \sum_{m \in \text{submodels}} P(d \mid m)P(m)$$

where $P(d \mid m)$ is the probability that submodel *m* generates data point *d*. This indicates that all submodels contribute to the probability of each data point. Using Bayes' rule, data point *d* assigned to a submodel *m* with probability $P(m \mid d)$ value can be determined. This methodology permits the model to fit the gathered information better when it is ambiguous which submodel should be utilized to describe the probability of a data point. After significant decrease and redundancy reduction as depicted, the features of a data point are conditionally independent in each submodel. For a data point *d* with *k* features after a dimensional decrease, the conditional probability of the data point on a submodel *m* is

$$P(d \mid m) = \prod_{i=1}^{k} P(d_i \mid m) \tag{2.14}$$

In the discrete Bayesian submodels used here, the values of each feature are placed in a finite number of intervals. The original value of a feature is replaced by the discrete indexes. To estimate the probability that a feature d_i takes a given value v based on the counted frequency in the training data set, the Bayesian expectation maximization (EM) algorithm is adopted.

$$P(d_i = v \mid m) = \text{count}(d_i = v \text{ and } m) / \text{count}(m)$$

$$P(m) = \text{count}(m) / \sum_{n \in \text{submodels}} \text{count}(n) \tag{2.15}$$

Count(.) represents the number of data points in the training data set that satisfy a specified condition.

$$\text{count}(d_i = v \text{ and } m) = \sum_{d \in \text{trainingset}} P(m \mid d).I(d_i, v)$$

$$\text{count}(m) = \sum_{d \in \text{trainingset}} P(m \mid d)$$

$$I(d_i, v) = \begin{cases} 1, & \text{if } d_i = v \\ 0, & \text{if } d_i \neq v \end{cases}$$

A number of submodels are selected to train the ensemble model. The submodel initialized the model by assigning the data points randomly. The EM algorithm is applied to determine the submodel and conditional data probability $P(m)$ and $P(d|m)$, respectively, then using Eq. (2.15) to calculate the data *probability*.

2.6.3 Supervised Failure Prediction by Decision Tree

In the previous section, we described the unsupervised learning method of failure detection. This method identifies the abnormal behavior of the datacenters. The report generated out of this analysis will be beneficial to decide the status of the cloud system, as failure or as normal. Details related to these data points will be labeled, which is valuable information about the cloud system status under failures. They ought to be exploited in failure detection [31]. The supervised learning technique explained in this section with the help of decision tree classification is helpful to forecast failure occurrence using health-related performance data with labels. Here the decision tree is a hierarchical non-parametric model with local regions identified in a sequence of recursive splits. The structure of a decision tree includes internal decision nodes n and terminal leaves. The internal decision node n implements a test function $f_n(d)$ and results in a discrete outcome labeling the branches. When the test hits a leaf node, the classification labeled on the leaf is output. Among the many techniques available for failure detection, the decision tree is not always the most viable classifier. It has the main advantage of a fast localization of the region covering information and yielding human interpretable outcome, which is significant if the strategy is to be received by the genuine cloud administrator.

Learning by means of a decision tree involves the selection of a specific branch of the tree, and the layers in it. For example, let x be the feature set. For binary classification

$$\text{The class label} \in \{0, 1\} \qquad \left| \begin{array}{ll} 1 & - \text{ failure} \\ 0 & - \text{ normal} \end{array} \right.$$

In a decision tree the root node maintains all of the health-related performance data. At each node the data set is split according to the value of one particular feature. Splits are chosen to expand the gain in information. This procedure continues until no additional split is conceivable or the node contains only one class. After the tree is constructed the sub-branches with low overall gain value are clipped to abstain from overfitting. The best part of the split is tested by impurity. A split is pure, if after the split, for all branches all the information taking a branch belongs to the same class. The value of impurity is quantified by means of entropy. The entropy for the nth node of a decision tree is

$$C_i \, H(n) = \sum_{i=1}^{j} P_n^i \log_2 P_n^i \qquad (2.16)$$

where P_n^i represents the probability of class C_i, its value is 0 or 1, given that a data point reaches node n and j is the number of classes. It denotes the failure or normal class ($j = 2$). The gain function G for feature x_i at node n is defined as

$$G(x_i, n) = H(n) - H(x_i, n) \qquad (2.17)$$

The second term in Eq. (2.17) indicates the sum of entropy of the sub-nodes after making the split based on feature x_i.

The decision tree algorithm works as follows:

■ The algorithm begins with the root node, which comprises all the features.
■ For every x_i values, the gain value from splitting x_i is obtained as $G(x_i, n)$.
■ The highest gain value is selected based on the feature x_{best}.
■ A decision node that split on x_{best} is created.
■ The pending process is repeated on the sub-list obtained by splitting x_{best} and adding those nodes as sub-nodes.

2.6.4 Proactive Failure Detection

Proactive failure detection using the decision tree process is repeated too deep into the tree, until all leaf nodes are not affected and there was no error during the process [31]. The sub-trees that cause overfitting are clipped off. From the initial labeled health-related data, the pruning data set is kept aside, unused in training. The sub-tree is replaced by a leaf node marked with the training data points covered by the sub-tree. In the event that the leaf node does not perform worse than the sub-tree on the pruning set, then prune the sub-tree and keep the leaf node, because the additional complexity of the sub-tree is not vital, or else keep the original sub-tree.

Once the decision tree is developed and pruned, it is used for failure detection. In the case of a new and unlabeled data point, the failure prediction traverses the decision tree from the root. The internal decision nodes are so important that in each such node the predictor reads the value of the feature associated with the node from the input data point and selects a path to a child node, consequently. This process is repeated in the entire depth of the tree until a leaf node is hit. As a result, the predictor outputs the label of the leaf as normal or failure. A better accuracy is achieved by means of an ensemble of trees. Finally, a failure prediction decision is made based on the voting by selecting the majority one.

2.6.4.1 Performance Analysis

The performance of the designed proactive failure management framework is analyzed by collecting runtime performance data. The data are collected by means of health-monitoring tools, and failure events are forecast by an ensemble of Bayesian predictor and decision tree classifiers [31]. In this section, the framework for the automatic performance failure management system discussed above is evaluated by using the data obtained from a production cloud system. The cloud infrastructure used for this to obtain the test data includes hundreds of high-performance servers in an institute-wide cloud computing environment. These servers comprise high configuration CPU and large memory units interconnected by higher bandwidth communication links and high-performance Ethernet switches. A set of large applications including large database application materials and metallodrugs property analysis applications, chemical kinetics simulations, genome and proteome analysis, molecular dynamics simulations, large database applications and so forth are also included. The cloud system also is open to receive a large set of sequential and parallel programs using a web-based interface. The data required for runtime performance are recovered periodically. A data record covers the statistics of key components of the cloud server elements including CPU usage, memory and swap space utilization, process creation, paging and page faults, task switching activity, input-output and data transfer, interrupts and network activity, power management and so forth.

As a first step of the process, the data are cleaned. The missing parameters of the features in the data are filled by the average of two adjacent values. Once the data are cleaned the training data set is parsed and passed for the feature selection component. The features selected for the process are %system, %user, %idle, kbbuffer, pgpgout/s, rxpck/s, lxpck/s, fault/s and tps. The redundancy among these selected features is reduced by using the PCA algorithm and reducing the dimension further to two. The failure detection and prediction are analyzed using the true positive rate and false positive rate as

$$true \ positive \ rate = \frac{true \ positive}{true \ positive + false \ negative}$$

$$false \ positive \ rate = \frac{false \ positive}{false \ positive + true \ negative}$$

Average prediction performance is achieved by considering a set of validations. In the training set, 10% of the normal data are used for cross-validation. The true-positive rate and false-positive rate are calculated to plot performance and failure detection as depicted in Figures 2.20 and 2.21, which provide the prediction accuracy with different threshold values in the receiver operating characteristic (ROC) curve. An optimum performance is observed in the performance curve, which is with a high true-positive rate and low false-positive rate. These curves are able to predict the failure in the health-related data set. Also, by using the eight features

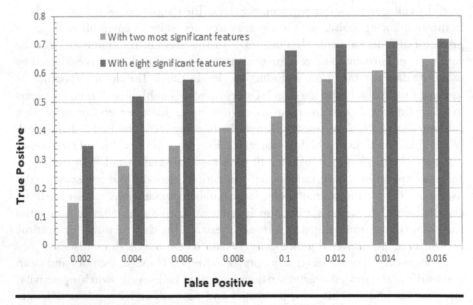

Figure 2.20   The ensemble of the Bayesian submodels.

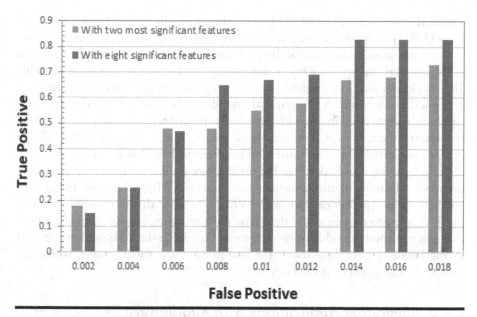

Figure 2.21 Decision tree classifiers.

mentioned above prediction accuracy is better than that by using only the two most significant features chosen from relevance and reduction procedures.

Failure detection performance failure detection performance.

2.7 HA at the Application Level

HA at the application level is based on deploying the SAForum middleware in the cloud. The SAForum solution involves a degree of difficulty that is not reasonable for the cloud model, which depends on the idea of rearranging the ease of usability features. In the following section, the middleware deployment aspect is explained first and then different solutions for simplifying the usability aspects.

2.7.1 Middleware

The middleware service in cloud computing supports the HA requirements of applications. Its objective is to manage how to operate the services, configure them and make decisions according to the information acquired. The cloud middleware is a set of software components collaborating to provide the cloud services. Those components include the management interfaces, scheduling, messaging, storage management and so forth. The VMs, although they run on the virtualization layer, are considered to be managed by the cloud middleware. OpenSAF is an open source system that suggests and implements the SAForum applications interface specifications (AIS). The AMF implemented by OpenSAF is a middleware that is responsible for sustaining service availability. It is also responsible for the implementation of the essential checkpoint services and storing the checkpoint data incrementally. The checkpoint data can be used to protect applications against HA middleware. The middleware monitors the physical and virtual resources in a datacenter and repairs or restarts them in case of failure. It also monitors the capability of the VMs and restarts them in case of failure, using the capabilities of a hypervisor. This is possible by establishing communication between the hypervisor and the HA middleware by using standard APIs. The middleware implementation will guarantee the service of the cloud middleware segment and the VMs, and provide HA. It will not remove the application within the VMs HA, since this implementation will not have access to the content of the VMs. The monitoring is possible by the implementation of another middleware implementation inside the VMs, which responds to the failure. Figure 2.22 shows the two middleware organizations, which are completely independent of each other.

2.7.2 Integrating Applications with Middleware

The three methods to integrate applications with the SAForum middleware are discussed below.

> *No integration:* This methodology is non-intrusive, and it does not require any changes to the application code. The integration is done through the AFM configuration alone by referring to the life cycle control (startup/end) contents. The middleware can identify the application failure by passively observing and quickly responding to these failures by restarting or failing

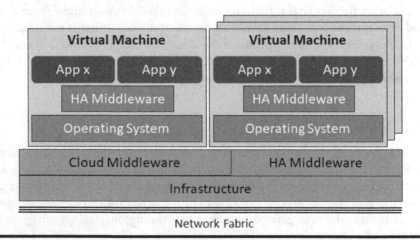

Figure 2.22 Middleware implementation inside VMs.

the application based on the configuration requirements. This mechanism is suitable for stateless applications that do not need to checkpoint their state.

Full integration: This mechanism is possibly a more interfering approach that requires the application to deploy the API essential for the middleware to enable two-way communication. With this methodology, the application can benefit from other middleware services like massage passing, checkpointing and so forth.

Proxied: In this method the application interacts with the middleware through an allotted proxy component that facilitates the interaction between them. The proxy is a completely integrated component that deploys the middleware APIs. The middleware cannot control the life cycle pattern of the proxied without the proxy.

The above three methods indicate that the application description is incorporated into the AMF configuration. These integrations are incorporated in runtime by defining an upgrade campaign, which enables it on the fly. To address the implementation issues of these complex middleware APIs, for the HA integration the cloud users are defined as two agents: (1) the integration agent, which dynamically upgrades the system configuration to update it to the middleware and make it aware of the added new applications, and (2) an HA agent that will interact with the stateful applications.

i. ***State-aware applications:*** In a state-aware application the integration only satisfies the service availability aspect but not the service continuity in case of failure. The state-aware application defined is simply an application that is aware of its state. This state information can be saved as needed. The state-aware application tries to acquire the last saved state information from an HA agent. If such a state does not exist, then the application will start from the default state; otherwise, it will continue executing from the last saved information as in Figure 2.23.

ii. ***Integration agent:*** This is a cloud user that provides the basic information, such as the script to instantiate/terminate its application, and the redundancy model according to which the middleware will protect the application. The user can also provide the instantiation scripts. This enables the standardized monitoring framework (SMF), which automatically deploys the applications on several nodes, without any operator intervention. This information is fed into two generators, the configuration generator and the upgrade-campaign generator.

The characteristic of the configuration generator is explained in [32]. It automatically generates the configuration XML file by gathering user input. The factors of these generators are extended to select the needed HA agents to maintain the state of the application, and include their information as instantiate-command arguments to the state-aware applications. The sate-aware application provides

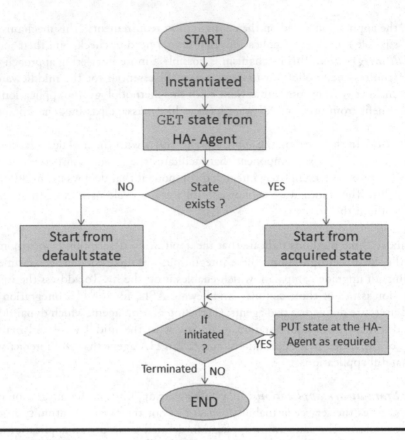

Figure 2.23 State-aware application.

the information that identifies its HA agent to acquire its state and then check-point its state.

The upgrade-campaign generator generates an upgrade campaign by gathering input from the AMF configuration file. It then acts as an input for the SMF framework of the middleware, which automatically installs the application and updates the system information model using information model management (IMM). The IMM will update the changes to the AMF; thereafter AMF will instantiate the application and maintain its availability. The same approaches are also used for future upgrades to the application with minimum service disruption. The integration agent workflow is shown in Figure 2.24.

2.7.3 HA Agent

The main objective of the presence of the HA agent is to abstract the composite middleware APIs that are needed for the state. The HA agent maintains the state of the state-aware applications. Software provides two interfaces, one

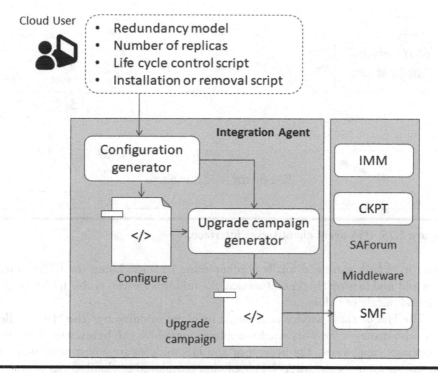

Figure 2.24   Integration agent workflow.

of which allows it to interact with the middleware. As a requirement of this, the software is fully integrated with the middleware and by the other interface, the state of the applications can be saved and retrieved by the state-aware application by means of the representational state transfer (REST) protocol. This process defines a client-server communication as shown in Figure 2.25, where the state-aware application functions as a client and the HA agent as a server.

The advantages of using REST are that it does not need to know the physical address of the server, which allows the replication of the HA agents across the cluster, and it uses the virtual address to connect the agent. The HA agent acts as a software component with the key functions such as accepting the application request in a generic format, processing them and responding to them in the specified format without utilizing much information concerning the application for which it is managing the state.

By implementing HA at the application, the user information pertaining to the application and its availability requirement is processed by the integration agent component and produces an upgrade campaign. This acts as an input to the middleware. It deploys the application and instantiates it and identifies its HA agent. The application then uses the REST interface to acquire its last state, executing it

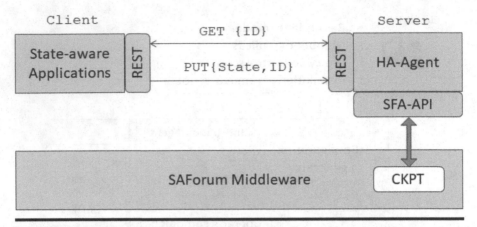

Figure 2.25 HA agent client-server interface.

from its default state and finally checkpointing its state. Using the REST interface and middleware checkpoint service, the middleware also is able to detect and respond in case of failure.

The HA of cloud service is achieved by cloud middleware. The HA middleware also manages the VMs stateless applications, which can be restarted using the hypervisor capabilities. The hypervisor and HA middleware will communicate to each other using a standard API. HA solution is deployed by cloud service providers at two levels: (1) in the cloud infrastructure level, which maintains the availability of the cloud middleware, and (2) in the cloud service, such as the PaaS level, the cloud users are allocated VMs with middleware and agents deployed. The cloud user's application now can be automatically implemented in the cloud datacenters and made highly available using integration agents.

2.8 Conclusion

Cloud computing systems are susceptible for the failure of infrastructure and software components. The effects of the systems are significant on both the system performance and administration. In this chapter, an effort has been made to analyze the different mechanisms for proactive failure management, such as monitoring, redundancy, failure detection and recovery, to achieve HA. The cloud service availability is evaluated based on the NIST orchestration model. The component-level availability is evaluated by defining the RBDs of the subsystems/components and their logical relationship among them. Once the anomalies are detected, the status of the system either as a failure or as normal and data gathered out of this are explored to forecast the future failure occurrence. Failure management for the application level is proposed for the cloud computing environment.

References

1. P. Heidari, M. Hormati, M. Toeroe, Y. Al Ahmad, and F. Khendek, "Integrating open SAF high availability solution with open stack," Services (SERVICES), 2015 IEEE World Congress on IEEE, pp 229–236, 2015. [Online]. Available: http://ieeexplore.ieee.org/document/7196529/?arnumber=7196529.
2. T. Dillon, C. Wu, and E. Chang, Cloud Computing: Issues and Challenges. New York: John Wiley & Son, Inc., 2010.
3. G. E. Gonçalves, P. T. Endo, T. Cordeiro, A. Palhares, D. Sadok, J. Kelner, B. Melander, and J. Mangs, "Resource allocation in clouds: Concepts, tools and research challenges," XXIX SBRC-Gramado-RS, 2011. [Online]. Available: http://sbrc2011.facom.ufms.br/files/mc/mc5.pdf.
4. OpenSAF. Availability management framework. [Online]. Available: http://devel.opensaf.org/SAI-AIS-AMF-B.04.01.AL.pdf. Accessed Oct 2016.
5. Y. Wu and G. Huang, "Model-based high availability configuration framework for cloud," Proceedings of the 2013 Middleware Doctoral Symposium. ACM. p. 6, 2013 [Online]. Available: http://dl.acm.org/citation.cfm?id=2541595.
6. Kanso, Lemieux, "Achieving high availability at the application level in the cloud," IEEE Sixth International Conference on Cloud Computing, 2013, ISBN:978-0-7695-5028-2.
7. A. Lenk, M. Klems, J. Nimis, S. Tai, and T. Sandholm, "What's inside the cloud? An architectural map of the cloud landscape," Proc. 2009 ICSE Work. Softw. Eng. Challenges Cloud Comput. CLOUD 2009, pp. 23–31, 2009.
8. G. Manno, "Reliability modelling of complex systems: An adaptive transition system approach to match accuracy and efficiency," Ph.D. thesis, University of Catania, Italy, 2012.
9. A. Zhou, S. Wang, Q. Sun, H. Zou, and F. Yang, "FTCloudSim: A simulation tool for cloud service reliability enhancement mechanisms," Proc. Demo Poster Track ACM/IFIP/USENIX Int. Middleware. Conf.,pp. 1–2, 2013.
10. R. Bauer and E. Adams, Reliability and Availability of Cloud Computing. Hoboken, NJ: Wiley-IEEE Press, 2012.
11. T. Thein and J. S. Park, "Availability analysis of application servers using software rejuvenation and virtualization," J. Comput. Sci. Technol., vol. 24, no. 2, pp. 339–346, 2009. [Online]. Available: http://link.springer.com/10.1007/s11390-009-9228-1.
12. H. Chan and T. Chieu, "An approach to high availability for cloud servers with snapshot mechanism," Proceedings of the Industrial Track of the 13th ACM/IFIP/USENIX International Middleware Conference. ACM. p. 6, 2012 [Online]. Available: http://dl.acm.org/citation.cfm?id=2405152.
13. F. M. Altukistani and S. S. Alaboodi, "An analytical model for availability evaluation of cloud service provisioning system," Int. J. Adv. Comput. Sci. Appl., vol. 8, no. 6, pp. 241–247, 2017.
14. Salvatore Distefano and Antonio Puliafito "Dynamic reliability block diagrams: Overview of a methodology," Terje Aven & Jan Erik Vinnem (eds), Risk, Reliability and Societal Safety, London: Taylor & Francis Group, 2007, ISBN 978-0-415-44786-7.
15. D. Bailey, E. Frank-Schultz, P. Lindeque, and J. L. Temple, III, "Three reliability engineering techniques and their application to evaluating the availability of IT systems: An introduction," IBM Syst. J., vol. 47, no. 4, pp. 577–589, 2008. [Online]. Available: http://ieeexplore.ieee.org/lpdocs/epic03/wrapper.htm?arnumber=5386507.

16. C. J. Colbourn, The Combinatorics of Network Reliability. New York, NY: Oxford University Press, 1987.

17. S. Sebastio, K. S. Trivedi, D. Wang, and X. Yin, "Fast computation of bounds for two-terminal network reliability," Eur. J. Oper. Res., vol. 238, no. 3, pp. 810–823, 2014. [Online]. Available: http://www.sciencedirect.com/science/article/pii/S0377221714003774.

18. R. D. S. Matos, P. R. M. Maciel, F. Machida, D. S. Kim, and K. S. Trivedi, "Sensitivity analysis of server virtualized system availability," IEEE Trans. Rel., vol. 61, no. 4, pp. 994–1006, Dec. 2012. [Online]. Available: http://ieeexplore.ieee.org/lpdocs/epic03/wrapper.htm?arnumber=6324402.

19. T. T. Lwin and T. Thein, "High availability cluster system for local disaster recovery with Markov modeling approach," Int. J. Comput. Sci. Issues, vol. 6, no. 2, pp. 25–32, 2009. [Online]. Available: http://arxiv.org/abs/0912.1835.

20. D. S. Kim, F. Machida, and K. S. Trivedi, "Availability modeling and analysis of a virtualized system," 2009 15th IEEE Pacific Rim International Symposium on Dependable Computing. IEEE. pp. 365–371, 2009 [Online]. Available: http://ieeexplore.ieee.org/lpdocs/epic03/wrapper.htm?arnumber=5368189.

21. W. E. Smith, K. S. Trivedi, L. A. Tomek, and J. Ackaret, "Availability analysis of blade server systems," IBM Syst. J., vol. 47, no. 4, pp. 621–640, 2008. [Online]. Available: http://ieeexplore.ieee.org/lpdocs/epic03/wrapper.htm?arnumber=5386524.

22. K. S. Trivede, R. Vasireddy, D. Trindale, S. Nathan, and R. Castro, "Modeling high availability," 2006 12th Pacific Rim International Symposium on Dependable Computing (PRDC). IEEE. pp. 154–164, 2006 [Online]. Available: http://www.computer.org/csdl/proceedings/prdc/2006/2724/00/27240154-abs.html, http://ieeexplore.ieee.org/lpdocs/epic03/wrapper.htm?arnumber=4041900, and http://ieeexplore.ieee.org/document/4041900/.

23. A. Alkasem and H. Liu, "Research article a survey of fault-tolerance in cloud computing : Concepts and practice," Res. J. Appl. Sci., vol. 11, no. 12, pp. 1365–1377, 2015.

24. T. Alexandrov and A. Dimov, "Software availability in the cloud," Proceedings of the 14th International Conference on Computer Systems and Technologies. ACM. pp. 193–200, 2013 [Online]. Available: http://dl.acm.org/citation.cfm?id=2516814.

25. Y. Wu and G. Huang, "Model-based high availability configuration framework for cloud," Proceedings of the 2013 Middleware Doctoral Symposium. ACM. p. 6, 2013 [Online]. Available: http://dl.acm.org/citation.cfm?id=2541595.

26. A. Imran, A. Ul Gias, R. Rahman, A. Seal, T. Rahman, F. Ishraque, and K. Sakib, "Cloud-Niagara: A high availability and low overhead fault tolerance middleware for the cloud," 2013 16th International Conference on Computer and Information Technology (ICCIT). IEEE. Pp. 271–276, 2014 [Online]. Available: http://ieeexplore.ieee.org/document/6997344/?arnumber=6997344.

27. A. Bessani, L. A. Cutillo, G. Ramunno, N. Schirmer, and P. Smiraglia, "The Tclouds platform: Concept, architecture and instantiations," Proceedings of the 2nd International Workshop on Dependability Issues in Cloud Computing. ACM. p. 1, 2013 [Online]. Available: http://dl.acm.org/citation.cfm?id=2506156.

28. F. Perez-Sorrosal, M. Patiño-Martinez, R. Jimenez-Peris, and B. Kemme, "Elastic SI-cache: Consistent and scalable caching in multi-tier architectures," The VLDB J., vol. 20, no. 6, pp. 841–865, 2011.

29. K. An, S. Shekhar, F. Caglar, A. Gokhale, and S. Sastry, "A cloud middleware for assuring performance and high availability of soft real-time applications," J. Syst. Arch., vol. 60, no. 9, pp. 757–769, 2014.
30. J. Behl, T. Distler, F. Heisig, R. Kapitza, and M. Schunter, "Providing fault-tolerant execution of web-service-based workflows within clouds," Proceedings of the 2nd International Workshop on Cloud Computing Platforms. ACM. p. 7, 2012 [Online]. Available: http://dl.acm.org/citation.cfm?id=2168704.
31. Q. Guan, Z. Zhang, and S. Fu, "Proactive failure management by integrated unsupervised and semi-supervised learning for dependable cloud systems," 2011 Sixth International Conference on Availability, Reliability and Security. IEEE. pp. 83–90, 2011.
32. H. Paul Barringer, Availability, Reliability, Maintainability, and Capability. Humble, TX: Barringer and Associated Inc., 1997.

Further Readings

R. Ghosh, F. Longo, F. Frattini, S. Russo, and K. S. Trivedi, "Scalable analytics for IaaS cloud availability," IEEE Trans. Cloud Comput., vol. 2, no. 1, pp. 57–70, 2014.
V. K. Katukoori, Standardizing availability definition. Thesis. New Orleans, LA: University of New Orleans, p. 21, 2007.
G. Ciardo, J. K. Muppala, and K. S. Trivedi, "Analyzing concurrent and fault-tolerant software using stochastic reward nets," J. Parallel Distrib. Comput., vol. 15, no. 3, pp. 255–269, 1992 [Online]. Available: http://www.sciencedirect.com/science/article/pii/0743731592-90007A.
M. Malhotra and K. S. Trivedi, "Power-hierarchy of dependability-model types," IEEE Trans. Rel., vol. 43, no. 3, pp. 493–502, 1994 [Online]. Available: http://ieeexplore.ieee.org/lpdocs/epic03/wrapper.htm?arnumber=326452.

Chapter 3

Engineering Resilient Microservices toward System Reliability: The Technologies and Tools

Pethuru Raj
Reliance Jio Platforms Ltd.

G. Sobers Smiles David
Bishop Heber College

Contents

3.5   Command Query Responsibility Segregation Pattern 91
        3.5.1   The Accelerated Adoption of Containers
                 and Orchestration Platforms...94
        3.5.2   The Emergence of Service Meshes and
                 API Gateways 94
                 3.5.2.1   API Gateways for Microservices Era 95
                 3.5.2.2   Resiliency and Fault Tolerance.......................................95
                 3.5.2.3   Why "Service Mesh?" 96
                 3.5.2.4   What Is a "Service Mesh?" 98
                 3.5.2.5   Service Mesh Implementations 101
                 3.5.2.6   Service Mesh: Pros and Cons 101
                 3.5.2.7   Service Mesh versus API Gateway..................................101
                 3.5.2.8   API Gateway and Service Mesh in Action 102
3.6   The Emergence of Serverless Computing toward
        the NoOps Era...104
        3.6.1   Reliable IT Infrastructures..105
        3.6.2   High Availability 105
                 3.6.2.1   Redundancy to Achieve Higher Availability 105
                 3.6.2.2   Fault Tolerance toward Higher Availability 106
                 3.6.2.3   Auto-Scaling Capability 107
                 3.6.2.4   Real-Time Scalability...107
3.7   Infrastructure as Code (IaC) 108
3.8   Conclusion 114
References 114
Further Readings..114

3.1 Introduction

The world is increasingly becoming connected. With the competent technologies and tools that continuously abound for establishing and sustaining deeper and extreme connectivity, our everyday entities and elements are getting connected with one another (locally as well as remotely) to interact and collaborate decisively and deeply. All kinds of physical, mechanical, electrical and electronics systems in our personal as well as professional environments are connected and integrated with the faster maturity and stability of digitization/edge technologies. There are powerful communication and data transmission protocols emerging and evolving fast to systematically link up everything and to empower them to team up together in a purpose-driven manner. Further, the power of digital technologies (cloud infrastructures and platforms for hosting and managing operational and transactional applications; big, fast and streaming data analytics platforms; path-breaking artificial intelligence [AI] algorithms and approaches to bring forth prognostic, predictive, prescriptive and personalized insights out of the Internet of Things [IoT] data; the pervasiveness of the microservices architecture [MSA] pattern; enterprise mobility and social networking; the surging popularity of fog or edge computing; blockchain, etc.) leads to the realization of knowledge-filled, service-oriented, event-driven, cloud-hosted, process-aware, business-centric and mission-critical software solutions and services. These services directly enable business automation and augmentation. The technologically enabled information technology (IT) adaptivity, agility and affordability enhancements overwhelmingly lead to the setting up and sustaining of intelligent business operations and bringing forth premium offerings.

With the unprecedented adoption of the cloud paradigm, the arrival of programmable, open and flexible IT infrastructures is speeding up. Previously, the cloud paradigm was primarily closed, inflexible and expensive IT infrastructures in the form of mainframe servers and monolithic applications. With the cloud-enablement strategy gaining prominence, we have additional infrastructural assets in the form of virtual machines (VMs) and containers. Cloud IT infrastructures are highly optimized and organized through the smart application of cloud technologies and tools. Because of segmenting physical machines/bare metal (BM) servers into multiple VMs and containers, the number of participating infrastructural modules is bound to rise rapidly. This creates a type of strategically sound partitioning of IT infrastructures (server machines, storage appliances and networking solutions) into a number of easily maneuverable and manageable, highly scalable, network-accessible, publicly discoverable, compassable and available IT resources. This transition definitely brings forth a number of business, technical and user advantages. However, there is a catch, that is, the operational and management complexities of modern IT infrastructures have gone up significantly. Also, for the connected world, the software solutions have to be made out of distributed and decentralized application components. To succulently meet evolving business requirements, software packages have to be nimble and versatile; thus hardware, software and services have to be creatively modernized and innately insight-driven.

Software complexity is on the rise consistently due to requirement changes and additions. The functional requirements of software applications are widely fulfilled, but the challenge is how to build software applications that guarantee the non-functional requirements (NFRs), which are alternatively termed as the quality of service (QoS) and quality of experience (QoE) attributes. The well-known QoS properties are scalability, availability, performance/throughput, security, maneuverability and reliability. For achieving reliable systems, we need to have reliable infrastructures and applications. Increasingly, we hear and read about infrastructure-aware applications and applications-aware infrastructures. Thus, it is clear that both infrastructure and application play a vital role in rolling out reliable software systems. This chapter is dedicated to detailing the best practices that empower software architects and developers to come out with microservices that are resilient. When resilient microservices are composed, we enjoy and experience reliable software systems.

3.2 Reliable IT Systems: The Emerging Technologies and Tools

Businesses across the globe mandate for reliability. IT reliability is the foundation for enabling business reliability. IT pundits have released a series of steps to be followed to arrive at reliable systems. There are architectural and design patterns, best practices, platform solutions, technologies and tools, methodologies, etc. to produce reliable systems that are resilient and elastic. Let us discuss them in detail in the subsequent sections. First, let us focus on the various noteworthy advancements happening in the IT space.

3.2.1 The Microservices Architecture Style

MSA is viewed as the next-generation application architecture style and pattern. There are several proven techniques for faster software development through a host of agile programming methodologies such as pair and extreme programming and Scrum among others. However, there is a lacuna on accelerated design of enterprise-class applications. MSA is being presented as the new agile application design method. Further, developing applications is also faster through the careful partitioning of legacy as well as modern applications into a number of easily implementable and manageable application components/services. That is, every software application gets segmented into a set of interactive microservices. Building microservices can be independently accomplished. Applications can be quickly formed out of distributed microservices through composition (orchestration and choreography) platforms. In other words, the era of software development from the ground up is gone forever. Instead, sophisticated applications are being made out of microservices through configuration, customization and composition techniques.

Thus, application design and development accelerate through the smart leverage of MSA concepts, tools, frameworks, design and integration patterns and best practices. Now, with the DevOps movement gaining a strong foothold across the IT industry, the goal of swift deployment of developed and tested application components is being fulfilled. With microservices positioned as the most optimal unit of software design, development and deployment, we will see microservices-centric applications ruling the business and IT services.

3.2.2 Microservices Design: The Best Practices

As microservices become established and elevated as the next-generation application building block, microservices design has to be done by leveraging the various patterns, practices and platforms. This section throws light on some of the best practices recommended by highly accomplished and acclaimed software architects. There are articles and blogs explaining the various best practices for efficient design of microservices. Precisely speaking, with the unprecedented adoption of MSA and the steady growth of the tool ecosystem, the risk-free realization of modular, service-oriented, extensible, event-driven, cloud-hosted, process-centric, business-critical, insight-filled, scalable and reliable applications is gaining momentum.

It is a widely accepted fact that MSA guarantees the much-needed agility in application design, development and deployment; however, there are a few challenges. Microservices can be weighed down due to the feebleness of distributed processing. For any worthwhile application, there is a need for integration and collaboration between all the participating microservices, legacy applications, data sources, etc. To overcome the abovementioned limitations, there are fresh approaches being recommended and rolled out.

3.2.3 Making Microservices More Resilient with Chaos Engineering

Chaos engineering (CE) [1] is defined as thoughtful, planned experiments designed to uncover hidden weaknesses in our systems. An appropriate metaphor is vaccination. A potentially harmful agent is injected into the body for the purpose of preventing future infections. In a similar way, the idea is to inject failure to understand the system's behavior and resiliency. These experiments are done as follows. First, form a hypothesis, carry out the experiment and see if it validates the hypothesis or not. The well-known failures to be injected into a system include shutting down hosts or containers, adding central processing unit (CPU) load or memory pressure and adding network latency or packet loss.

3.2.3.1 Forming a Hypothesis

The first step in performing a CE experiment is forming our own hypothesis. The hypothesis clearly describes the impact we expect on the system from the failures we inject. This is done because we are trying to test the resiliency of our systems. Generally, our hypothesis is that the system will be resilient to the types of failures we inject. Sometimes we find that our hypothesis is not correct. This helps us to think through the ways and means of improving the system's resilience.

For example, say that we have a stateless Hypertext Transfer Protocol (HTTP) service running on Nginx web server that exposes a representational state transfer (REST) application programming interface (API) to some of our other services. Suppose we are running an instance of this service on 10 hosts in our production environment to comfortably handle user and data loads. We can check whether the system is able to continuously function if one or two hosts are taken out. In this case, our hypothesis is "The system is resilient to the failure of a host – there will be no impact on other services or the people using the system".

3.2.3.2 Blast Radius, Magnitude and Abort Conditions

These are the important concepts to keep in mind when planning experiments. *Blast radius* is the proportion of hosts (or containers) on which we run the experiment. This is a very important concept as we need to minimize the potential impact of the experiments on users. The best practice is that we start with a small blast radius (like one host or container) and then increase the blast radius steadily.

Magnitude is the amount of stress or disruption we apply to the individual hosts or containers. For example, if we are testing the effect of a CPU attack against a Nginx web server, we might start off by adding 20% more CPU load (the magnitude) and increase that over time. This helps to get to know the effect of increasing CPU load on service metrics like response time and to understand how large an attack the system can withstand before performance becomes unacceptable.

Abort conditions are the conditions that cause us to halt the experiment. It is good to have an idea in advance of what kinds (or amount) of effects on the system make the experiment too disruptive to continue. Those could be an increase in your error rate or latency, or perhaps a certain alert generated by your monitoring software.

3.2.3.3 Verifying Dependencies with Blackhole Attacks

We know that with MSA in place, there will be additional dependencies created and managed. Any enterprise system comprises hundreds of microservices, which have to find, bind and use others to be right and relevant to users. Some services are internal and others may be external. What happens when those external or internal dependencies fail? We need proper safeguards to compensate or mitigate any kind of faults and failures. The standard approaches such as timeout and retry logic have to be well-tuned. Verifying all of these in production environments needs CE experiments.

Blackhole attacks are a great way to test whether you are in a position to deal with failed dependencies. A blackhole attack blocks a host or container's access to specific hostnames, IP addresses and/or ports to simulate what would happen if that resource was unavailable. This is a great way to simulate network- or firewall-related outages, as well as network partitions.

In the case of an external dependency [1], let us imagine that we are operating a service that sends short message service (SMS) messages to customers using the Twilio API. We know that our communications with Twilio might be interrupted at any time, so we have designed our microservice to read messages from a queue, and to delete them from the queue only after they are successfully sent to Twilio via the Twilio API. If the Twilio API is unavailable, the messages queue up on our end (possibly using a message bus like Kafka or ActiveMQ), and they will eventually be sent once communication with Twilio resumes. Sounds great, right?

But how do we know our service actually behaves when our network connection to Twilio is severed, until we actually test it? How do we know that what we drew up on the white board when we designed the service is how it is actually operating in production? By running a blackhole attack in which we block that service's access to the Twilio API, we can see how it actually behaves. This can help us answer the following questions: Do the messages queue properly? Is the timeout we have set appropriate? Does the service continue to perform well as the message queue grows? Instead of looking at the code and making educated guesses at the answers to these questions, we can actually inject that failure and see what happens. In this case our hypothesis might be "Messages queue correctly while the network connection is down, and are delivered properly when it resumes." We either prove or disprove that hypothesis when we run the blackhole attack. If we disprove it, we likely learn some things that will help make our system more resilient.

A blackhole attack also can be used to verify what happens when internal dependencies fail, and to discover hidden dependencies. A hidden dependency happens when someone adds a new dependency on a service, but it is not documented or communicated well within the organization. By periodically running blackhole attacks on your services, you can surface these hidden dependencies. Blackhole attacks are great for seeing how resilient your service is to dependency failures, but there are also other useful experiments to test in a microservices environment. Shutting down hosts, adding latency or packet loss, breaking domain name server (DNS) resolution and adding CPU or memory pressure are all great things you can do to test the resilience of your microservices.

3.3 The Relevance of Event-Driven Microservices

To enhance the scalability and reliability of microservices-centric applications, a number of options are being reviewed. The combination of event-driven architecture (EDA) and MSA is found to work wonders in the pursuit of designing and deploying reliable applications. This section throws light on the importance of event-driven microservices and how they can be implemented and composed to produce reliable systems. Let us start with the need for asynchronous communication.

Events have become an important ingredient to have not only scores of integrated systems but also intelligent systems for succulently automating business activities and people tasks. Enterprise applications are increasingly event-driven. For example, we have varied events through various business operations. An airline service provider delays a flight, a doctor prescribes a medicine, a consignment has just arrived, an invoice is not paid in time, a threshold break-in in the electricity meter and so forth. Events link different and distributed applications and services to do integrated operations. A monitoring, measurement and management service can receive and analyze a stream of events emitted by other applications to discover whether the pattern of events sticks to its normal course. If there is any deviation, then it has to be detected and used for taking any appropriate counter measures.

3.3.1 Why Asynchronous Communication?

Microservices can communicate in a synchronous and asynchronous manner. However, as things evolve, there is an insistence for event-driven microservices, which, in turn, ask for asynchronous interactions. This section discusses some of its motivations.

We have been fiddling with synchronous communications. We are more comfortable with the Transmission Control Protocol (TCP), HTTP and File Transfer Protocol (FTP), which intrinsically support synchronous communication and have certain advantages. The overwhelmingly used interaction model of request and response (R&R) is accomplished through a synchronous communication pattern. However, the world tends toward an asynchronous communication pattern. If the server application is heavily loaded, then clients have to wait to get the response from the server. How can this situation be handled? That is, how can a long-running business process on the server machine be elegantly communicated to the client? If a server-side service is not available due to one of the typical reasons, then how can the client handle this scenario? As there are redundant service instances, how can the client be empowered to take a different route to the functioning service to handle the client request? How the guaranteed server or service response time can be ensured for the client is another huge challenge in this extremely connected world, but there are other challenges too.

Asynchronous communication is expected to relieve us from these pains. Long-running tasks, unavailable or unresponsive servers, service transparency, request reordering and prioritizing, etc. can be easily accomplished through asynchronous communication. Now let us discuss the nitty-gritty of the EDA pattern.

An *EDA* consists of *event producers* that generate a stream of events, and *event consumers* that listen for the events. Events are delivered in near real time, so consumers can respond immediately to events as they occur. Producers are decoupled from consumers. An EDA can use a pub/sub model or an event stream model.

- **Publish/subscribe:** We have detailed this below. Due to the production of a staggering amount of events, competent messaging middleware solutions abound to precisely keep track of event subscriptions. That is, when a tangible event gets published, the messaging infrastructure sends the event to each of its subscribers. Once an event is received, it cannot be replayed again. Further on, new subscribers cannot see the event.
- **Event streaming:** Events are streamed and written in a log in an orderly manner. Events are persisted to be durable. Clients do not subscribe to the event stream; instead, a client can read any part of the stream. A client can join at any time and replay events.

Events may be simple or complex as defined below. Lately there have been a number of streaming analytics platforms and event processing engines to make sense of event streams. Today, the application design is increasingly event-centric. Events have acquired such a dominant position in the business and IT worlds. Data-centricity is steadily tending toward event-centricity. The enterprise and cloud IT teams are tasked to have event platforms in place to succulently extricate beneficial associations and patterns, fresh possibilities and opportunities, outliers/anomalies, risks and rewards, etc.

1. **Simple event processing:** An event immediately triggers an action in the consumer.
2. **Complex event processing:** Complex events are typically a series of events, and a consumer is supposed to process complex events searching for actionable insights in the event data.
3. **Event stream processing:** It is all about using an event streaming platform, such as Apache Kafka, as a pipeline to ingest events and feed them to one or more stream processors. The stream processors process or transform the stream accordingly.

3.3.2 Why Event-Driven Microservices?

There is a connection between asynchronous communication and event-driven microservices. Events are emerging as the unit of integration in the increasingly decentralized and distributed IT world. Microservices and their applications have to be deftly enabled to capture and crunch event messages to be intelligent in their actions and reactions. Business and people-centric applications are expected to be sensitive and responsive (S&R). The mode of pulling information from servers is to be replaced with servers pushing their information and capabilities to several clients across; that is, the push mode is getting star attraction these days. Client agents and services fire and forget until the server services respond back with all the asked details. There are simple and complex events, and the IT systems have to have the appropriate competency to intelligently respond to various events in time. Simple events are being clubbed together to create complex events.

To attain the real agility through microservices, there is a need to embrace the distinct capabilities of the EDA pattern. It is all about getting the right event to the right service to produce the right response at the right time. Events have to be systematically captured and acted upon immediately and intelligently to produce real-time, situation-aware, people-centric and adaptive applications. Thus, microservices, to generate real-world applications, have to be sensitive to all kinds of events. While designing next-generation systems and environments, the event-centric thinking has to be the key for renowned success as the device ecosystem continuously evolves with the addition of a dazzling array of slim and sleek, handy and trendy wearables, implantables, handhelds and mobiles; portable, nomadic and wireless devices; edge and digitized entities, etc. As we prepare ourselves for the ensuring era of IoT systems and environments, there is a need for knowledge-filled, event-sensitive and device-centric microservices. For fulfilling any useful activity, there is a need for microservices to find, bind and leverage one another in an insightful manner. Thus, for integrating microservices, the proven and potential methods of service orchestration and choreography play a very bountiful and beautiful role.

Event-driven design is a way of extending applications without modifying them in an MSA. Each microservice is designed as a fine-grained and self-sufficient software that fulfills a single business activity. This means, for implementing a use case or process, there may be a need to visit many microservices several times; that is, for integrating and composing microservices, eventing and asynchronous messaging are preferred as they guarantee scalability and resiliency. There are message-oriented middleware (MoM) and message brokers from the open source community as well as from commercial vendors. For events, there are event stores and hubs to stock events. Events emitted by publishing applications are meticulously captured, stored and delivered by these middleware solutions to the consuming applications. Because of these intermediaries, events and messages are kept in a secure place. For internal communications, Apache Kafka is a popular product. For external communications, the HTTP-based middleware solutions such as WebSockets and webhooks are used.

We have leveraged several enterprise integration patterns for producing integrated systems. However, the distributed nature of microservices demands decentralized messaging; that is, there is a shift from centralized integration bus architecture to smart microservices with dumb pipes. The required intelligence is stuffed with all the participating services instead of accumulating them in a central integration hub such as an enterprise application integration (EAI) hub and enterprise service bus (ESB). Today we have a database for each of the microservices; that is, we are heading toward polyglot and decentralized persistence. In a similar line, we need to embrace decentralized polyglot messaging infrastructure for enabling microservices to find, bind and compose to produce process-aware, business-centric and composite services.

3.4 Asynchronous Messaging Patterns for Event-Driven Microservices

Here are a few popular asynchronous messaging patterns that enable the faster realization of event-driven and asynchronous messaging microservices.

> ***Event sourcing (see Figure 3.1):*** Today events are penetrative and pervasive and occur in large numbers due to the broader and deeper proliferation of multifaceted sensors, actuators, drones, robots, electronics, digitized elements,

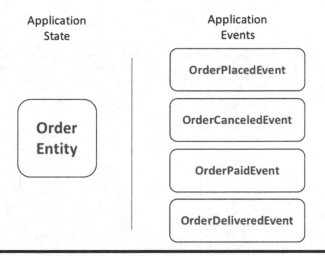

Figure 3.1   Event sourcing.

connected devices, factory machineries, social networking sites, integrated applications, decentralized microservices, distributed data sources and stores, etc. Thus, events from varied and geographically distributed sources get streamed into an event store, which is termed as a database of events. This event store provides an API to enable various consuming services to subscribe to and use authorized events. The event store primarily operates as a message broker.

Event sourcing persists in the state of a business entity such as order service as a sequence of state-changing events. Whenever there is a change in the state of the business entity, a new event gets triggered and is meticulously appended to the list of events. This is similar to how log aggregation works. Event sourcing is an excellent way to add visibility to what is happening to a service. The application can easily reconstruct a business entity's current state by replaying the events.

The most common flow for an event sourcing is as follows:

- *Message receiver* receives and converts the incoming request into an event message.
- *Event store* stores the event messages sequentially. It notifies the listeners/consumers.
- *Event listener* represents the code in charge of executing the respective business logic according to the event type.

Apache Kafka is the widely used event store. Events are grouped into multiple logical collections called Topics. Topics are subsequently partitioned toward parallel processing. A partitioned Topic functions like a queue; that is, events are delivered to their consumers in the order they were received. However, unlike a queue, events

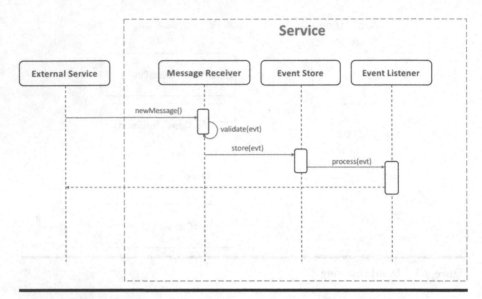

Figure 3.2   Common flow for an event.

are persisted to be made available to other consumers. Older messages get automatically deleted based on the Stream's time-to-live (TTL) setting. Event consumers can consume the event message at any time and replay the messages any number of times. Apache Kafka can scale quickly to handle millions of events per second.

The idea is to represent every application's state transition in the form of an immutable event as shown in Figure 3.2. Events are then stored in a log or journal form as they occur. Events can also be queried and stored permanently. This ultimately shows how the application's state, as a whole, has evolved over time.

> ***Publisher/subscriber:*** This is emerging as the way forward to accomplish asynchronous real-time data distribution. The producer does not know about the subscribers. This pattern is to comprehensively decouple microservices. Subscribers register to receive a message without any knowledge of the publishers. This pattern is primarily for ensuring applications to scale to handle any number of subscribers. The middleware broker guarantees the required scalability. MSA is capable of creating loosely and lightly coupled microservices. Hence, independently deploying and updating along with horizontally scaling microservices is quite easy. However, while composing microservices using service orchestration, we get sticky microservices and, hence, experts want service choreography. This pattern is vividly illustrated in the Figure 3.3.
>
> In this example, the Portfolio service, as shown in Figure 3.4, has to add a stock position. Rather than calling the Accounts service directly, it publishes an event to the "Position Added" event stream. The Accounts microservice has

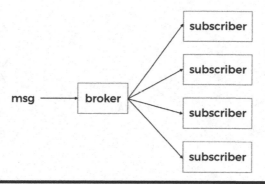

Figure 3.3 Broker-subscriber.

subscribed to that event stream so it gets the notification. This indirect and intermediary-enabled asynchronous communication ensures that the participating services are totally decoupled. This means services can be replaced and substituted with other advanced services. The services can be quickly scaled out by additional containerized microservice instances. The only flaw here is that there is no centralized monitoring and management system in place.

Event firehose pattern: When a greater number of events are being produced by several producers and there are many consumers waiting for event messages, there is a need for a common hub to exchange messages. The event messages get exchanged via topics. As indicated below, in the case of asynchronous command calls, the exchange happens via queues. The common implementation of this pattern looks a little something as shown in Figure 3.5.

Asynchronous command calls: There are certain scenarios mandating proper orchestration over asynchronous calls. These are usually done for local integration use cases. The other prominent use cases include connecting closely related microservices to exchange messages with a delivery guarantee. Here, microservices interact in an asynchronous manner. In this pattern, messages

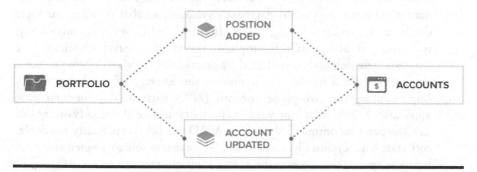

Figure 3.4 Portfolio services.

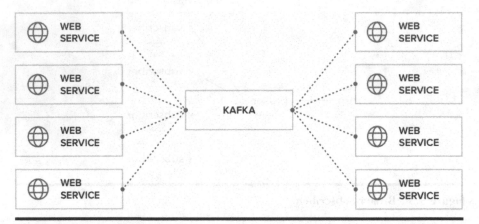

Figure 3.5 Kafka event services.

are typically exchanged using queues. Queues facilitate messages to be exchanged in a point-to-point manner. Most of the conversations here are short-lived. It is a traditional broker-centric use case but it is reliably connecting end points through asynchronous communication.

This pattern is demanded when one microservice has to publish an event for a second microservice to process and then has to wait to receive and read an appropriate "reply" event from that second microservice. Consider the abovementioned Portfolio example. A standard REST API call tells the Portfolio service to add a stock position. The Portfolio service posts an event to the Position Added queue for the Accounts service to process. The service then waits for the Accounts service to post a reply event to the Account Updated queue so that the original REST API call can return data received from that event to the client service.

Saga pattern: We all know that each microservice is empowered through its own database. However, some business operations involve multiple services. Each atomic business operation that spans multiple services may involve several transactions on a technical level. The challenge here is how to ensure data consistency in a multi-database environment; that is, when multiple databases are to be accessed, the traditional local (atomicity, consistency, isolation, durability) ACID-compliant transaction is not sufficient. The situation here demands distributed transactions. One viable option to solve this problem in a hassle-free manner is the leverage of the XA protocol implementing the two-phase commit (2PC) pattern. But for web-scale applications, 2PC may not work well. To eliminate the disadvantages of 2PC, experts recommended trading ACID for BASE (basically available, soft state and eventually consistent). The experts tell to implement each business transaction that spans across multiple services as a saga; that is, a saga is presented as a sequence of local transactions. Sagas are viewed as an application-level distributed coordination of multiple transactions. Each local transaction updates the database and publishes an event message to the next local transaction in the saga. If a local transaction fails for one or multiple reasons, then the saga executes a series of compensating activities that undo the changes that were made by the preceding local transactions.

The role of EDA to produce reactive applications: These are also called event-driven applications. Predominantly, instead of service orchestration, service choreography is preferred to build event-driven applications. As per the Reactive manifesto, reactive applications have to have the following characteristics: be responsive, resilient, elastic and message-driven. Reactive systems are bound to respond instantaneously to any kind of stimulus. This is the opposite of the traditional R&R model, which is generally blocking. This pattern turns out to be an excellent way to use the available resources in a better manner. Also, the system responsiveness gets a strong boost. Instead of blocking and waiting for computations to be finished, the application starts to handle other user requests in an asynchronous manner to make use of all the available resources and threads.

In conclusion, we are heading toward a deeply and extremely connected world. Any noteworthy event and incident, state or status changes, threshold break-ins, etc. are being collected and conveyed to all the consuming systems in time to take immediate countermeasures with confidence and clarity. Our applications have to be designed to appropriately respond and reciprocate for varied events from distributed sources; that is, event-driven application architecture is gaining a strong foothold in the IT and business worlds. Integrated systems such as business workloads, operational systems and IT services are adequately empowered and stuffed with required logic to be S&R to events. There are event stores/hubs, MoM, message brokers and event streaming platforms and databases to facilitate the EDA goals. As we have described in the previous sections, microservices emerge as the unique and nimble building block for building and deploying event-driven applications. For truly enabling the digital transformation initiatives, business houses and IT organizations have to meticulously invest their time, talent and treasures on event-driven microservices to harvest handsomely in due course of time.

3.5 Command Query Responsibility Segregation Pattern

Command query responsibility segregation (CQRS) is an important pattern to realize decoupling at the database level. This pattern actually helps us to use different models to update and read data, as vividly illustrated in Figure 3.6. This segregation comes in handy as we embrace microservices, which are event-driven. CQRS

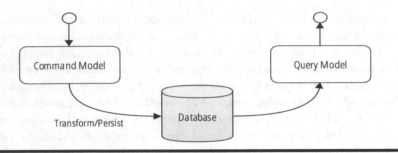

Figure 3.6 CQRS – event-driven architecture.

is acquiring a special significance because domain events are the inputs in the EDA era. However, the database expects a domain object, which is structurally different from a domain event. Here is a domain model object representing an account. The example is taken from the article "Building Event-Driven Microservices Using CQRS and Serverless" (see http://www.kennybastani.com/2017/01/building-event-driven-microservices.html).

Example 1. Account Aggregate

```
{
"createdAt": 1481351048967,
"lastModified": 1481351049385,
"userId": 1,
"accountNumber": "123456",
"defaultAccount": true,
"status": "ACCOUNT_ACTIVE"
}
```

When a service queries for an account, the database expects this model to be input. However, the requirement at hand is to update the current status to ACCOUNT_SUSPENDED by using a domain event. There is a need for a kind of transformation. The following is a snippet of a domain event to transition the state of the account from ACCOUNT_ACTIVE to ACCOUNT_SUSPENDED.

Example 2. Account Event

```
{
"createdAt": 1481353397395,
"lastModified": 1481353397395,
"type": "ACCOUNT_SUSPENDED",
"accountNumber": "123456"
}
```

The need is to process this domain event and apply the update to the query model. The command contains the model of the domain event and uses it to process the update to the account's query model as shown in Figure 3.7.

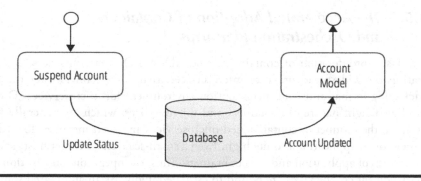

Figure 3.7   Account query model.

CQRS and microservices: When CQRS combines with microservices, things become complicated as illustrated in Figure 3.8.

A single microservice is partitioned into three services (Command, Event Processor and Query Services). These services can be deployed independently. CQRS is vital for the increasingly event-driven microservices world.

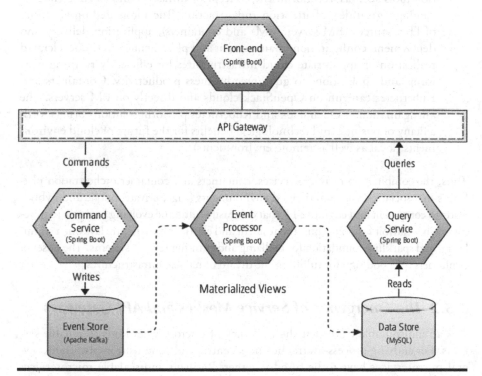

Figure 3.8   Implementation of the CQRS pattern.

3.5.1 The Accelerated Adoption of Containers and Orchestration Platforms

The faster proliferation of containers, especially the Docker containers, is accelerating the widespread usage of microservices; that is, containers offer the best packaging format and runtime/execution environment for microservices. Due to the lightweight nature of containers and microservices, which are generally fine-grained, the number of containerized microservices and their instances for redundancy for an application is quite high. Even a small-scale cloud center hosts several thousands of application and data containers. Thus, the operation, observation and management complexities are bound to escalate rapidly. As an automated solution for this predicament, there are container life cycle management solutions such as Kubernetes, Docker Swarm and Marathon. These solutions simplify and speed up container clustering, orchestration and management activities.

> *The emergence of containerized clouds:* With the growing tool ecosystem of Kubernetes, setting up and sustaining containerized cloud environments have been greatly simplified and streamlined. With the flourish of configuration management (CM) tools such as Chef, Puppet, Ansible and cloud orchestration tools such as Terraform, the concept of infrastructure as code (IaC) is gaining a great deal of attention and attraction. The automated provisioning of IT resources (BM server, VMs and containers), application delivery and deployment, configuration, management and placement eases the accelerated realization of appropriate cloud infrastructures for efficiently running platforms and applications to guarantee business productivity. Containers and Kubernetes can run on OpenStack clouds and directly on BM servers. The amalgamation of OpenStack and Kubernetes platform solutions brings forth a litany of business and technological benefits for the future of cloud environments (local as well as remote environments).

Thus, the combination of microservices, containers and container orchestration platforms in association with multi-cloud environments (edge, private, public and hybrid) leads to competent and cognitive IT that can easily fulfill the evolving business requirements in an adroit fashion. Thus, the resilient and elastic infrastructure lays out a stimulating and sparkling foundation for realizing and running reliable systems. The onset of containers is a good sign for fulfilling the dream of reliable infrastructures.

3.5.2 The Emergence of Service Meshes and API Gateways

It is an indisputable truth that the resiliency of microservices leads to reliable systems. For crafting process-aware, business-centric and composite applications, several microservices have to be fused together. Resilient and scalable microservices collaborate with one another leading to the realization of reliable software systems.

3.5.2.1 API Gateways for Microservices Era

Trying to keep track of all those microservices, and knowing when and how to use each of them are not easy tasks for service developers. The need to continuously track microservices and make them easier to use is the primary reason to use an API gateway. Using an API gateway makes your collection of microservices look like a custom API, which is developed to meet your application's specific needs. From the front, it looks like an API, but from the back, it uses individual microservices to perform tasks – you get the best of both worlds. The key differentiators of API gateways are:

- ■ ***Decoupling:*** API gateways enable you to route based on path, hostname, headers and other key information enabling you to decouple the publicly facing API end points from the underlying microservice architecture.
- ■ ***Reduce round trips:*** Certain API end points may need to join data across multiple services. API gateways can perform this aggregation so that the client does not need complicated call chaining and reduce the number of round trips.
- ■ ***Security:*** API gateways provide a centralized proxy server to manage rate limiting, bot detection, authentication, cross-origin resource sharing (CORS), etc. Many API gateways allow setting up a data store such as Redis to store session information.
- ■ ***Cross-cutting concerns:*** Logging, caching, and other cross-cutting concerns can be handled in a centralized manner rather than deployed to every microservice.

Service mesh and API gateways are two simplifying and streamlining artifacts in the microservices world. The complexity induced by the multiplicity and heterogeneity of containerized microservices is substantially lessened through the smart application of these two products. Increasingly these products are being integrated into one product as there are several overlaps in these products.

Building and packaging Java microservice is one part of the story. How do we make microservices resilient? How do we introduce health checks, timeouts, retries, ensure request buffering or reliable communication between microservices? Some of these features are built into the microservices framework, but often they are language specific, or you have to accommodate for it in your application code. How do we introduce it without changing the application code? Service mesh architecture attempts to solve these issues. Istio provides an easy way to create this service mesh by deploying a control plane and injecting sidecar containers alongside your microservice.

3.5.2.2 Resiliency and Fault Tolerance

Istio adds fault tolerance to your application without any changes to the code. Some resiliency features it supports are:

- ■ Retries/timeouts
- ■ Circuit breakers

- Health checks
- Control connection pool size and request load
- Systematic fault injection

3.5.2.3 Why "Service Mesh?"

Most people think that microservices are the perfect answer to all the problems they had with previous architectures such as service oriented architecture (SOA)/ESB. However, when we observe the real-world microservices implementations, we can see that most of the functionalities that a centralized bus (ESB) supports are now implemented at the microservices level. So, we are more or less solving the same set of fundamental problems, but we are solving them at different dimensions with microservices.

For example, let us take a scenario in which you need to call multiple downstream services in a resilient manner and expose the functionality as another (composite) service. As shown in Figure 3.9, with the ESB architecture, you can easily leverage the inbuilt capabilities of the ESB for building virtual/composite services and functionalities such as circuit breakers, timeouts and service discovery and so forth, which are useful during interservice communication. When you implement the same scenario using microservices, then you no longer have a centralized integration/ESB layer but a set of (composite and atomic) microservices. So, you have to implement all of these functionalities at the microservices level.

Therefore a given microservice, which communicates with other services (Figure 3.10), is comprised of:

- *Business logic* that implements the business functionalities, computations and service composition/integration logic.
- *Network functions* that take care of the interservice communication mechanisms (basic service invocation through a given protocol, apply resiliency and stability patterns, service discovery etc.) These network functions are built on top of the underlying operating service (OS)-level network stack.

Now think about the effort involved in implementing such microservices. Implementing the functionalities related to service-to-service communication from scratch is a nightmare. Focusing on the business logic, you will have to spend a great deal of time on building service-to-service communication functionalities. This is even worse if you use multiple technologies to build microservices (such as multiple programming languages as shown in Figure 3.9), because you need to duplicate the same efforts across different languages (e.g., the circuit breaker has to be implemented on Java, Node, Python etc.). The most complex challenge in realizing microservice architecture is not building the services themselves, but the communication between services. Since most of the interservice communication requirements are quite generic across all microservices implementations, we can

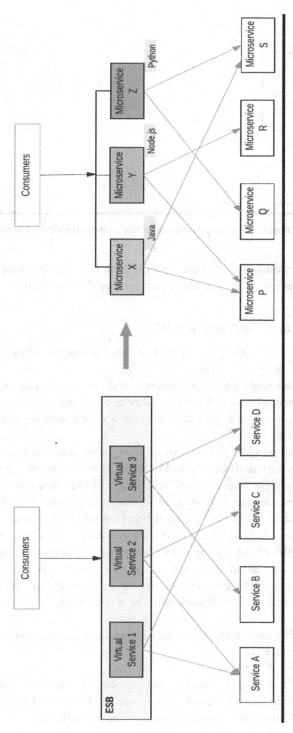

Figure 3.9   From centralized integration/ESB to microservices.

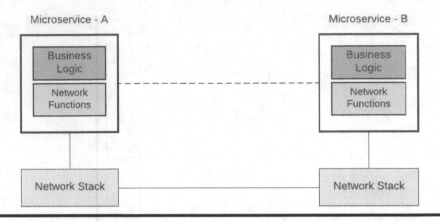

Figure 3.10 Microservice components and service-to-service communication.

think about off-loading all such tasks to a different layer, so that we can keep the service code independent. This is where "service mesh" comes into the picture.

3.5.2.4 What Is a "Service Mesh?"

In a nutshell, a service mesh is an interservice communication infrastructure.

- With a service mesh, a given microservice will not directly communicate with the other microservices. Rather, all service-to-service communications will take place on top of a software component called service mesh (or sidecar proxy).
- Service mesh provides the built-in support for some network functions such as resiliency, service discovery and so forth. Therefore, service developers can focus more on the business logic while most of the work related to the network communication is off-loaded to the service mesh. For instance, you do not need to worry about circuit breaking when your microservice calls another service anymore because it is already part of the service mesh.
- Service mesh is language agnostic: Since the microservice-to-service mesh proxy communication is always on top of the standard protocols such as HTTP1.x/2.x, gRPC and so forth, you can write your microservice from any technology and it will still work with the service mesh.

Let us try to further understand the service interactions and responsibilities, which are shown in Figure 3.11.

Business logic: The service implementation should contain the realization of the business functionalities of a given service. This includes logic related to its business functions, computations, integration with other services/systems

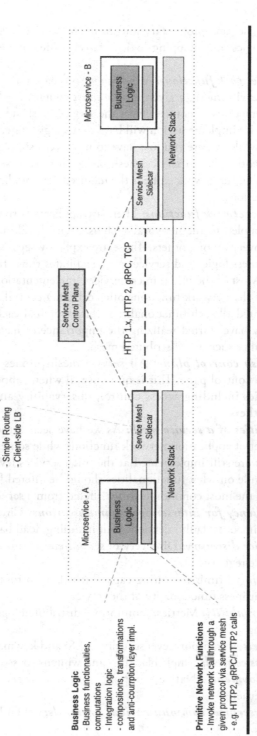

Business Logic
- Business functionalities, computations
- Integration logic
- compositions, transformations and anti-courrption layer impl.

Applicaiton Network Functions
- Circuit breaker
- timeouts / retries / budgets
- Service Discovery
- Simple Routing
- Client-side LB

Primitive Network Functions
- Invoke network call through a given protocol via service mesh
- e.g. HTTP2, gRPC/-TTP2 calls

Figure 3.11 Service-to-service communication with service mesh.

(including legacy, proprietary and SaaS) or service compositions, complex routing logics and mapping logic between different message types among others.

Primitive network functions: Although we off-load most of the network functions to service mesh, a given service must contain the basic high-level network interactions to connect with the service mesh/sidecar proxy. Hence, a given service implementation will have to use a given network library (unlike the ESB world, where you just have to use a very simple abstraction) to initiate network calls (to service mesh only). In most cases, the microservices development framework embeds the required network libraries to be used for these functions.

Application network functions: There are application functionalities that are tightly coupled to the network, such as circuit breaking, timeouts and service discovery among others. Those are explicitly separated from the service code/business logic, and service mesh facilitates those functionalities out of the box. Most of the initial microservices implementations simply ignore the gravity of the network functions offered from a central ESB layer, and they implemented all such functionalities from scratch at each microservice level. Now they have started realizing the importance of having a similar shared functionality such as a distributed mesh.

Service mesh control plane: All service mesh proxies are centrally managed by a control pane. This is quite useful when supporting service mesh capabilities including access control, observability and service discovery among others.

Functionalities of a service mesh: As we have seen earlier, the service mesh offers a set of application network functions while some (primitive) network functions are still implemented at the microservices level. There is no hard and fast rule on what functionalities should be offered from a service mesh. These are the most common features offered from a service mesh:

- ***Resiliency for interservice communications:*** Circuit-breaking, retries and timeouts, fault injection, fault handling, load balancing and failover
- ***Service discovery:*** Discovery of service end points through a dedicated service registry
- ***Routing:*** Primitive routing capabilities, but no routing logics related to the business functionality of the service
- ***Observability:*** Metrics, monitoring, distributed logging and distributed tracing
- ***Security:*** Transport-level security (TLS) and key management
- ***Access control:*** Simple blacklist- and whitelist-based access control
- ***Deployment:*** Native support for containers and Docker and Kubernetes
- ***Interservice communication protocols:*** HTTP1.x, HTTP2 and gRPC

3.5.2.5 Service Mesh Implementations

Linkerd and Istio are two popular open source service mesh implementations. They both follow a similar architecture but different implementation mechanisms.

3.5.2.6 Service Mesh: Pros and Cons

Let us have a quick look at the pros and cons of service meshes.

Pros

- Commodity features are implemented outside microservice code and they are reusable.
- Solves most of the problems in MSA from which we used to have ad hoc solutions such as distributed tracing, logging, security, access control and so forth.
- More freedom when it comes to selecting a microservices implementation language. You do not need to worry about whether a given language supports or has libraries to build network application functions.

Cons

- ***Complexity:*** Having a service mesh drastically increases the number of runtime instances that you have in a given microservice implementation.
- ***Adding extra hops:*** Each service call has to go through an extra hop (through a service mesh sidecar proxy).
- ***Service meshes address a subset of problems:*** Service mesh only addresses a subset of interservice communication problems, but there are a great deal of complex problems, such as complex routing, transformation/type mapping and integrating with other services and systems, to be solved at your microservice's business logic.
- ***Immature:*** Service mesh technologies are relatively new to be declared as full production ready for large-scale deployments.

In summary, service mesh addresses some of the key challenges when it comes to the realization of microservice architecture. They give you more freedom to select a diverse set of microservices implementation technologies as well as to focus more on business logic rather than investing more time on network functions between services. However, service mesh will not solve any of the business logic–related or service integration/composition–related problems.

3.5.2.7 Service Mesh versus API Gateway

To differentiate API gateways and service mesh, let us have a closer look at the key characteristics of API gateways and service mesh.

API gateway: The key objective of using an API gateway is to expose your (micro) services as managed APIs. So, the API or Edge services that we develop at the API gateway layer serve a specific business functionality.

■ API/Edge services call the downstream (composite and atomic) microservices and contain the business logic that creates compositions/mash-ups of multiple downstream services.
■ API/Edge services also need to call the downstream services in a resilient manner and apply various stability patterns such as circuit breakers, timeouts and load balancing/failover. Therefore, most of the API gateway solutions have these features built in.
■ API gateways also come with inbuilt support for service discovery, analytics (observability: metrics, monitoring, distributed logging and distributed tracing) and security.
■ API gateways closely work with several other components of the API management ecosystem, such as the API marketplace/store and API publishing portal.

Service mesh: Now let us look at how we can differentiate service mesh.

■ Service mesh is a network communication infrastructure that allows you to decouple and off-load most of the application network functions from your service code.
■ Hence when you do service-to-service communication, you do not need to implement resilient communication patterns such as circuit breakers or timeouts in your service code. Similarly, service mesh provides other functionalities including service discovery and observability among others.

3.5.2.8 API Gateway and Service Mesh in Action

The key differentiators between API gateways and service mesh are that API gateways are a key part of exposing API/Edge services, whereas service mesh is merely an interservice communication infrastructure that does not have any business notion of your solution. Figure 3.12 illustrates how API gateways and service mesh can exist. As we discussed above, there are also some overlapping features (such as circuit breakers, etc.), but it is important to understand that these two concepts are serving fundamentally different requirements.

As shown in Figure 3.12, service mesh is used alongside most of the service implementations as a sidecar and it is independent of the business functionality of the services.

On the other hand, the API gateway hosts all the API services (which have a clearly defined business functionality) and it is a part of the business functionality of your solution. API gateways may have in-built interservice communication capabilities,

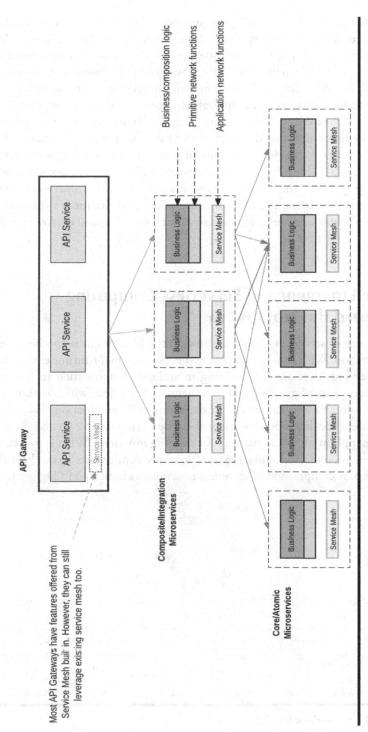

Figure 3.12 API gateways and service mesh in action.

but that does not prevent the API gateway from using service mesh to call down-stream services (API Gateway→service mesh→microservices). At the API management level, you can either use the in-built interservice communication capabilities of the API gateway or API gateway can call downstream services via service mesh by off-loading application network functions to service mesh.

Service resiliency is achieved through the leverage of service mesh solutions such as Istio, Linkerd and Conduit. Forming service meshes is the way forward to ensure the much-demanded service resiliency while services interact with one another. The faster maturity and stability of service mesh–enabling solutions goes a long way in establishing resilient microservices, which, when composed together, form reliable systems. Thus, containerized microservices, container orchestration platforms such as Kubernetes and the incorporation of service mesh solutions blend well to add a robust and versatile foundation for producing and deploying reliable systems.

3.6 The Emergence of Serverless Computing toward the NoOps Era

The emergence of serverless computing toward the NoOps era is another interesting phenomenon. With containers gaining the most optimal runtime environment, cloud service providers are able to bring in additional automation in infrastructure provisioning, configuration and management. Serverless, which is also termed *FaaS* (Function as a Service), assists in deploying code as functions fast. That is, there is no need for developers to worry about optimally setting up and managing appropriate application infrastructures for running functions. What is the relationship between microservices and serverless functions? A microservice can be realized through a smart composition of serverless functions as indicated in Figure 3.13.

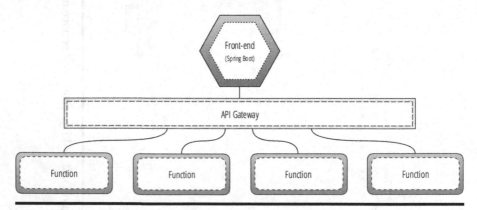

Figure 3.13 Serverless functions.

Being serverless lends well to increasing the velocity with which microservices get updated and deployed in production. It does so by moving much of the workflow management out of the core components and into small composable functions that can be independently upgraded and deployed. Thus, faster deployment of microservices gets fulfilled through the serverless computing.

The goal of NoOps can be enabled through serverless computing; that is, infrastructure setup and management are being taken care of programmatically. Hence, there is a possibility for any kind of operational errors. There is less dependency on human instruction, interpretation and involvement.

3.6.1 Reliable IT Infrastructures

As indicated in the beginning, to arrive at reliable systems, we need to have reliable applications and infrastructures. We have discussed previously the various ways and means of bringing forth reliable applications. Now, we need to dig deeper and detail the best practices to be followed to craft and use reliable infrastructures.

3.6.2 High Availability

3.6.2.1 Redundancy to Achieve Higher Availability

The first and foremost tip is for architect software applications to be redundant. Redundancy is the duplication of any system to substantially increase its availability. If a system goes down for any reason, the duplicated system comes to the rescue. That is why we often hear and read that software applications are generally deployed in multiple regions as indicated in Figure 3.14. Lately, applications have been constructed out of distributed and duplicated application components. Thus, if one component or service goes down, then its duplication comes in handy in sustaining and elongating the application lifetime. MSA eventually leads to distributed systems, which are highly available and scalable.

Table 3.1 shows why the redundancy turns out to be a crucial need for business and IT systems. With duplication in place, we can easily attain 99.999% availability of systems and software.

If a component is guaranteed to fulfill 99% availability, and if we have the component in two geographically different places, then the total availability goes up to 99.99%. With more instances, we are bound to get a higher availability of systems. To design such an architecture across multiple availability zones and regions, applications have to be stateless and an elastic load balancer (cluster to avoid single point of failure) needs to be used to intelligently route requests from different sources to the back-end applications and their clones. Not all requests are going to be stateless. Some requests demand stickiness; hence, there are several options being rolled out to involve stateful applications.

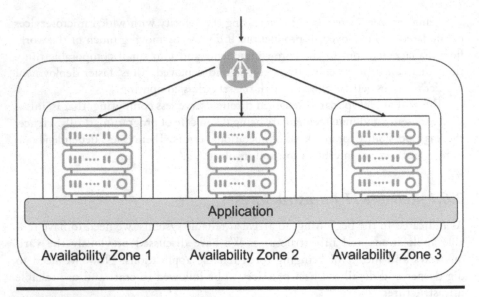

Figure 3.14 Microservice architecture.

3.6.2.2 Fault Tolerance toward Higher Availability

Fault tolerance relies on a specialized mechanism to proactively detect a fault/risk in one or more of the components of any IT hardware system and instantaneously the system gets switched to a redundant component to continue the service without any delay. The failed component may be the motherboard, which typically comprises the CPU, memory and connectors for input and output devices; power supply or a storage component. Software downtime is another issue due to faults in software packages. Recently, there has been a litany of techniques and tools to help developers build fault-tolerant software systems.

Table 3.1   Percentage Availability and Downtime

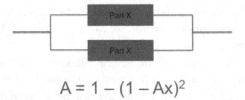

$$A = 1 - (1 - Ax)^2$$

Component	Availability	Downtime
X	99% (2-nines)	3 days 15 hours
Two X in parallel	99.99% (4-nines)	52 minutes
Three X in parallel	99.9999% (6-nines)	31 seconds

Also, software testing and analysis methods through automated tools come handy when eliminating any kind of deviations and deficiencies in software libraries. In the recent past, with the faster maturity and stability of containers, errors or attacks on containerized microservices could be easily identified and contained within their containers toward the goal of fault isolation. Through this isolation, any kind of misadventures and misdemeanors can be stopped on their way preemptively, which means a compromised component need not affect other components within the system. This avoids the complete shutdown of the system. Failed services can be rectified and restarted or the redundant service instances can be leveraged to ensure the business continuity. The fault-tolerance capability of IT systems guarantees that there is no service interruption. Systems are innately empowered to continuously deliver their assigned functionalities in the event of internal failures and external attacks.

3.6.2.3 Auto-Scaling Capability

As defined elsewhere in this book, reliability is resiliency plus elasticity; that is, IT infrastructures ought to be extremely elastic. They have to be application aware to meet up any kind of spikes in user and data loads, and infrastructure modules and assets have to be elastic. The popular compute instances such as VMs and containers have to be automatically provisioned in addition to the existing ones to tackle extra load. Similarly, other infrastructural components such as networking solutions and storage appliances have to be enabled to auto-scale in when necessary. These are coarse-grained IT resources. The fine-grained IT resources such as memory, processing power and input-output capability also need to have the power to be self-scaling in an on-demand manner. Thus, any spike in load can be met by IT resources in an automated manner with less intervention, involvement and interpretation of human resources. In the cloud era, additional IT modules can be provisioned across nearby availability zones by taking the location constraints into account. The intelligent capacity planning and management acquires special significance here. Infrastructures as well as applications have to be architected and designed in such a manner to support auto-scaling intrinsically. There are patterns, procedures and practices that have come out with highly scalable applications and services. With the deployment of web-scale applications and as the traffic varies quite frequently in a big way, the auto-scaling feature must be available these days.

3.6.2.4 Real-Time Scalability

Provisioning additional resources to meet increasing demands is being sped up through the leverage of application containers. Containers, as articulated in other chapters, are lightweight so bringing forth additional containers concurrently is faster and easier. Thus, the goal of a real-time scalability facility is being realized through the containerization movement. Containers typically take a couple of seconds to be alive, whereas VMs need a few minutes. BM servers take several minutes to be ready to receive clients' requests. Thus, considering the limitations of physical and VMs, horizontal scalability has gained prominence recently.

3.7 Infrastructure as Code (IaC)

The widely quoted benefit of IaC is repeatability and reproducibility. There are a number of components (server, network, security, storage etc.) in any data center to be configured to deploy applications. In cloud environments, there are thousands of such components to be configured. If all configurations are done manually, then the time taken is huge and error-prone. Further, there are possibilities for creeping in configuration differences and drifts. Humans are not great at undertaking repetitive and manual tasks with 100% accuracy, but machines are very good at doing repetitive, redundant and routine tasks at scale and speed. If we produce a template and input it into a machine, the machine can execute the template a thousand times without making any error. This template-centric approach for infrastructure provisioning, configuration and application deployment has gained wider attraction and attention these days. Infrastructure optimization and management get elegantly simplified through the leverage of well-designed templates. With the concept of IaC picking up steadily, the infrastructure setup and sustenance is being streamlined with ease and elegance. With enhanced visibility, controllability and observability, IT infrastructures are manipulated as we do programming software applications. The infrastructure life cycle management activities are automated through a host of advancements happening in the pioneering IaC space.

> *Immutable infrastructure:* Instead of getting updated, immutable components are being replaced for every deployment; that is, no updates are being performed on live systems. It is all about provisioning a new instance of the resource. Containers are the best example for immutable infrastructure resources. Similarly, fresh instances of various Amazon web services (AWS) images are being created and deployed instead of updating the existing instances.
>
> *Tip:* To support application deployment in an immutable infrastructure, the canary deployment is recommended. The canary deployment reduces the risk of failure when new versions of applications go to production environments. It helps to gradually roll out the new version to a small set of users and then to expand it to make it available to everyone. This is vividly illustrated in Figure 3.15.
>
> The real benefit of canary deployment is that it is possible to roll back the new version if there is any issue. Thus, faster yet safer deployment of applications with real production data is facilitated through the canary deployment model.

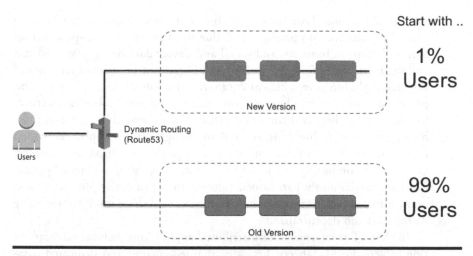

Figure 3.15   New versions for a small set of users.

Stateless applications: As articulated elsewhere, for enabling auto-scaling, applications have to be stateless. For immutable infrastructures, the stateless feature is important; that is, any request can be expertly handled by any resource. Stateless applications respond to all client requests independently of prior requests or sessions. There is no need for the applications to store any information in memory or in local disks. Keeping state information in the application server may lead to performance degradation when there is a huge number of requests from different users. Generally, sharing state information with any resources within the auto-scaling group has to be accomplished through in-memory databases (IMDBs) and in-memory data grids (IMDGs). The popular products are Redis, Memcached and Apache Ignite among others. Thus, to have reliable infrastructure and application, we need IaC, stateless application, immutable infrastructure, automation through DevOps tools, etc.

Avoiding cascading failures: Generally, any error/misbehavior in one component of any system gets quickly propagated across the system to bring down the whole system. Thus, it is mandatory to unearth and use competent techniques that intrinsically help to avoid those cascading failures. A classic example of a cascading failure is overload, which is when one component is stressed due to heavy load and is in utter distress. All of the other components depending on the stressed component may be made to wait exorbitantly, that is, when precious and expensive resources are being exhausted and resultantly, the whole system may be out of work. Thus, fault identification and isolation in a preemptive manner is vital for the intended success of any complicated and sophisticated system. There are a few widely accentuated approaches and algorithms to avoid cascading failures.

Distributed systems: Due to various business evolutions, we are heading toward distributed computing. First, due to the varying size, speed, structure and scope of business, and social and device data being generated and collected, we need highly optimized and organized IT infrastructures and integrated platforms for efficient data virtualization, cleansing, storage and processing. We aspire to have path-breaking platforms and infrastructures for performing big, real-time and streaming data analytics. Second, we have a great deal of highly integrated and insight-driven applications, that is, we are destined to have both data- and process-intensive applications. Distributed computing is the way forward. Large-scale complex applications are meticulously partitioned into a number of easily producible and manageable application components/services, and these modules are being distributed and decentralized.

The key IT components for distributed applications include web/application servers; load-balancers; firewalls; sharded, shared and dedicated databases and DNS servers among others. There are a few crucial challenges associated with distributed systems. The security, service discovery, service integration, service availability and reliability, network latency, etc. are the widely circulated issues of distributed computing. Experts and evangelists have studied these problems thoroughly and have recommended a series of best practices, evaluation metrics and architecture and design patterns among others.

Having understood the significance of resiliency engineering, there is a set of resiliency patterns to come out with reliable systems. Also, there are resiliency-enablement frameworks, platform solutions, programming models, etc. to sufficiently enhance system and service reliability.

Retry: The one standard technique for tackling the issues related to the famous distributed computing is to apply the proven "retry" method. In this method, the service requesters attempt to redo the failed operation as soon as an error occurs. The issue is when there are a large number of requesters, the network can start to feel the stress, that is, the network bandwidth will be completely drained and resultantly the system is bound to collapse. To avoid such scenarios, back-off algorithms such as the common exponential back-off are recommended to be used. The exponential back-off algorithms gradually increase the rate at which retries are performed. This way, the network congestion can be greatly avoided.

Timeouts: Timeouts are another resiliency-guaranteeing method. Suppose there is steady baseline traffic, and all of a sudden the database slows down and INSERT queries take more time to respond. The baseline traffic has not changed so the sudden slowdown occurs because more request threads are holding the database connections. Resultantly, the pool of database connections has shrunken significantly. There are no connections left out in the pool to serve any other API so other APIs start to fail. This is a classic example of cascading failure. If the API was timing out instead of clinging to the database, the service performance could have been completed; instead, there was an unwanted complete failure. Thus, the timeout phenomenon has to occur to achieve service resiliency.

Idempotent operations: This is an important facet in ensuring data consistency and integrity. If a client request is sent out as a message over the HTTP to an application, due to a transient error there can be a timeout reply from the application. The request message could have been received and processed by the application. Still, because of the timeout response, the user goes for the retry option.

Suppose the request is an INSERT to the back-end database. When the retry option is applied again, there is a possibility for a repeat insertion of the same data. These errors can be avoided if the application implements idempotent operations. An idempotent operation is the one that can be repeated any number of times, and this repetition does not affect the application in any way. Importantly, the same result will be delivered even if repeatedly tried.

Service degradation and fallbacks: Instead of a complete shutdown, an application can be allowed to degrade to provide a lower-quality service; that is, the application response may be a bit slow, or the throughput of the application is on the lower side. This is a kind of trade-off to be made instead of application failure. One or other fallback options have to be employed.

Let us see what happens if it is a database. If INSERT queries become slow, then it is prudent to go for timeout and then fall back to the read-only mode on the database until the issue with the INSERT gets sorted out. If the application does not support the read-only mode, then the cached content can be returned to the user.

Resilience against intermittent and transient errors: With cloud environments emerging as the one-stop IT solution for business processes and operations automation, augmentation and acceleration requirements, enterprise-class applications are meticulously modernized and migrated to clouds to reap all the originally expressed and eulogized benefits of the flourishing cloud idea. Building and deploying application components in a distributed manner with centralized governance becomes the new normal as the aspect of hybrid IT is gaining its grip on IT in general. There are several problems cropping up with large-scale distributed systems in cloud environments. Due to the exorbitant rise in the size and the complexity (heterogeneity and multiplicity-induced) of the systems and the architecture used, the occurrence of intermittent errors is not ruled out. The well-known intermittent errors include transient network connectivity, request timeouts, input-output operations and the dependency on external services, which becomes overloaded.

Hence, there is a clarion call for a producing resilient system that can intelligently come back to its previous and preferred state if attacked and affected. The best practice is to design systems to fail not to be fail-proof. The complications of modern IT systems demand that we need to design, develop and deploy resilient and versatile applications. Applications have to be designed to be extremely fault-tolerant to continuously deliver their ordained functionality. One expert idea is to collect the statistical data about the various intermittent errors and, based on that information, define a threshold that can trigger the correct reaction to errors.

Circuit breaking: This is a widely implemented resiliency technique by various web-scale service providers. This technique is all about applying circuit breakers to failing method calls to avoid any kind of catastrophic and cascading failure. As reported earlier, timeout, back-off, allowing service degradation, fallbacks and intermittent error handling are the key methods to prevent cascading failures.

A circuit breaker monitors for the number of consecutive failures between a producer and a consumer. If the number passes over a failure threshold, the circuit breaker object trips, and all attempts by the producer to invoke the consumer will fail immediately, or return a defined fallback. After a waiting period, the circuit breaker allows few requests to pass through. If those requests successfully pass a success threshold, the circuit breaker resumes its normal state; otherwise, it stays broken and continues monitoring the consumer. Figure 3.16 shows an example of a circuit breaker with timeouts.

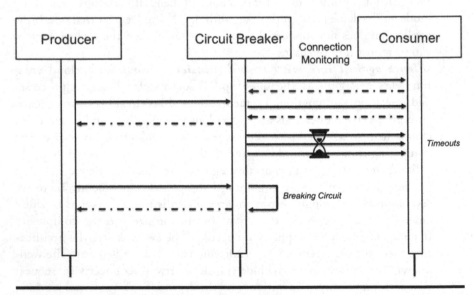

Figure 3.16   Circuit breaker monitoring the failure.

Circuit breaking is being presented as one of the key resilient methods, and such resiliency-enabling mechanisms inspire software architects and engineers to incorporate the resiliency measures while designing and building software systems. There are free implementations such as Hystrix and they can be incorporated in the source code to arrive at resilient applications.

Load balancing: This is another resiliency aspect widely used in enterprise and cloud IT environments. With a larger number of services and their instances being stuffed into any IT environment, there is a need for load balancers for distributing application and device requests to multiple instances of one or more application components by understanding the latest load scenario of each application component. How every instance is occupied is taken into consideration by the load balancer to route client requests so as to balance the load. This clearly helps in maintaining the system resiliency. There are hardware and software load balancers on the market. Consistent and continuous health checks of microservices are extremely vital for their continued service delivery. Load balancers are capable of doing a health check, as depicted in Figure 3.17. Load balancers are continuously probing their service instances and, if a service is not available for fulfilling service requests, then load balancers will redirect service requests to one of the functioning service instances. As articulated somewhere, there can be several reasons for services to go down or unable to fulfill their obligations in time. The service database may not be responding, the service may be overwhelmed with too many service requests or the network may not be available transiently.

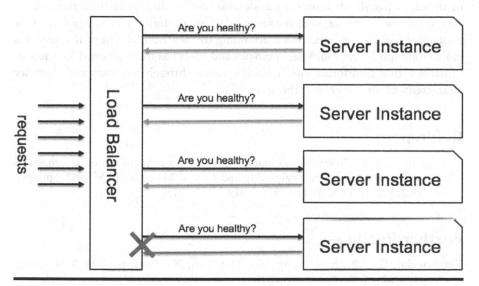

Figure 3.17 Load balancer monitoring server instances.

With the multiplicity of microservices, services and their communications have to be guaranteed for resiliency. There are several straightforward ways and means of ensuring service resiliency as articulated in the above sections. When we have resilient services, through the various composition methods, resilient services lead to reliable systems.

As we all know, enterprise-scale and mission-critical applications are made out of distributed and decentralized microservices. With the adoption of containerized microservices, the availability of microservices is significantly increased through the deployment of multiple instances of the services. That is, multiple instances of the same microservice are being deployed through the leverage of containers, which emerge as the most optimal runtime/execution environment for microservices. When one service experiences some difficulties, its instance can be asked to deliver the expected functionality. The API gateway works as the mediator and coordinator of microservices. The location intelligence along with the network latency plays an extremely vital role in finalizing service instances in place of the service.

3.8 Conclusion

With the role and responsibility of IT continuously rising in elevating business operations and people tasks, the complexity induced by the multiplicity and heterogeneity of IT systems is on the rise consistently. There are a number of noteworthy advancements in IT that have resulted in a variety of business processes becoming optimized, simplified and automated. Business agility is being fulfilled through the IT agility mechanisms. Business deployment and service models have gone through a few delectable transitions in the recent past with faster maturity and stability of the cloud paradigm. Business transformations are directly enabled through IT transformation; however, with the faster adoption of digital technologies, the new concept of digital transformation is becoming the new normal. The goal of business reality through IT reliability technologies and tools has to be attained for the sustainable digital transformation. Reliable systems through resiliency and elasticity characteristics are the need of the hour.

References

1. Martin Garriga, "Towards a Taxonomy of Micro-services Architectures," International Conference on Software Engineering and Formal Methods SEFM 2017, Springer, 203–218, 2017, DOI: 10.1007/978-3-319-74781-1_15.

Further Readings

Yin Kanglin, Du Qingfeng, Wang Wei, Qiu Juan, Xu Jincheng, "On Representing and Eliciting Resilience Requirements of Micro-service Architecture Systems," arXiv:1909.13096v2 [cs.SE] 22 Jun 2020.

Andre van Hoorn, Aldeida Aleti, Thomas F. Dullmann, Teerat Pitakrat, "ORCAS: Efficient Resilience Benchmarking of Micro-Service Architectures," 29th IEEE International Symposium on Software Reliability Engineering (ISSRE 2018), IEEE, 2018.

Roberto Pietrantuono, Stefano Russo, Antonio Guerriero, "Run-Time Reliability Estimation of Micro Service Architectures," 2018 IEEE 29th International Symposium on Software Reliability Engineering (ISSRE), IEEE, 2018, DOI: 10.1109/ISSRE.2018.00014.

Nuha Alshuqayran, Nour Ali, Roger Evans, "A Systematic Mapping Study in Micro-Service Architecture," 2006 IEEE 9th International Conference on Service-Oriented Computing and Applications, IEEE, 2016, DOI 10.1109/SOCA.2016.15.

Armin Balalaie, Abbas Heydarnoori, Pooyan Jamshidi, "Migrating to Cloud-Native Architectures Using Micro-Services: An Experience Report," arXiv:1507.08217v1 [cs.SE] 29 Jul 2015.

Inna Vistbakka, Elena Troubitsyna, "Modelling Autonomous Resilient Multi-robotic Systems," *Springer Nature Switzerland AG 2019, SERENE 2019, LNCS 11732*, 29–45, 2019, DOI: 10.1007/978-3-030-30856-8_3.

David Ebo Adjepon-Yamoah, "Reactive Middleware for Effective Requirement Change Management of Cloud-Based Global Software Development," *Springer Nature Switzerland AG 2019, SERENE 2019, LNCS 11732*, 29–45, 2019, DOI: 10.1007/978-3-030-30856-8_4.

Jacopo Parri, Fulvio Patara, Samuele Sampietro, Enrico Vicario, "JARVIS, A Hardware/Software Framework for Resilient Industry 4.0 Systems," *Springer Nature Switzerland AG 2019, SERENE 2019, LNCS 11732*, 29–45, 2019, DOI: 10.1007/978-3-030-30856-8_6.

Sukhpal Singh Gill, Rajkumar Buyya, "Failure Management for Reliable Cloud Computing: A Taxonomy, Model, and Future Directions," *Computing in Science & Engineering*, 22(3), 52–63, 2020.

Zeida Solarte, Juan D. Gonzalez, Lyda Peña, Oscar H. Mondragon, "Microservices-Based Architecture for Resilient Cities Applications," *Springer Nature Switzerland AG 2021, ETA 2019, LNEE 685*, 423–432, 2021, DOI: 10.1007/978-3-030-53021-1_43.

Paul de Vrieze, Lai Xu, "Resilience Analysis of Service-Oriented Collaboration Process Management Systems," *Service Oriented Computing and Applications*, 12, 25–39, 2018, DOI: 10.1007/s11761-018-0233-5.

Nabor C. Mendonça, Carlos M. Aderaldo, Javier Camara, David Garlan, "Model-Based Analysis of Micro-Service Resiliency Patterns," 2020 IEEE International Conference on Software Architecture (ICSA), IEEE, 2020, DOI: 10.1109/ICSA47634.2020.00019.

Elena Troubitsyna, "Model-Driven Engineering of Fault Tolerant Micro-Services," *ICIW 2019*, Fourteenth International Conference on Internet and Web Applications and Services, ARIA, 2019, ISBN: 978-1-61208-728-3.

Denise Ratasich, Faiq Khalid, Lorian Geissler, Radu Grosu, Muhammad Shafique, Ezio Bartocci, "A Roadmap Toward the Resilient Internet of Things for Cyber-Physical Systems," *IEEE Access*, 7, 13260–13283, 2019, DOI: 10.1109/ACCESS.2019.2891969.

Javad Ghofrani, Daniel Lübke, "Challenges of Micro-Services Architecture: A Survey on the State of the Practice," Proceedings of the 10th ZEUS Workshop, Dresden, Germany, 2018.

Cleber Santana, Leandro Andrade, Brenno Mello, Ernando Batista, José Vitor Sampaio, Cássio Prazeres, "A Reliable Architecture Based on Reactive Micro-Services for IoT Applications," 2019 Proceedings of the 25th Brazilian Symposium on Multimedia and the Web, ACM, 2019, DOI: 10.1145/3323503.3345027.

Hulya Vural, Murat Koyuncu, Sinem Guney, "A Systematic Literature Review on Microservices," Springer International Publishing AG 2017, *ICCSA*, 2017, Part VI, LNCS 10409, 203–217, 2017, DOI: 10.1007/978-3-319-62407-5_14.

Nane Kratzke, "A Brief History of Cloud Application Architectures," *Applied Sciences*, 8, 1368, 2018, DOI: 10.3390/app8081368.

Ron Ross, Victoria Pillitteri, Richard Graubart, Deborah Bodeau, Rosalie Mcquaid, "Developing Cyber Resilient Systems: A Systems Security Engineering Approach," *Computer Security*, NIST Special Publication, 800–160, *Volume 2, Nov* 2019, DOI: 10.6028/NIST.SP.800-1 60v2.

Chapter 4

Service Resiliency in Cloud and Network Function Virtualization

---

Rathnakar Achary

Alliance University

Contents

4.1 Introduction

Companies providing cloud service have developed an approach for increasing cloud resiliency by identifying and analyzing potential failures. Generally, the traditional software systems are embedded with fault prevention mechanisms. This enables the isolation of the customers on premises deployment. The cloud service system is typically run as a highly complex distributed system supporting many customers. It is designed to always be available and is normally built by using commodity hardware and is dependent on third-party applications to run them. The services are deployed to the end customers by means of a global network such as the Internet.

Persistent failures of these networks are another challenge to deliver uninterrupted cloud services to customers, so designers need to develop and incorporate managing mechanisms into the cloud service design and the software system to minimize the harmful effects of such failures. These failures are categorized as spectrum failure, such as a natural disaster (most infrequent), and common failures, such as failure of hardware systems, failure of Internet connectivity, software failure due to software imperfection or failure due to human error. Among these the former ones are inevitable, whereas the latter one is most frequent. Most importantly failure existence and effect must be factored into the service during the design phase of the cloud systems. This enables the software systems designed with an inbuilt fault-tolerant resilient mechanism to minimize the impact of failure [1]. Figure 4.1 represents the spectrum of failure ranging from uncommonly increasing failure to common failure and the common resilient mechanisms.

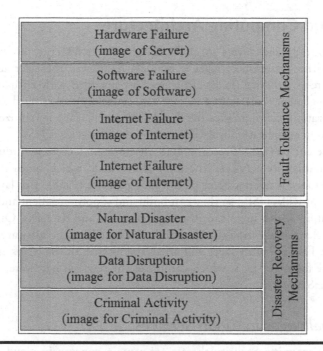

Figure 4.1 Different failover techniques.

If the failure of cloud services is inevitable, then the designers of the cloud services systems must design to extend time between failure (TBF) and design to minimize the time to recover (TTR) from failure. If the failures are from a common source and common place, they must be considered with utmost importance to detect them quickly and build handling techniques that minimize the effects on customers. Resiliency is defined as the capacity of a system or an infrastructure or a business to remain reliable, failure tolerant, survivable, dependable and secure in case of any malicious or accidental malfunctions or failures that result in a transitory or permanent service distraction.

Resiliency in cloud computing is classified into two major categories:

1. Infrastructure-based resilience
2. Application-based resilience

Infrastructure-based resilience mainly targets the physical and virtualization layer, whereas the application-based resiliency minimizes the downtime and its impact on cloud services. Cloud services include the application of resilience in the areas of

1. Developing resilient application
2. Resilient application collaboration
3. Resilient application management

4.2 Cloud Computing Architecture

There are four distinct layers in cloud computing architecture as illustrated in Figure 4.2. The bottommost layer is physical resources. The layer above this is infrastructure as a service (IaaS). This layer is embedded with virtualization and system management tools. Cloud infrastructure usually comprises the datacenters and virtualization techniques for the cloud deployment. IaaS maximizes the use of physical resource application isolation and quality of service (QoS).

The different services offered by IaaS are normally accessed through a set of user-level middleware services. The layer above IaaS, which binds all user-level middleware tools, is referred to as platform as a service (PaaS). This layer supports PaaS service providers (SPs) so they can build and supply a resilient and optimized environment on which users can install applications and data sets. On the top of this user-level are applications that are built and hosted on the software as a service (SaaS) layer. Failure in any layer will affect the services of the layers above it. For example, the failure of IaaS, which comprises the physical hardware, will impact PaaS and SaaS layers.

4.2.1 Challenges in Cloud Services

1. *Cloud security:* Security threats are a main concern in cloud computing. Malicious or unintended actions can cause damage at many levels in a cloud computing system. The attack surface of cloud services is higher than the traditional service model. This can be addressed by a variety of approaches to mitigate these threats. One of the common threats to cloud computing is distribute denial of service (DDoS). A number of techniques are proposed to prevent these kinds of threats like traffic isolation or access control lists to create rules that define the permissions of a component with several levels of granularity. Researchers also proposed intelligent solutions to detect intrusions in cloud deployment.

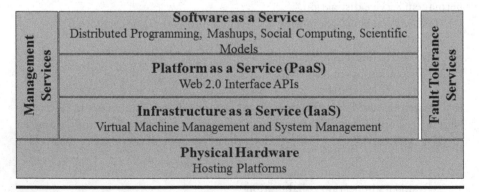

Figure 4.2   Layered architecture of cloud computing.

2. ***Resilience and cloud availability:*** Similar to other traditional systems, cloud computing system availability is also not free from failure. Resiliency is the ability to handle failures gracefully and recover the whole system. This is one of the main challenges for providing uninterrupted services and applications where the components compete for resources. The purpose of an efficient cloud resilience system is to detect, fix and recover the damage. To support this, tools are available to simulate random failure, from hardware issues to massive external attacks. This even includes failed deployments or unused software behavior. Some of the basic techniques used to increase the resiliency of cloud computing system are as follows:
   - ***Checking and monitoring:*** An independent process continuously reviews the system and meets the minimum specification behavior. This technique, although simple, is key to detect failures and reconfiguration of resources.
   - ***Checkpoints and restart:*** The status of the entire system or the key status variables are saved based on certain circumstances. System failure shows a process of restoration to the latest correct checkpoint and the system recovery.
   - ***Replication:*** Data in a cloud storage are always replicated to ensure durability and high availability. Storage replication copies a tenant's data so that they are protected from planned and unplanned events ranging from transient hardware failure, network or power outage, massive natural disaster and so forth. Tenants can choose to replicate the data within the same datacenter or in multiple datacenters.
3. ***Cloud data management:*** Another interesting challenge to traditional cloud management is data management. Today there are innumerable cases related to data management because of the requirements of handling different types of databases, such as document databases, big table databases and graph and column databases. The main requirement is to maintain data consistency. Cloud management also needs to aggregate, extend, transform and analyze the data based on several contexts. Another important aspect of data management to be addressed is the consistency of the data. This means that all the users of the cloud application should see the same data at the same time.

4.2.2 Cloud Service Disruption

In this section we provide an overview of the disruptions of cloud services. Various causes for disruptions are categorized as follows:

1. ***Physical failure (failure of infrastructure):*** It represents failure of the infrastructure and the resources. The physical failure is spread along the length and breadth of the cloud infrastructure. It starts from the physical layer and then affects the functions of the virtualization and application layers. This also affects the multiple servers and resources in the cloud infrastructure.

2. **Software failure:** These are caused by errors in the software, software aging, software bugs, errors due to the application design and malicious software programs.
3. **Human error:** This is mainly due to human actions. It is categorized as intentional or unintentional. Unintentional actions are due to accidentally deleting a file or accidental modification of programs. This can be controlled and fixed. Intentional errors like espionage and identity theft are produced by attacks or sabotage to destroy or disrupt the cloud services and data storage.
4. **Disaster:** These can be natural disasters or human-induced ones. Natural disasters such as tornadoes, earthquakes, tsunamis and so forth may destroy infrastructures like datacenters and networking links. Human-induced disasters are caused by terrorist attacks or mob destruction attacks. Failure due to disaster often has a higher impact on cloud services. They can even spread as a cascade of hardware and software failure.

4.2.2.1 Impact of Cloud Service Disruption

The impact of service disruptions is classified into four categories:

1. **Masked disruption:** The cloud SP can recuperate effected cloud instances without causing any service distraction for the end users.
2. **Degraded service:** In this case the tenants are able to receive the service, with compromised QoS. The service disruptions may incur penalties.
3. **Unreachable service:** In this case the intended services by the tenants are available on the server, but they cannot access the services. These service disruptions are common in the case of network communication failure.
4. **Corrupted services:** In this type of service disruption, the service cannot be recovered and tenants lose critical data. This may lead to revenue loss and legal action against the cloud SP for breach of the service-level agreement (SLA).

4.2.2.2 Consequence of Cloud Service Disruptions

Cloud service disruption incurs losses in different ways to different tenants. This includes the following:

1. **Repair cost:** To bring the system up to the cloud, SPs must have a budget for the repair of the servers and network functions [2].
2. **Penalty cost:** Disruption of the cloud service increases the penalty cost for the cloud applications and cloud infrastructure [2, 3].
3. **Business revenue loss:** Dependence on the cloud is rising year by year. In 2015, 25% of companies used IaaS as their primary environment, and that

percentage is expected to increase by 12% in 2018. Cloud service disruption results in cloud service outage. The business loss due to service disruption is expected to rise to 37% in the United States.

4.3 Classification of Cloud Resilience Approaches

The different resilience approaches in cloud computing are classified as resiliency strategy, metrics for resiliency objectives and categorization of surveyed cloud resiliency approaches [4].

4.3.1 Resiliency Strategy

The cloud SP has to have an appropriate resiliency strategy. This strategy addresses the resiliency from the traditional classification of network resiliency and the resiliency of datacenters. A broad classification to cover all the resilience techniques is addressed in [5]. This taxonomy includes failure projecting and exclusion, protection and restoration.

1. ***Failure forecasting and removal:*** This strategy deals with proactively assessing the probability of failure and its consequences for the system and application. For cloud infrastructure and resource providers an effective failure forecasting mechanism helps to minimize the effect of the failure and the cascading effect of the same on cloud infrastructure [3]. The fault predictive and mitigation technique is classified as proactive and reactive fault tolerance.

   A proactive fault tolerance technique avoids extra effort for recovering the failed nodes, tasks and so forth by predicting faults before they happen and replacing them with other elements. Reactive fault tolerance is when the actual fault occurs in the system; this technique helps to reduce the impact of failures on the active systems. Some of the techniques under the proactive fault tolerance scheme are software rejuvenation, self-healing and preemptive migration. The types of reactive fault tolerance are checkpointing, replication, job migration, task resubmission, reuse workflow and so forth.

2. ***Protection:*** Protection provides pre-deploying redundant or standby computational capacity and communication capacity to recover the service in case of failure.

   a. ***Replication:*** The replication method provides duplicate or alternative facilities in partial or complete duplication of capacity. This provides protection of the resources in case of failure. Replication can be classified as passive or active.

   Passive replication: In this scheme a working component and a dedicated backup replica are in use, where the backup is activated in case of failure of the working component to avoid disruption.

> *Active replication:* An active replication maintains multiple copies and updated versions of programming both for storage and networking.
>
> b. *Check pointing:* It periodically saves the system stakes. In case the original instance fails, in this case it can be restored.

3. *Restoration:* It is one of the most common and best effort schemes. This technique reloads the failed application component when the system reboots.

4.3.2 Resiliency Techniques for Cloud Infrastructure

Cloud infrastructure encompasses multiple datacenters, interconnected by redundant communication facilities. Resiliency practices can ensure the availability of the infrastructure for the cloud users. The cloud computing infrastructure with different layers and their interconnection by communication network [6] is shown in the Figure 4.3. The resiliency technique for cloud infrastructure is categorized into six groups as illustrated in Figure 4.4. The first two groups (I, II) deal with the resiliency inside the cloud infrastructure and specifically with resiliency facilities for the key components of datacenters such as power generating plants and resiliency of servers.

Categories III and IV include the resiliency in the inter datacenter communication networks and resiliency of the combination of network links with the servers. The last two groups (V and VI) focus on higher level components to deal with resiliency of middleware and some measurement and estimation techniques for resiliency.

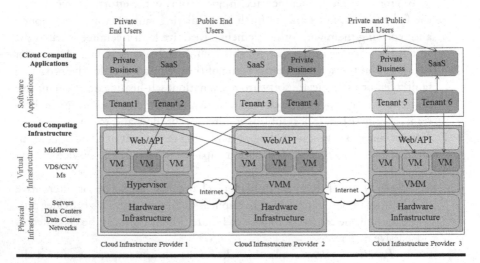

Figure 4.3 Cloud computing infrastructure. API, application programming interface; CN, Computer Networks; VD, Virtual Desks; VM, virtual machine.

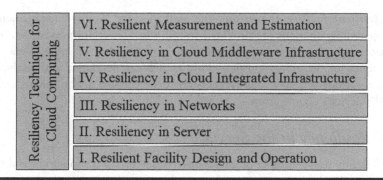

Figure 4.4   Resiliency techniques for cloud computing.

4.3.3 Design of Resilient Facility

The primary function of the cloud server companies is to protect the cloud computing infrastructure. This includes the resiliency of datacenters from the different types of threats. Among these the physical threats are disaster, sabotage, terrorist attack, human error, hardware trip, energy blackouts [7] and weapons of mass destruction (WMD) attacks. The different types of logical threats are hackers and terrorism. Datacenter resiliency is classified into four tiers. This classification is based on the resiliency requirements. Tier 1 represents loose requirements and tier 4 includes the stringent requirements. To reach tier 4, the cloud infrastructure provider must provide resiliency at the cloud resources. Some of these types of resiliency are described as follows:

1. ***Resiliency of power supply:*** Energy supply is an important facility for a cloud computing system. Power resilience has given its critical dependency on the cloud facility [7]. A backup power supply mechanism protects the cloud facility against temporary power interruptions. These outages may be due to malicious attacks, power grid accidents and bad weather conditions. An uninterrupted power supply and an emergency power generation system can minimize the impact of these vulnerabilities. The quality of the power supply also may be degraded due to sudden power fluctuations, surges or spikes. Cloud facilities are also protected from the effects of poor-quality power supply. A quality power supply can be provided to a datacenter by a secured power distribution unit (PDU) and an uninterrupted high-voltage DC distribution (HVDC) system to provide a quality power supply [8]. The cloud infrastructure requires a continuous cooling system to protect the devices from overheating. A redundant cooling system can minimize the effect due to heat accumulation.
2. ***Resilient facility access:*** This mechanism protects the cloud infrastructure from the physical and cyber access of malicious users.

3. **Resilient facility operation:** The staff at cloud facility management and operations divisions are provided training for detection, prevention, mitigation and recovery in case of malicious attacks. Most of the resiliency techniques for the protection of a cloud facility are developed and analyzed for the various industry requirements with the support and standardization of the device's organization.

4.3.4 Resiliency in the Server

A cloud facility uses a number of interconnected servers for computation and storage purposes. Resiliency in servers is implemented in two ways, in the physical and/or in the virtualization layer. The resiliency in the physical sever covers the resiliency techniques for the physical server and storage units; whereas the resiliency in the virtual server (VS) covers the resiliency technique for virtual machines (VMs) and virtual storage. The taxonomy of resiliency [5] in server technique is illustrated in Figure 4.5.

4.3.4.1 Resiliency in the Physical Sever

The resiliency in a datacenter supports the recovery from failure and the protection of the tenant's data at different levels, such as servers, hardware components, running processes and the data. The resiliency in the physical server and the VS are different in nature. The physical failure isolation technique provides failure removal in the physical machine (PM) components and process and VS resiliency includes resiliency in VMs and virtual storage.

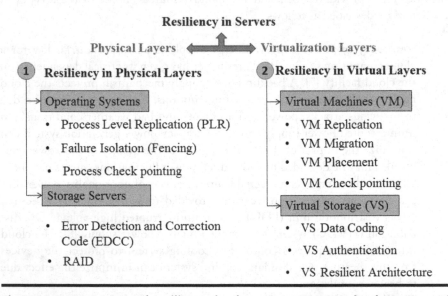

Figure 4.5 Taxonomy of resiliency in the server. RAID, redundant array of independent disks.

The failure of the physical server enforces the removal of failures in PM components and processes, while in the process level replication the resiliency enforces failure protection and process checkpointing. This provides failure recovery in the process level. There are different techniques for fault tolerance and data retrieval. The very popular ones are redundant array of independent disks (RAID) and error detection and correction codes (EDCC) [9]. Failure propagation due to the failed hardware components and processes is prevented by failure fencing and isolation. The fencing used in multiprocessor architecture in the failure contention and component retirement is explained in [10].

Process-level replication (PLR): PLR uses the software-centric model of transient fault detection. It replicates the Application and Library codes, global data, heap, stack, file descriptor table and so forth. PLR leverages the operating systems to schedule the redundant processes to take advantage of the hardware resources. With the availability of the multicore hardware infrastructure, the PLR provides a way to utilize the redundant hardware resources for transient fault tolerance.

Failure isolation (fencing): This is the process of separating the failed hardware and software process, which includes the failed components, links or software process. The fencing technique used in a multiprocessor architecture includes the failure contention and component retirements.

Providing checkpoints: This mechanism re-initializes the process or an operating system when a failure occurs. The cloud management tools use reset/reboot to deal with a failed process in PMs or VMs [11].

EDCC: This technique is used to detect and correct the error in data stored on memory and storage devices. Generally, memory storage uses one-bit correction code and two-bit detection code. This periodic parity check method is used to detect and correct uses of one bit per byte. The practical parity check method includes Hamming code and Reed-Solomon code, which are commonly used with EDCC [12]. The main limitation of EDCC is that it consumes large resources for processing.

Redundant array of independent (or inexpensive) disks: RAID uses several independent and relatively small disks in combination with a large-size single storage. A RAID enables expansion of storage capacity by combining many small disks. A RAID mechanism can be implemented by hardware, software or a hybrid of both. Software RAID uses the server's operating systems to virtualize and manage the RAID array [9]. The cloud infrastructure provider configures the RAID in the server in different ways (RAID0 to RAID6).

These levels of RAID use the following methods of storing data in the array:

1. *Striping:* This consists of splitting the flow of data into blocks of a certain size, then writing these blocks across the RAID one by one.

2. *Mirroring:* In mirroring identical copies of the data are stored on the RAID members simultaneously.
3. *Parity:* This is a storage technique that utilizes stripping and checksum methods.

4.3.4.2 Resiliency in the Virtual Server

Resiliency in the VS is mainly due to the VMs that provide server virtualization. The protection of the VS is provided by VM replication in the cloud datacenter; it is a type of VM protection mechanism. VM replication takes a copy of the VM as it is right now and copies it to another VM. This replication is done whether the VM is on the same host or on the remote host. The VS recovery is provided by VM relocation and VS data coding. As mentioned in this section, the resiliency approach in VS is a combination of VS protection, recovery and failure removal VM checkpointing and VM placement mechanisms. This mechanism of resiliency is done by *replicating VMs* in multiple PMs in homogeneous and heterogeneous environments (both for PMs and operating systems), whereas VM migration is the process of complete relocation of VM content from a defective PM to a non-defective PM. This mechanism is considered a best effort and low cost recovery mechanism. The two approaches used in *VM migrations* are pre-copy and post copy, where the former one relocates the full VM contents of both memory and storage before initiating the user's reconnection. This induces a significant amount of service downtime. The latter one progressively reproduces the content of the VM without effecting the user connectivity [13]. The *VM checkpointing* technique periodically saves the entire state of the system without shutting it down. One of the main limitations of VM checkpointing is the synchronization overhead. It also requires a large number of VMs. Generally, similarity compression reduces the storage space by using compression algorithms. A page caching technique is used to minimize the storage space required with high-speed and capacity-efficient VM checkpoints

> *VM placement:* VM placement is the process of selecting the appropriate PM for a given VM [13]. A placement technique aims to determine the most optimal VM to PM mapping whether it is an initial VM placement or a VM migration for placement re-optimization [11]. The different algorithms are used for VM placement techniques. These algorithms are classified based on the goal of placement and on the type of principle approach used.

> ■ Based on the goals of placement, VM placement techniques are classified as a power approach and a QoS-based approach. The former one aims to obtain VM-PM mapping, which results in a system that is energy efficient with extreme resource utilization. The latter one ensures maximal fulfillment of QoS requirements [7].
> ■ Based on the types of principal approach used to attain a desirable VM-PM mapping, the placement technique is classified as constraint programming,

bin packing, stochastic integer programming and genetic algorithms. Appropriate placement techniques are selected based on the resources used [central processing unit (CPU), memory and network band width], their achieved goals and their locations. The pre-migration technique consists in pre-defining a migration location for a VM in case the physical server failure keeps an empty VM as a substitute. The main limitation of this approach is the determination of the point of migration. However, this method minimizes the migration time of baseline. In the second method of resiliency a clustering of VM replicas are distributed in multiple PMs. This avoids the problem of single point failure. In the third system VM assignment can be attained based on the specific resiliency demands of each application. This adaptive fault tolerance is the requirement of real-time cloud computing. It also reduces the downtime.

■ Data coding is a technique for recovering the data of virtualized storage in case of physical failures. If there is a server failure the recovery process uses a scalable Reed-Solomon approach [12]. Using this approach minimizes the resource consumption such as processing time, storage space and bandwidth required for the recovery process. VS authentication ensures data consistency to prevent data losses and unauthorized access of the resources during the failure or attack. The resiliency required is enforced in virtual and cloud storage by adding a specialized layer in the VS resilient architecture design. Two such approaches suggested by the researchers for VS resilient mechanisms developed are cloud storage with minimal trust (Depot) and high availability and integrity layer (HAIL). Both of these techniques enforce data recovery and authentication. The HAIL design adds a layer with a proof-of-irretrievability module in each server to mitigate data losses due to server failure. Depot adds two more layers for the VS architecture. These two layers have specific purposes: the first layer implements data replication and the second layer implements protocols for data consistency and recovery functionalities.

4.4 Datacenter Network Topology

Most of the datacenters use Ethernet switches to interconnect the servers, and there are many datacenter network topologies. These topologies are characterized by different resource requirements aiming to bring enhancements to the performance of the datacenters. A datacenter network (DCN) topology is represented as a graph with servers and switches as the vertices with the wired links as edges. The taxonomy of a DCN topology is seen in Figure 4.6, where there are n number of ports in a switch, k number of ports in the server and N is the total number of servers inside the DCN. Also note that n and k may differ according to the position of the nodes.

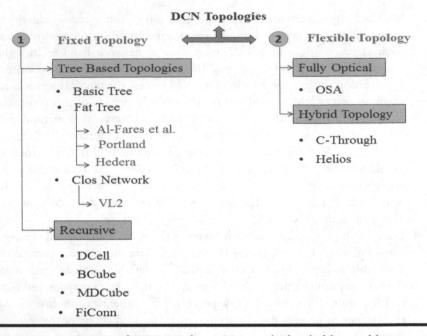

Figure 4.6 Taxonomy of DCN topology. OSA, optical switching architecture.

4.4.1 Classification of DCN

DCN topologies are basically classified as fixed and flexible. A fixed topology is not modifiable after deployment, whereas the flexible topologies are modifiable. The fixed architecture is divided into two categories: tree based and recursive. Tree-based architecture and its variants are extensively used in the design of DCNs. The DCN with flexible architecture mainly uses optical switching technologies [14, 15]. Optical technology provides higher bandwidth and has significant flexibility of reconfiguring the topology during operation.

4.4.1.1 Tree-Based Topology (Fixed Architecture)

Fixed architecture includes tree-based topologies. Different types of tree-based topologies are used for the design of DCNs.

> ***Basic tree:*** This topology includes two or three layers of switches or routers, with servers as the leaves. A three-level topology consists of the core tier at the root, aggregation at the middle and edge tiers of the switches connected to the servers. The switches used in this tier should have higher performance and reliability. The number of servers connected in the edge tier depends on the number of ports on the switches.

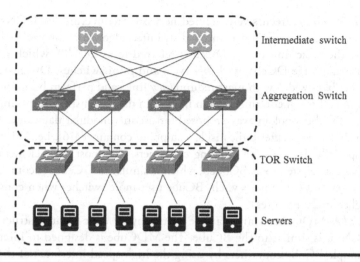

Figure 4.7   DCN architecture with Clos topology.

Fat tree: Fat tree topology is selected to resolve the problem of the network bottleneck and prevent single node failure. It includes three layers, with a core layer, aggregation layer and edge layer. Implementation of the fat tree topologies is a cost-effective solution because it replaces the expensive and more advanced switches in a DCN.

Clos network: This is a multi-rooted tree topology as illustrated in Figure 4.7. When a Clos network is implemented it consists of three levels of switches called input, middle and output. In this network, top-of-rack (TOR) switches are directly connected to the servers, the aggregation switches are connected to TOR switches and the intermediate switches are connected to the aggregation switches. The requirements of the number of switches are determined based on the number of ports available in both the intermediate and aggregation switches. If n is the number of ports in each switch, then the number of aggregation switches is n and the number of intermediate switches is $n/2$. Each intermediate switch and aggregation switch are connected by one link. The remaining $n/2$ ports on each aggregation switch are connected to $n/2$ different TOR switches. Each TOR switch is connected to two different aggregation switches, and the other ports of TOR switches are connected to servers. There are $n^2/4$ TOR switches, and these switches are connected to $(n^2/4)n_{TOR}$ servers in the network.

4.4.1.2 Recursive Topology

The basic difference between a tree-based topology and recursive topology is that in a tree-based topology the servers are connected as leaf nodes. However, in recursive topology the servers may be connected to switches in different levels or even to other servers. The servers in recursive topology consists of multiple ports.

DCell: DCell is a recursively defined network architecture for DCNs. It uses servers and mini switches and a distributed algorithm for packet forwarding. The basic unit of the DCell is referred to as DCell0, which is used to construct large DCells, with n-servers and mini switches. DCells provide a higher bandwidth with mass redundancy links and perform better in one-to-all and all-to-all communication models in data-intensive computing [10].

BCube: BCube topology was proposed for use in a modular datacenter (MDC), which is a datacenter built inside a shipping container [16], i.e., this topology is specially designed for shipping containers. The most basic elements of the BCube is referred to as BCube0, which is similar to DCell0. It connects to an n-server and one n-pot switch. BCube uses more switches when constructing higher level structures.

MDCube: MDCube is an example of the hyper cube–related structure of a DCN; it is similar to the BCube. The MDCube is designed to interconnect multiple BCube containers by using the high-speed interfaces of the BCube switches [16]. These switches contribute to the high-speed interfaces as virtual interfaces for its BCube containers, and they are treated as virtual nodes. The switches can observe only those servers that are directly connected to them, such as the directly connected peer switches and the servers connecting to those peer switches. Hence, MDCubes are considered as server centric and the switches as dumb crossbars.

FiConn: FiConn is the modified DCell architecture; it is a traditional commercial server network that uses two network adapters. One of the adapters is used for receiving data and forwarding, and another adapter is used for redundancy. FiConn is used to reduce the mass redundancy caused by this architecture. FiConn structure uses a compound graph to accommodate a large number of servers (Figure 4.8) for a level 1 FiConn architecture. For a level 4 FiConn with a 16-port switch, the number of servers is 3,553,776. FiConn uses idle ports of the switches and servers and switches to connect with other devices, which reduces the number of redundancy links and the network adapters on the server. One of the main advantages of FiConn compared with DCell is that it minimizes the overhead when establishing the network by decreasing performance [17].

VL2: VL2 is a tree-based architecture that connects all servers through a virtual two-layer Ethernet [18] as illustrated in Figure 4.9. The network is located in the same local area network (LAN) with servers. It uses Clos topology to establish the connectivity and Valiant load-balancing (VLB) as the routing mechanism for load balancing. To forward the data over multiple optimal paths and resolve the problem of address redistribution in VM migration, VL2 uses equal cost multipath routing (ECMR) techniques. The main challenge in VL2 architecture is that it does not contribute to enhance the reliability of the DCN [18, 19]. There are also issues related to scalability and single node failure.

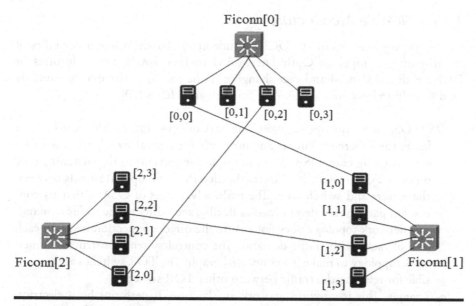

Figure 4.8   Level 1 FiConn architecture.

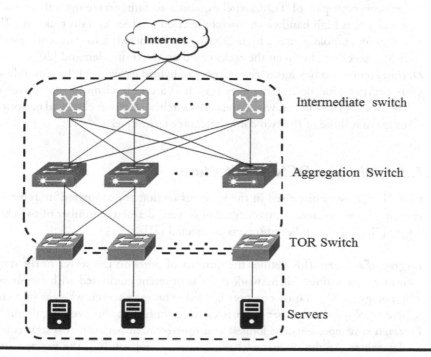

Figure 4.9   DCN architecture using VL2 topology.

4.4.1.3 Flexible Architecture

Important requirements of any DCN include higher bandwidth and flexibility of reconfiguring the topology. Optical networks have these two important features for DCNs with unbalanced and ever-changing traffic patterns. The most commonly used flexibly architectures are OSA, c-Through and Helios [20].

> *OSA:* OSA is a fully optical switching network [14, 15], which means that it leaves the Ethernet switches and uses only the optical switches to construct the switching core. OSA allows multiple connections to the switching core on each TOR switch. It converts the electrical and optical signals between the servers and switch core. The main advantages of OSA is that its connection patterns are determined as flexible according to the traffic demand. The network topology does not ensure the direct connection between each pair of racks with traffic demand. The control system constructs the network topology to make it a connected graph. The TOR switches are responsible for relaying the traffic between other TOR switches.
>
> *c-Through:* This is a hybrid network architecture. It performs both electrical packet switching and optical circuit switching. It is also called a hybrid packet and circuit (HyPaC) network. The required switching function is performed in two ways: as a tree-based electrical network, which maintains connectivity between each pair of TOR switches, and a reconfigurable optical network, which offers high bandwidth interconnection between certain racks [6]. The c-Through topology uses a high-capacity optical network to transiently establish connectivity between the racks based on the traffic demand [20].
>
> *Helios:* Helios also belongs to the category of hybrid networks; it functions both as electrical and optical switches [15]. It is a two-level multi-rooted tree of core and TOR switches, where the core switches are either electrical or optical to make full use of the two complementary techniques.

4.4.2 Analysis of DCN Architecture

The DCN topologies discussed in the previous section are compared in Table 4.1 by referring to parameters such as degree of servers, diameter, number of switches, number of links and number of servers connected [21].

> *Degree of servers:* This defines the number of ports on the server in the datacenter. The number of network ports is different compared with tree-based topology in which only one port is needed on each server, whereas in recursive topology the number of ports varies according to the levels required.
>
> *Diameter:* It represents the longest and shortest path between two servers in a datacenter. As the diameter changes latency and routing, the performance also changes.

Table 4.1   Comparison of DN Topologies

	Fat Tree	BCube	DCell	FiConn	DPillar
Degree of servers	1	$k+1$	$k+1$	2	2
Bisection width	$\dfrac{N}{2}$	$\dfrac{N}{2}$	$\dfrac{N}{4\log_n N}$	$\dfrac{N}{4 \times 2^k}$	$\dfrac{N}{n}$
Number of switches used	$6\dfrac{N}{n}$	$(k+1)\dfrac{N}{n}$	$\dfrac{N}{n}\log_n N$	$\dfrac{N}{n}$	$m\dfrac{N}{2}$
Number of links	$N\log_2 \dfrac{N}{2}$	$\left(\dfrac{k}{2}+1\right)N$	$N\log_n N$	$\left(2-\dfrac{1}{2^k}\right)N$	$\left(\dfrac{n}{2}\right)^m$
Number of servers	$\dfrac{n^3}{4}$	$\dfrac{n^3}{4}$	n^{k+1}	$2^{k+2}\left(\dfrac{n}{4}\right)^{2^k}$	$m\left(\dfrac{n}{2}\right)^m$
Cost of connectivity	$5\dfrac{U_s}{n}$	$(k+1)\dfrac{U_s}{n}$	$\dfrac{U_s}{n}$	$\dfrac{U_s}{n}$	$2\dfrac{U_s}{n}$
Disjoint paths	1	1	$k+1$	1	$\dfrac{n}{2}$
Traffic balance	Yes	Yes	No	No	No
Switch upgrade	Yes	Yes	No	No	Yes
Bandwidth	High	High	Very High	High	High

Parameters: k is the depth of recursion in building the network (for BCube, DCell and FiConn); m is the number of server columns in DPillar; N is the total number of servers; n is the number of ports in each switch and U_s is the unit price of an n-port switch.

Number of switches: The number of switches varies from one topology to another. Generally, basic tree topology uses a minimum number switches compared with other architectures.

Number of links: This represents the electrical connectivity levels, while deploying a datacenter. All of the architectures mentioned in the above section use an equal number of connectivity links. Comparing BCube and DCell, it is clear that BCube uses a greater number of wired links than DCell, which shows the wiring complexity of BCube. The bandwidth of the wiring links in the aggregation level is 10 Gbps, whereas in the edge level it is 1 Gbps.

Number of servers N: This represents the scalability of different architecture with the same value of n and k. It is evident that the DCell architecture scales up much faster than other architectures in terms of the number of servers. The number of servers in DCell architecture grows exponentially with k.

4.5 Resilient Cloud Networks

Today's cloud infrastructure consists not only the servers and storage elements, but they are also interconnected by strong communication networks. Software defined networks (SDNs) and network function virtualization (NFV) technologies enable network function utilization, where the basic functions of the network must be available during attack or failover. The other essential requirements of network elements are to provide sufficient QoS and reliability to customer's services that need to be optimized in an end-to-end fashion. Reliability of the network infrastructure is the primary concern for both cloud SPs and tenants. Another requirement is a fast and efficient means of recovering from the localized outages and major disasters. One of the approaches used by most of the cloud SPs is network virtualization with a combined control of network and cloud resources.

Network virtualization is seen as a key enabler of the cloud infrastructure. By virtualization we can decouple the services from the underlying physical infrastructure. This permits all parts of the physical infrastructure to be virtualized [3]. The virtual network imitates the functionalities of the physical network and on top of that it also offers more flexibility in the network design due to an overview of different physical network and cloud domains.

4.5.1 Network Virtualization Architecture

The cloud network architecture is illustrated in Figure 4.10. In Figure 4.11 we define the functions into three layers: physical infrastructure provider (PIP), virtual network operator (VNO) and SP. The PIP provides the required physical infrastructure, which includes fixed or mobile networks and computing and storage resources. The communication networks in cloud infrastructure are different types: wavelength division multiplexing (WDM), back bone networks, optical fiber links, Ethernets, Internet Protocol (IP) and many more. The PIP layer can fully control and monitor its resources. This can use a generalized multiprotocol label switch (GMPLS) control plane or an SDN-based approach like open flow (OF). An infrastructure provider is expected to have its own DCN with various interconnected services. The interface between the datacenter and network depends on the technologies used on both sides. For example, if OF is used in the datacenter, the OF controller can communicate with other OF controllers and with the GMPLS. In case multiple label switching is used in the datacenter, it can be easily connected to a GMPLS wide area network (WAN) with, for example, a hierarchical label-switched path (LSP) or LSP switching.

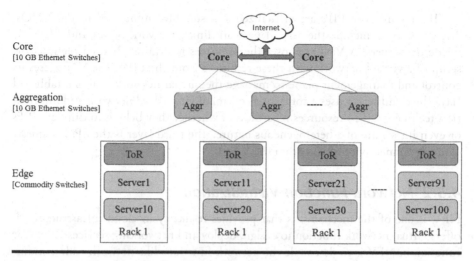

Figure 4.10 Cloud network architecture.

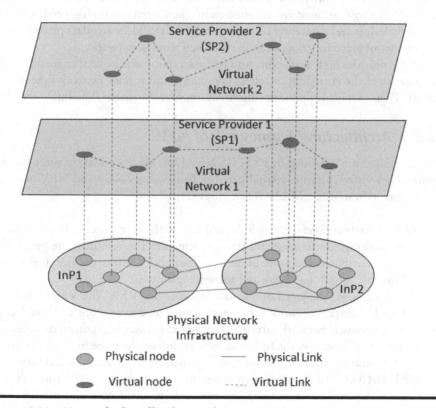

Figure 4.11 Network virtualization environment.

The resources of PIPs are virtualized and suitably announced to the VNOs. These resources include the virtual network links, network nodes and the VMs inside the servers. A VNO chooses the resources it requires. It then requests the setup of a virtual network with these resources from the PIPs. The VNO uses its control and management plane to manage the virtual network that is established [11]. The cloud server uses a combined control of virtualized network and information technology (IT) resources regardless of whether they belong to different PIPs or even if they are of a heterogeneous nature. The third layer is the SP. It requests cloud or connectivity service from the VNO.

4.5.2 Network Function Virtualization

NFV is one of the mechanisms that provides resiliency in cloud infrastructure. It offers virtual network function to design, deploy and networking services. The basic function in NFV is to de-couple the network functions like network address translation, domain name system (DNS) and security services. A high availability and resiliency of network functions can be achieved from proprietary hardware systems so they can run in any software and commodity servers. To provide better performance, an NFV uses sophisticated visualization technologies that run on high configuration network devices and datacenter components. NFV is valid for any data plane processing or control plane function, both in wired and wireless networks.

NFV provides high availability and resiliency, but there are challenges due to the complexity of the virtualization, cloud computing and various network functions. A cloud SP has to quickly provide connectivity, transfer the data and maintain the QoS.

4.5.3 Architectural Framework of NFV

NFV architecture is defined by ETSI GS NFV [20], which consists of three components: NFV infrastructure, virtual network functions (VNFs) and NFV management and orchestration (MANO) functions [11].

NFV infrastructure: This includes important cloud resources such as physical networking, computing and storage elements. The resources are geographically distributed and available as a common NFV infrastructure. It is a combination of both hardware and software resources.

VNFs: These are deployed on virtual resources like VMs. The VNF is liable to handle a certain network function that runs on one or more VMs on the top of the physical network infrastructure like cloud servers, routers, switches and gateways. To deliver the full-scale networking services, the individual virtualized modules are combined together, providing the essential scalability.

NFV MANO: This is used to manage the virtualized infrastructure. Various tools required for managing the life cycle of the VNFs and orchestrating virtual infrastructure and network functions are provided to combine end-to-end network services.

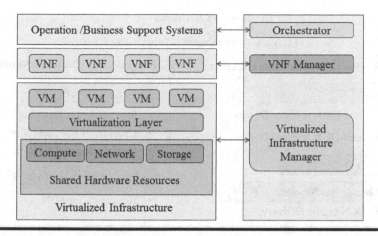

Figure 4.12   VNF instances.

One of the major advantages of NFV is that it provides the opportunity for a flexible system design. Existing network services are supported by diverse network functions that are connected in a static way. The framework for the actual deployment of VNF instances [22] is illustrated in Figure 4.12.

4.6 Resilient Virtual Network Design

Along with the design and operation of resilient datacenter facilities, cloud provider management also designs virtualized communication services from carrier and/or Internet SPs. This enables the cloud SP to provide multi-tenancy and geo-distribution services. However, the virtual network environment is prone to failure disruptions. A failure in one single physical element of this communication link leads to the detachment of a large number of virtual links from different tenants and applications. Individual cloud SPs adopt different resiliency techniques for their datacenter networks and virtualized networks. The different resiliency techniques adopted by the cloud SPs for the network are given in Figure 4.13.

4.6.1 Resilient Network in the Datacenter

This technique is classified into three types: intra-datacenter network (intra-DCN), inter-datacenter network (inter-DCN) and DCN.

Intra-DCN resiliency design: The intra-DCN connects several enterprise datacenters and then brings their traffic via a high-speed optical link to the closest colocation point. These datacenters are then managed by a single management system. Large enterprises deploy the backup datacenters to ensure the reliability of their most critical data connectivity and corporate compliance requirements. These multiple datacenters are gathered and back-hauled to the disaster recovery site where all data are replicated

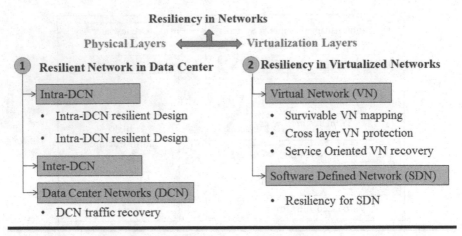

Figure 4.13 Classification of network resiliency.

Analogous to any other network infrastructure, datacenters also suffer from network failure. The most essential components of datacenters such as switches and servers in the network may fail independently. A typical datacenter may encounter hundreds of switch failures and thousands of individual server failures each year. These failures disrupt the entire cloud services. If these issues are not addressed correctly and efficiently the performance of the cloud may be severely impacted. The failure of the switches and nodes may result in loss of routing paths and availability of the cloud services. Such failure may lead to re-routing or congestion in the network; hence, network bandwidth is likely to be lost. As a result, there may be imbalance of the load among nodes. Hence, it is an essential requirement of any cloud SP to improve the robustness of cloud center networks to fit the reliability of the cloud services.

The DCN must be robust enough to dynamically access all of the interconnected datacenters, and in the case of a catastrophic event ensure that all the data are available and secure [23]. Most datacenter management systems and cloud SPs adopt these design strategies for meeting these requirements.

4.6.2 Switch Redundancy

In an intra-DCN the switch redundancy consists of an additional backup TOR and/or aggregation (Agg) and/or core switches. Some of the popular architectures enabling this scheme are fat tree, VL2, and QFabric.

> *Switch redundancy in fat tree*: A fat tree architecture has similar trends in telephone switches, which led to designing a topology with high bandwidth by interconnecting smaller commodity switches. A fat tree-based architecture (Figure 4.14), for a k-array, has three layers, core, aggregation and edge, where each pad consists of $(k/2)^2$ servers and two layers of $k/2$, k port switches.

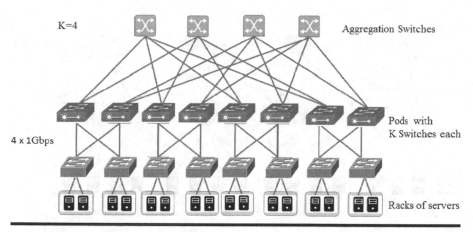

Figure 4.14   Fat tree topology.

Each edge switch connects to $k/2$ servers and $k/2$ aggregate switches. Each aggregate switch connects to $k/2$ edge and $k/2$ core switches. Each $(k/2)^2$ core switch, each connects to k pods.

One of the common problems in the fat tree mechanism is bottleneck up and down the fat tree. Other problems include packet re-ordering, which occurs if layer 3 blindly takes advantage of path diversity; further load may not necessarily be well balanced and there is writing complexity in large networks.

Switch redundancy in BCube: A BCube architecture is a secure-centric network structure [23] with servers with multiple network ports connected to multiple layers of common off-the-shelf (COTS) switches. The servers act as not only end hosts, but also relay nodes for each other. BCube supports various bandwidth-intensive applications by spending up one-to-one, one-to-several and one-to-all traffic patterns and providing high network capacity for all-to-all traffic. The performance degradation is a common problem in the BCube switch due to server/or switch failure [24]. The (n, k) BCube uses n-port switches and $k + 1$ levels. Each server has $k + 1$ ports. The server provides $k + 1$ parallel paths between any two servers.

BCube is used in a server-centric approach to provide an MDC using commodity switches. There are two types of BCube topologies: the server with multiple ports and switches that connect a fixed number of servers. In general, *BCube0* is simply connected to *N*-servers using the n-port switch, *BCube$_k$* is constructed with n *BCube$_{k+1}$* having $nk-1$ switches each connecting the same index server from each *BCube$_{k-1}$*. A *BCube$_3$* with eight-port minimum switches can support up to 4096 servers. *BCube* with $n = 4$ and with two levels is depicted in Figure 4.15.

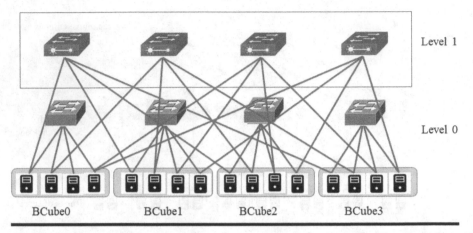

Figure 4.15 BCube (4, 1) topology.

Switch redundancy in QFabric: This architecture provides a simplified networking environment that reduces most challenging issues faced by datacenter operators. It is a highly scalable, distributed, layer 2 and layer 3 networking architecture that provides high performance, low latency and certified interconnect solutions. QFabric topologies are flexible and more scalable so they can meet the needs of small-, medium- and large-sized datacenters.

4.6.3 Server Port Redundancy

Server port redundancy is a server-centric architecture that allows a higher level of redundancy. The different topologies in this architecture are DCell, BCube, FiConn, DPillar, small-world datacenter (SWDC) and Scafida.

Server-centric DCell: DCell is a server-centric hybrid DCN architecture in which one server is directly connected to many other servers (Figure 4.16). These servers are mounted with multiple network interface cards (NICs) as shown in DCell topology [17]. The *cell0* is the basic unit of a *DCell* topology.

The topology is arranged in multiple levels, where the higher level cell contains multiple lower layer cells. *Cell0* contains "n" servers and one commodity network switch. This switch is used to connect the server within the *cell0*. A DCell contains $k = n + 1$ *cell0* cells and a *cell2* contains $k*n + 1$ cells. With this combination of servers and switch a DCell can be built to connect a large number of servers (more than 3.26 million) with $k = 3$ and $n = 6$.

Server-centric DPillar: This uses only commodity hardware and can easily scale to a large number of servers. There are no restrictions in terms of the number of servers to be connected in a DPillar network; the number of ports in each server is always fixed. Having a symmetric structure DPillar

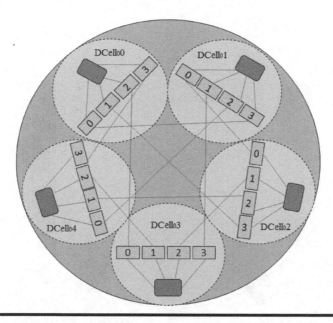

Figure 4.16 **DCell1 network when *n* = 4, composed of five DCell0s, forming a fully connected graph.**

eliminates any network bottleneck at the architecture level. The symmetric structure architecture provides a high-performance routing mechanism. The servers in the process of forwarding messages does not maintain any routing table, and this minimizes the overhead. Instead, the server computes the next hop in $O(1)$ time complexity on its own address and the destination address of the packet being forwarded. A DPillar network built by using devices such as dual-port servers and *n*-port switches is shown in Figure 4.17. The server and switches are logically arranged into *k*-equal size server columns with $(n/2)^k$ switches and *k*-equal size switch columns with $(n/2)^{k-1}$ switches.

Small-world routing small-world 2D small world 3D hexagonal

Server-centric SWDCs: SWDC network topology has many different instantiations. The configuration of this network defines the dimension of the underlying lattice, the number of random links, degree of each node and so forth. For easy deployment and cost-effectiveness the following SWDC network is discussed. Based on the number of regular versus random links the network has caused different properties for these topologies. For example, the topology small-world ring with a relatively high number of random links and a smaller number of regular ones can render the topology better suited for a datacenter-wide search. The opposite weighting, as in the case of a small-world 3D hexagonal, structure is shown in Figure 4.18. It can yield better performance when searching local nodes.

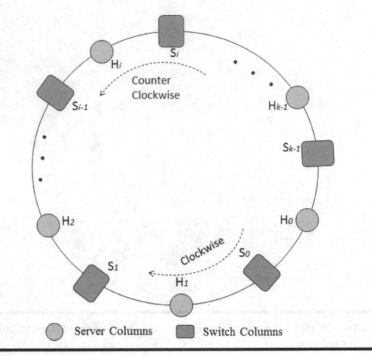

Figure 4.17 Vertical view of pillar.

Server-centric Scafida: It is an assignment-scale free datacenter network topology with high error tolerance. Scafida is used to build short-distance network links. The important characteristics of a scale-free network is small diameter and high resistance to random failures. The network uses a heterogeneous set of switches and hosts in term interconnecting ports or links. The topology is built incrementally by adding nodes and then randomly connecting all available empty ports.

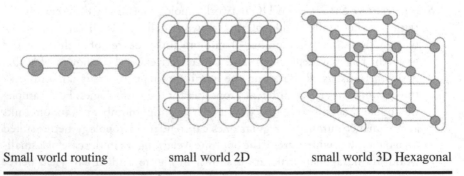

Small world routing   small world 2D   small world 3D Hexagonal

Figure 4.18 SWDC network topologies.

Inter-DCN traffic protection: This mechanism provides a redundant system to maintain network traffic in case of failure [19]. This consists of three approaches: pre-configured path, pre-configured graph and failure-aware provisioning

Pre-configured path: This path provides a dedicated backup path protection (DBPP). As a result, there is a dedicated backup for each working path and a shared backup path protection. This allows sharing of the backup path between different working paths.

Pre-configuration graph: The redundant capacity using this traffic protection method is realized by using graph topologies like pre-configured tree (*p*-tree), pre-configured cycle (*p*-cycle) and pre-configured prism (*p*-prism).

DCN-traffic recovery: Different DCN architecture uses different types of recover mechanisms [19]. This technique provides fast traffic re-routing in case of failure in the networks. For example, in intra-DCN failure, it provides traffic-aware routing (TAR).

4.6.4 Resiliency in Virtual Networks

A major challenge in virtual networks is that the effect on one section of the network might disconnect many virtual networks. One of the common techniques to deal with the issue is survivable virtual network embedding (SVNE). The resiliency technique suggested in DCNs is either proactive or reactive in nature [25]. Most of these methods deliver resiliency in a single-node or single-link failure. Some techniques like resilient software-defined networks, cross-layer backup and cut-disjoint deliver higher resiliency in case of multiple node failures [26].

Survivable VN mapping: This method provides the technique of mapping a virtual network over a physical network and not disconnecting the virtual network. Survivable VN mapping is classified into three types: virtual topology augmentation, topology cut avoidance and traffic disruption avoidance.

Virtual topology augmentation: This technique also includes virtual link and/ or nodes to protect or recover from possible failures. The earlier technique used in place of this is virtual network topology augmentation for survivable virtual optical network (SVON) mapping (*aug-* SVON mapping), where non-SVON mapping is augmented to become survivable. The *aug*-SVON mapping recognizes the single and multiple connectivity failure and provides the recovery. The design approaches proposed by the researcher [9] minimize the retrieval time and allow multiple topology augmentation for one and multiple virtual networks or multi-user VNs, which is the key requirement for cloud infrastructure providers.

Topology cut-avoidance: This method performs the virtual network mapping by avoiding the failure due to the disconnected network. Here the defective virtual topology is mapped on the same physical link. One of the earlier techniques provided for this is cut-disjoint mapping for SVONs in IP-over WDM networks. This type of mapping is an extension of routing and wavelength assignment (RWA). It is also referred to as RWA cut-disjoint. Compared with other approaches, the cut-disjoint approach offers more scalable resiliency than path disjoint approaches. For a single physical link and dual-link failure, the RWA cut-disjoint provides near-full VON survivable and best effort resiliency, respectively.

Traffic disruption avoidance: The purpose of this mechanism is for analyzing the probability of link failure and mapping the virtual network to avoid a specific link failure and/or traffic interruptions. Two such techniques of this type are failure-aware routing in topology augmentation scheme (*ext-aug*-SOVN) and a technique that attempts to limit the congestion while performing failure-aware routing as routing-allocation-SVON. The former one also provides the post-failure fast recovery capabilities, whereas in the latter one the capacity can be minimized by optimizing the IP and optical-level routing. *Ext-aug*-SVON provides higher resiliency and recovery from large numbers of failures, and routing-allocation-SVON provides higher cost-efficiency.

Cross-layer VN protection: In the physical and logical network levels the protection of VN is provided through the cross-layer design of the backup capacity [26]. This mechanism is subdivided into two types. The first type is related to the physical layer backup sharing, which focuses on efficient use of backup capacity in the physical network. Between the virtual networks the backup capacity sharing can be enabled using the shared backup network provision for SVN (SBPV) or SBPSV for SVON (SBPSVO) to provide a more capacity-efficient survivable VN mapping.

The other type of two-layer backup optimization is a process of interchanging the backup resources between the physical network and the VN. This is also an extension of the cross-layer protection scheme to provide resiliency in case of layer failure [26]. This method is the inter-layer common backup path in [27] that exploits the two-layer backup pool, where the shared backup pool includes either standby physical or virtual links that can be used to recover different types of failures.

Service-oriented VN recovery: This technique adopts the service-level objectives while performing the VN recovery for different tenants. The approaches proposed in this scheme are QoS VN map, overlay VN mapping, heuristic overlay VN mapping and VN configurable survivability [28] as illustrated in Figure 4.19.

1. ***QoS VN map:*** It uses the service-level objective needed to assign the backup capacity required to meet the exact recovery time of each cloud service.
2. ***Overlay VN mapping:*** The main constraint of this approach is that it is not scalable for cloud infrastructure with multi-tenants.
3. ***Heuristic overlay VN mapping:*** It provide scalability while maintaining the service-level objective targets and quasi-optimality of the results.
4. ***VN configurable survivability:*** The purpose of this approach is to intelligently route the traffic in each link and allow adaptable protection and recovery during node or link failure.

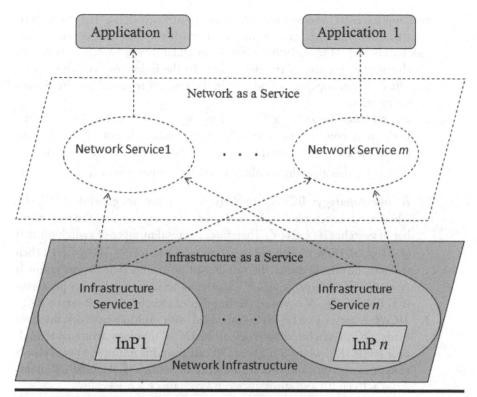

Figure 4.19 Service-oriented network virtualization.

Resiliency for SDNs: The objective of adopting an SDN is to provide the resiliency for the interaction between the data plane and control plane. The resiliency in SDNs needs replication of the centralized controller and careful placement of these replicas. The control plane recovery mechanism proposed in [10] is a physical replication of the logically centralized controller, which minimizes the recovery time. The complexity of resiliency in network virtualization is for the integration with other resiliency techniques in cloud infrastructure.

4.6.5 Performance Comparison

In this section we will define and obtain performance metrics for each of the topologies discussed.

Scalability: This is the ability of a system to handle the growing amount of demand of services and the ability of the cloud services to support this growth. Scalability is evaluated based on the demand of a particular topology; it quantifies the bandwidth sharing among all the hosts. By referring to the survey conducted [4] on the different topologies, we set the demand ratio top for each topology for comparison purposes as 1:1. This ratio indicates that all the hosts can communicate with the other hosts with a full link bandwidth. The main impairment to scalability is switch port count, which specifies the size of the datacenter. In the following section we analyze the different topologies and obtain parameters required for the performance metrics.

1. **Fat tree topology:** For a fat tree topology the demand ratio is 1:1. If f is the port count of each switch, with a bandwidth of 10 GigE, then the relationship between the number of hosts and switch port count is $N = \frac{1}{4} f^3$. This gives the number of switch ports per host as $N = \frac{\frac{4}{5}f^2 \times f}{\frac{f^3}{4}} = 5$.

2. **BCube topology:** BCube topology is analyzed in general as $BCube_k$ where $k = 2, 3, 5$, with n as the port count of the switch, and the total number of switches is $(k+1)n^k$. Therefore, the total number of switch ports is $(k+1)n^k \cdot n$. If the number of switch ports per host is $\frac{((k+1)n^k \cdot n)}{n^{k+1}} = k+1$ then the relationship between the number of hosts and switch port count is $N = n^{k+1}$. For $BCube_2$, $k = 2$, $N = n^3$, the number of switch ports per server is 3. For $BCube_3$, $N = n^4$ and the number of switch ports per server is 4.

3. **DCell:** A server in a DCell is embedded with multiple network interface cards. $DCell0$ is a building block of the DCell topology arranged in multiple levels [17], where a higher level cell contains multiple lower cells. It contains n servers and one commodity network switch. A cell contains $k = n + 1$ cell (0) and similarly a cell2 contains $k \times n + 1$ cells.

4. **Clos network:** The Clos network allows the formation of a large switch from smaller switches.

DCNs utilize the hardware redundancy to get better performance. This is adopted by scheduling and multi-path routing [29]. The different performance enhancement schemes for DCN topologies are given in the Table 4.2.

Table 4.2 Performance Enhancement Schemes for DCN Topologies

	Fat Tree	BCube	FiConn	MDCube	VL2
Flow scheduling algorithms	Re-assign paths for large flows	Metric-based routing	Matric-based routing	Random path selection	Random path selection
Decision maker of multi-path selection	Central scheduler	Source node	Intermediate node	Intermediate node	Source node

4.6.6 *Resilient Routing of DCN Topologies*

Due to the prolonged use of datacenter resources such as servers, switches, routers and links, it is unavoidable for the systems to have faults throughout their lifetimes. Some of the common datacenter outage problems are DNS configuration problems, storage services faults, errors during data migration and Hypertext Transfer Protocol (HTTP) load balancer blip. The datacenter must be designed with an appropriate self-healing mechanism to recover automatically from such common failures. Most of the DCN design includes redundant links and components to ensure connectivity in case of hardware failure. In this section we analyze the fault models and then discuss some of the resiliency techniques that can be adopted in the aforementioned DCN architecture.

> *Routing techniques:* Routing in DCN architecture changes from one topology to another. It can be implemented in different layers, and the routing function can be classified as centralized or distributed. Table 4.3 explains the routing techniques in different DCN topologies.

4.6.7 *DCN Architecture Fault Models*

The default models discussed in this section help to figure out the features of different failures and methods to detect and deal with certain types of failures [30].

> *Taxonomy of DCN failure:* The taxonomy of the DCN failure model is given in Figure 4.20, where one category of failure can be classified into multiple modes [5].
>
> *Failure types:* It identifies what types of DCN components or events consist of the failure. A single component or a link failure is catastrophic in cloud services. The impact of failure varies from one type of DCN architecture to another. The impact of the failure of a node with a single link and the failure of a node with multiple links is different. The failure of a node with multiple links can be considered as a link failure for all its links. Based on the survey conducted on the network event logs, we analyzed the hardware failure in the DCN [4].
>
>> With this we could differentiate these failures into two types.
>>
>> 1. *Link failure:* This type of failure occurs when the connection between the two nodes fails. A Simple Network Management Protocol (SNMP) monitoring mechanism can detect this failure.
>> 2. *Device failure:* The node or the device considered here includes the routers/switches, which are interconnected by the links. This occurs when these devices are unable to route or forward the signals. Device failure may occur due to various reasons such as the device being power interrupted or down due to hardware or software errors.

Table 4.3 Routing Techniques in Different DCN Topologies

	Fat Tree	BCube	DCell	FiConn	MDCube	VL2
Address level	IP	MAC/IP	MAC/IP	MAC/IP	MAC/IP	MAC/IP
Route decision	Intermediate	Source	Source	Source	Source	Intermediate
Address resolution	Distributed	Distributed	Distributed	Distributed	Distributed	Centralized
Compatibility with different topologies	Specialized	Specialized	Specialized	Specialized	Specialized	Compatible

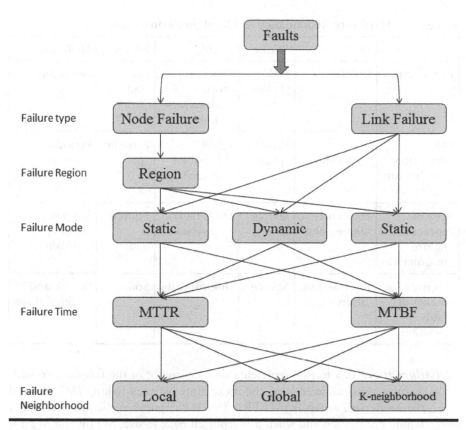

Figure 4.20   Taxonomy of DCN failure.

Failure region: Faulty regions define the place where multiple related component failure occurs. In a cloud infrastructure, a rack can be considered for the
failure region. The position of the components depends on the physical and
logical architecture of the datacenter. The common failures in a rack are from
power failure or due to protocols. Both can detour the failure of whole rack.

Failure neighborhood: This feature provides the details about the dissemination of the information related to failure with the neighboring nodes. It is
classified into three modes: *global*, *local* and *n-neighborhood*. In the global
mode every node in a network will receive the updates about the failure.
Using this information, the traffic can be re-routed effectively. In local mode
only the local devices will receive the failure information. The resiliency system can respond faster to manage the failure, whereas in *n*-neighborhood
mode, the information about a faulty node from a specific coverage area on
distance is tracked. It can make a decision to handle the fault by referring to
the two extreme conditions.

Table 4.4 Hardware Redundancy to Maintain Performance

	Fat Tree	BCube	DCell	FiConn	MDCube
Failure type	Link failure	Link failure	Link failure/ server failure/rack failure	Link failure	Link failure
Failure detection mechanism	BFD (periodic probes)	Periodic probes	DCell broadcast (reactive probes)	Periodic probes	Periodic probes
Area of spreading failure information	Edge/core/ aggregation	Source	Local/rack/ inter-rack	Source	Source/ inter-container
Decision maker of fault reaction	Intermediate source	Source	Intermediate	Source	Source and intermediate

Failure time: This feature represents the occurrence of the failure. Two such features are considered here: the mean time between failures (MTBF) and the mean time to repair (MTTR). This is computed as the time between a failure notification and when it is reported back to live. MTBF and MTTR are close for one kind of component, whereas in a datacenter there will be multiple concurrent failures of components. The value of MTBF and MTTR also depends on the types of hardware used in the datacenter. Different DCN architectures utilize the hardware redundancy to maintain performance in the presence of failure as indicated in Table 4.4.

Resiliency in fat tree: In fat tree architecture, there is no redundant link between a computer and an edge switch. The only way to provide resiliency in such cases is by adding extra links between the edge switches and the computers. There are two types of failure between the switches: between edge switches (lower in a pod) and failure between aggregation switches and core switches.

Link failure between the edge switches: Link failures in this case effect three kinds of traffic:

1. The outgoing traffic originated by a computer connected to the edge is detected by the switch. If there is a link failure the cost of the link is selected as infinity and an alternative link will be selected [2].
2. In an intra-pod the traffic connecting to the aggregation switch from the core switch is effected and causes the link failure. To mitigate

this the aggregation switch detects the link failure and will broadcast this failure to edge switches in the pod, and they will try to deviate this link.

3. The effect is on the traffic coming to the aggregation switch from a core switch. The aggregation switches will detect the link failure and disseminate the information to all the core switches. The core switches in turn communicate to the aggregation switches so that they will deviate the effected core switch when sending traffic to the subnet connected to the edge switch.

Link failure between an aggregation switch and a core switch: Traffic affected due to this failure include:

1. ***Outgoing inter-pod traffic:*** The aggregation switch detects the failure. It will then set the link as unavailable and select the link to another core switch.

2. ***Incoming inter-pod traffic:*** Here the failure is detected by the core switch. This information is disseminated to all other aggregation switches connected to it. Based on this link failure information the aggregation switch will denote the core switch when trying to send traffic to the pod.

Resiliency in DCell: The resiliency function in DCell uses DCell routing and DCell broadcast [17]. DCell resiliency defines three types of failure and three mitigation techniques. These failures are server failure, rack failure and link failure. The mitigation techniques are local re-route, local link state and local link state jump-up to deal with these failures, respectively.

Local deviation: In this case the architecture will make a decision to bypass a link where a failure occurs. The decision will be made at one of the two ends of the failed link. If the failed link (n_1, n_2) is a level 1 link, n_1 will choose a node in another $DCell_{k-1}$ that does not contain n_2 as its proxy, as long as all links from n_1's $DCell_{k-1}$ to another $DCell_{k-1}$ are failed, such a proxy can always be found. After the proxy is selected, DCell routing will be executed on the proxy to find the path to the destination.

Local link state: This method uses the link state information gathered with DCell broadcast to bypass node failure. By means of DCell broadcast a node in a DCell can know the status of all the links connecting its own $DCell_b$ to another $DCell_b$. A node will then calculate the route inside its DCell local, using link state information and Dijkstra's algorithm. When a link state happens, the node will invoke a re-route to find a proxy. Since the decision is made on the link state of the whole $DCell_b$ number matter, whether or not the link failure implies a potential mode failure, the failed node can be bypassed.

Jump-up: In DCell this scheme explains the rack failure, and it leads to the failure of the whole DCell. In a local link state if this failure occurs, the packet will be re-routed endlessly around the DCell. Generally, when a link failure is detected the first attempt to re-route to another path in a DCell$_b$ is unsuccessful; it will be assumed that the whole DCell$_b$, i.e., the whole of reach is down. The receiver of the re-routed packet will jump up to a higher level DCell to bypass the whole failed DCell. The issue related to unending re-routing can be avoided by using a time-to-live (TTL) filed into every packet.

4.7 Conclusions

The growing ubiquity of cloud infrastructure, big data and a system of engagement is driving significant changes in how cloud computing services are defined and delivered. As cloud computing continues to evolve, organizations will need to reassess how they approach resiliency from system, storage and network design to recovery processing. The complexity of cloud computing network architecture is due to the diverse nature of the cloud services. In this chapter we crudely refer to the diverse cloud resiliency techniques to indicate the performance and fault tolerance capabilities among the cloud services and networking topologies [30].

Survivability of cloud infrastructure generally depends on the server and network resiliency [28]. The amount of the resiliency differs based on the architectures used in the DCN. An insignificant resiliency level is achieved by protecting against the cloud infrastructure failure. To provide an end-to-end resiliency the designers add resiliency functionalities for physical devices, storage systems, operating systems and applications. A higher degree of resiliency is achieved through server and network virtualization.

Resiliency through non-virtualization in a network is achieved through redundancy. The redundancy at the network topology level is achieved at the switch or ports, and it improves its resiliency. Looking at the fault tolerance, traffic re-routing is used to minimize the effect of failure. DCN designers are still proposing potential new topologies for future DCNs. Any topologies designed in this way have to strike a balance between performance, cost and sustainability.

References

1. M. Grottke, R. Matias, and K. Trivedi, "The fundamentals of software aging," in *Proc. IEEE International Conference on Software Reliability Engineering Workshops*, Nov. 2008.
2. CA Technologies, "Research report, the avoidable cost of downtime," Tech. Rep., Nov. 2010. [Online]. Available: http://m.softchoice.com/ files/pdf/brands/ca/ACOD REPORT.pdf.

3. T. W. Pitt, J. H. Seader, and V. E. Renaud, "Datacenter site infrastructure tier standard:topology," Uptime Institute, The Global Datacenter Authority, Tech. Rep., 2010.

4. P. Cholda, A. Mykkeltveit, B. Helvik, O. Wittner, and A. Jajszczyk, "A survey of resilience differentiation frameworks in communication networks," *IEEE Communications Surveys and Tutorials*, vol. 9, no. 4, pp. 32–55, Dec. 2007.

5. V. Panagiotis, S. Vera, D. Panagiotis, C. Scott, G. Slawomir, and I. Demosthenes, "Ontology and taxonomies of resilience," European Network and Information Security Agency (ENISA), Tech. Rep. V1, Dec. 2011.

6. J. W. Dally and B. Towles, *Principles and Practices of Interconnection Networks*. Morgan Kaufmann, San Francisco, CA, 2004.

7. R. Aldrich and G. Mellinger, "Cisco energy management: A case study in implementing energy as a service," July 2009, white paper. [Online]. Available: https://datacenters.lbl.gov/sites/default/files/CiscoEMSWhitePaper_2010.pdf.

8. A. Fukui, T. Takeda, K. Hirose, and M. Yamasaki, "HVDC power distribution systems for telecom sites and data centers," *in Proc. International Power Electronics Conference (IPEC'10)*, pp. 874–880, June 2010.

9. A. Leventhal, "Triple-parity RAID and beyond," *Communications of the ACM*, vol. 53, no. 1, pp. 58–63, Jan. 2010.

10. R. Jain and S. Paul, "Network virtualization and software defined networking for cloud computing: a survey," *IEEE Communications Magazine*, vol. 51, no. 11, pp. 24–31, Nov. 2013.

11. J. Panneerselvam, L. Liu, R. Hill, Y. Zhan, and W. Liu, "An investigation of the effect of cloud computing on network management," *in Proc. IEEE 9th International Conference on High Performance Computing and Communication, IEEE 14th International Conference on Embedded Software and Systems (HPCC-ICESS'12)*, pp. 1794–1799, June 2012.

12. S. B. Wicker, *Reed-Solomon Codes and Their Applications*. IEEE Press, Piscataway, NJ, 1994.

13. D. J. Scales, M. Nelson, and G. Venkitachalam, "The design of a practical system for fault-tolerant virtual machines," *ACM SIGOPS Operating Systems Review*, vol. 44, no. 4, pp. 30–39, Dec. 2010.

14. K. Chen, A. Singla, A. Singh, K. Ramachandran, L. Xu, Y. Zhang, X. Wen, and Y. Chen, "Osa: An optical switching architecture for data center networks with unprecedented flexibility," *in Proc. of the 9th USENIX conference on Networked Systems Design and Implementation. USENIX Association*, 2012, pp. 18–18.

15. N. Farrington, G. Porter, S. Radhakrishnan, H. Bazzaz, V. Subramanya, Y. Fainman, G. Papen, and A. Vahdat, "Helios: a hybrid electrical/optical switch architecture for modular data centers," in *ACM SIGCOMM Computer Communication Review*, vol. 40, no. 4, pp. 339–350, 2010.

16. I. Egwutuoha, S. Chen, D. Levy, and B. Selic, "A fault tolerance framework for high performance computing in cloud," in *Proc. 12th IEEE/ACM International Symposium on Cluster, Cloud and Grid Computing (CCGrid'12)*, pp. 709–710, May 2012.

17. C. Guo, H. Wu, K. Tan, L. Shi, Y. Zhang, and S. Lu, "Dcell: A scalable and fault-tolerant network structure for data centers," in *Proc. ACM SIGCOMM Conference (SIGCOMM'08)*, pp. 75–86, Aug. 2008.

18. A. Greenberg, J. R. Hamilton, N. Jain, S. Kandula, C. Kim, P. Lahiri, D. A. Maltz, P. Patel, and S. Sengupta, "VL2: A scalable and flexible data center network," *Communications of the ACM*, vol. 54, no. 3, pp. 95–104, March 2011.

19. R. Niranjan Mysore, A. Pamboris, N. Farrington, N. Huang, P. Miri, S. Radhakrishnan, V. Subramanya, and A. Vahdat, "Portland: a scalable fault-tolerant layer 2 data center network fabric," *ACM SIGCOMM Computer Communication Review*, vol. 39, no. 4, pp. 39–50, 2009.
20. G. Wang, D. Andersen, M. Kaminsky, K. Papagiannaki, T. Ng, M. Kozuch, and M. Ryan, "c-through: Part-time optics in data centers," in *ACM SIGCOMM Computer Communication Review*, vol. 40, no. 4, pp. 327–338, 2010.
21. M. Al-Fares, A. Loukissas, and A. Vahdat, "A scalable, commodity data center network architecture," *ACM SIGCOMM Computer Communication Review*, vol. 38, no. 4, pp. 63–74, Aug. 2008.
22. C. Guo, G. Lu, D. Li, H. Wu, X. Zhang, Y. Shi, C. Tian, Y. Zhang, and S. Lu, "BCube: A high performance, server-centric network architecture for modular data centers," *SIGCOMM Computer Communication Review*, vol. 39, no. 4, pp. 63–74, Aug. 2009.
23. A. Avizienis, J.-C. Laprie, B. Randell, and C. Landwehr, "Basic concepts and taxonomy of dependable and secure computing," *IEEE Transactions on Dependable and Secure Computing*, vol. 1, no. 1, pp. 11–33, Oct. 2004.
24. C. Guo, G. Lu, D. Li, H. Wu, X. Zhang, Y. Shi, C. Tian, Y. Zhang, and S. Lu, "BCube: a high performance, server-centric network architecture for modular data centers," in *ACM SIGCOMM*, pp. 63–74, Aug. 2009.
25. Q. Zhang, M. Zhani, M. Jabri, and R. Boutaba, "Venice: Reliable virtual data center embedding in clouds," in *Proc. 33rd IEEE International Conference on Computer Communication (INFOCOM'14)*, pp. 289–297, April 2014.
26. N. Carter, H. Naeimi, and D. Gardner, "Design techniques for cross layer resilience," in *Proc. IEEE Design, Automation Test in Europe Conference Exhibition (DATE'10)*, pp. 1023–1028, March 2010.
27. C. Guo, G. Lu, D. Li, H. Wu, X. Zhang, Y. Shi, C. Tian, Y. Zhang, and S. Lu, "Bcube: A high performance, server-centric network architecture for modular data centers," *ACM SIGCOMM Computer Communication Review*, vol. 39, no. 4, pp. 63–74, 2009.
28. J. P. Sterbenz, D. Hutchison, E. K. Cetinkaya, A. Jabbar, J. P. Rohrer, M. Schller, and P. Smith, "Resilience and survivability in communication networks: Strategies, principles, and survey of disciplines," *Elsevier, Computer Networks*, vol. 54, no. 8, pp. 1245–1265, June 2010.
29. M. Al-Fares, S. Radhakrishnan, B. Raghavan, N. Huang, and A. Vahdat, "Hedera: Dynamic flow scheduling for data center networks," in *Proceedings of the 7th USENIX Conference on Networked Systems Design and Implementation. USENIX Association*, p. 19, 2010.
30. L. Chen and A. Avizienis, "N-version programming: A fault-tolerance approach to rellablllty of software operatlon," in *Proc. 25th International Symposium on Fault-Tolerant Computing, Highlights from Twenty-Five Years*, June 1995.

Further Readings

N. Aggarwal, P. Ranganathan, N. P. Jouppi, and J. E. Smith, "Configurable isolation: Building high availability systems with commodity multi-core processors," *ACM SIGARCH Computer Architecture News*, vol. 35, no. 2, pp. 470–481, June 2007.

L. A. Barroso, J. Clidaras, and U. Hölzle, "The Datacenter as a Computer: An Introduction to the Design of Warehouse-Scale Machines, Second Edition, *ser. Synthesis Lectures on Computer Architecture.* Morgan & Claypool Publishers, San Rafael, CA, May 2013.

P. Chan, M. Lyu, and M. Malek, "ReliableWeb services: Methodology, experiment and modeling," *in Proc. IEEE International Conference on Web Services, (ICWS'07),* pp. 679–686, July 2007.

S. Potter and J. Nieh, AutoPod: Unscheduled system updates with zero data loss," *in Proc. IEEE Second International Conference on Autonomic Computing, (ICAC'05),* pp. 367–368, June 2005.

D.-J. Kan, A. Narula-Tam, and E. Modiano, "Lightpath routing and capacity assignment for survivable IP-over-WDM networks," *in Proc. 7th International Workshop on Design of Reliable Communication Networks, (DRCN'09),* pp. 37–44, Oct. 2009.

S. Osman, D. Subhraveti, G. Su, and J. Nieh, "The design and implementation of Zap: A system for migrating computing environments," *ACM SIGOPS Operating Systems Review,* vol. 36, pp. 361–376.

A. Shye, J. Blomstedt, T. Moseley, V. Reddi, and D. Connors, "PLR: A software approach to transient fault tolerance for multicore architectures," *IEEE Transactions on Dependable and Secure Computing,* vol. 6, no. 2, pp. 135–148, April 2009.

D. Sun, G. Chang, C. Miao, and X. Wang, "Analyzing, modeling and evaluating dynamic adaptive fault tolerance strategies in cloud computing environments," *Journal of Supercomputing,* vol. 66, no. 1, pp. 193–228, March 2013.

K. V. Vishwanath and N. Nagappan, "Characterizing cloud computing hardware reliability," *in Proc. 1st ACM symposium on Cloud Computing (SoCC'10),* pp. 193–204, June 2010.

Chapter 5

Achieving Reliability of Quantum State in Cloud Infrastructure

Chetan Shelke and P. Mano Paul
Alliance University

I. Diana Jeba Jingle
CHRIST (Deemed to be University)

Contents

5.1 Introduction

Cloud computing is a developing business foundation for a resource-sharing world view that guarantees that companies and institutes equip resource backups in different backup streams. Using virtualization and asset time sharing, a huge user base service with a single set of physical resources must be furnished. The current commercial clouds have been built to work out multimedia file database approaches, which are distinct from other scientific approaches [1]. Cloud computing is becoming an increasingly important technology; it is also called parallel computing, distributed computing and grid system design [2]. Basic providers of the cloud, such as computing resources as storage (Amazon S3), a central processing unit (CPU, Amazon EC2) or databases, can actuate as web services, which can be subscribed or consumed on a pay-as-you-go model deprived in agreements [3].

However, these multimedia databases in text, audio and video form require specific techniques for processing in the cloud. Cloud computing services frequently give online business applications that are received from an Internet browser, while the product and information are put away on the servers [4]. As shown in Figure 5.1, the "cloud" generally incorporates services in the following way [5, 6]:

> *Infrastructure as a Service (IaaS)* – IaaS is a design paradigm that offers the computing infrastructure itself as a service. Instead of purchasing the server, software and silos of a datacenter or equipment over the network, clients would now be able to purchase those assets as completely redistributed help. This design offers web-facilitating and virtual server contributions at the following level. The purchaser can control the working framework, stockpiling and conveyed applications and perhaps organizing parts, such as a load balancer and firewalls [4, 7].

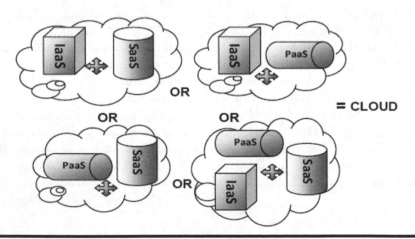

Figure 5.1   Services of cloud computing.

Platform as a Service (PaaS) – PaaS offers the computing platform or solution stack as a service. Consumers need not deploy or manage the applications and the underlying software layers as they are completely assisted by the PaaS service available in the cloud services. Purchasers can utilize a facilitating situation for their applications to control the applications that run in that condition, yet need not control the working operating system (OS), equipment or system foundation on which they are running. The executable is ordinarily an application-structured framework [8].

Software as a Service (SaaS) – In the SaaS model, software is facilitated by a seller or specialist organization and made accessible to clients over a network system. The customer utilizes an application, yet does not control the working OS, equipment or system foundation infrastructure.

Mobile cloud computing (MCC) [9, 10] is one of the business trendy expressions and has received a significant conversation string in the information technology (IT) world since 2009. As per [11], "By 2015, in excess of 240 billion clients will use distributed computing administrations through cell phones, driving incomes of $5.2 billion" [11]. According to the study, among all the portable information traffic over the world, 66.5% will be just video-related until 2017. This was just 51% in the last review. As cell phones are restricted by calculation, memory and vitality, they may not fill in as stages for rich media, for cloud applications and administrations. It is estimated that cloud applications will represent 84% of the all-out portable information traffic in 2017 [12]. The rapid evolution of mobile computing (MC) has become a powerful inclination for the development of the IT sector and other important fields. The combination of the cloud with cell phones has radically decreased the requirement for cutting-edge handsets. It is truly energizing to realize that a component telephone with constrained usefulness and only a program to get to the cloud will do the trick to play out any sort of broad handling task. The principle target of MCC is to provide a helpful and fast technique for clients to get to and get information from the cloud; such an advantageous and quick strategy implies getting to distributed computing assets successfully by utilizing cell phones [13].

However, these mobile devices face a number of challenges while providing services to users with their storage assets, for example, battery life, backups, transmission capacity, mobile security and its services [14, 15]. MCC incorporates cloud computing and MC processes to provide rich computational services to mobile users, network operators and cloud computing providers. But in providing multimedia services, MCC is still at the developing process, as there are too many obstacles such as memory, bandwidth, battery problems and so forth, while sending data accurately and rapidly in the mobile environment [16].

Video streaming refers to the continuous transmission of video files from a remote server to a client. Mobile streaming permits purchasers to watch video anytime and anyplace, and it is turning into an increasingly more famous approach to share video content [17]. In cloud infrastructure, the video that is being played is stored on a cloud server and is transmitted within a few seconds from the cloud server when requested by the client. On-demand service recordings are viewed through different video technological service innovations in cloud services. Video streams in the cloud despite everything have challengeable research issues as they are greatly utilized in inter-clouds. Since streaming is a real-time process, the cloud is more efficient than downloading video content. Video streaming principally relies on encoding convention and the buffering component. The video codec utilizes a scope of encoded/decoded strategies to fit recording signals into the dispensed channel transfer speed. These encoding strategies can impact the nature of the video to be spilled. This framework is all the more impressive for giving video as a service (VaaS) in well-known cell phones. Video encoding is done through different backup designs. The MP4 position has been generally utilized for this reason, and it has been used extensively due to features such as real-time transport protocol (RTP) headers, packetization boundaries and transmission times. Companies want to send the client video services by encoding video information so that its consumption uses lower bandwidth for cell phone use [18]. Although the existing encoding mechanisms are efficient, they still lack reliable streaming of video content.

The User Datagram Protocol (UDP) is used along with the Internet Protocol (IP) as UDP/IP for streaming video content from the cloud server to the mobile device. Since the video is streamed through UDP/IP, it cannot be delivered in a reliable manner, but it can be delivered without any delay when compared with Transmission Control Protocol (TCP)/IP. Factors such as network problems like latency and congestion and bandwidth problems may slow down the video streaming process.

The proposed framework is capable of delivering reliable video content to users with distinct configurations and delivering their needs over qualitative data contents to the user. Accessing the web services on mobile devices affects the video quality due to the heterogeneous nature of the devices and because they demand high processing and memory requirements. In most cases, the servers are not able to provide efficient service to the clients due to the processing overhead at the cloud server and the heterogeneity of data formats at the client device, thereby resulting in delayed responses. This is why the cloud computing concept is used for data accessed through mobile devices that were stored in the cloud environment. The video content from the cloud server is available whenever it is needed. MCC provides better memory capacity, battery reinforcement and less equipment and programming for portable mobile user clients. Right now, portable clients get fast video productively and reliably with minimum buffering time.

5.2 Literature Review

Several existing methods are available for mobile multimedia to access the multimedia content from the cloud server. While streaming video, the cloud server faces a number of challenges to meet reliability and time. Figure 5.2 shows how video

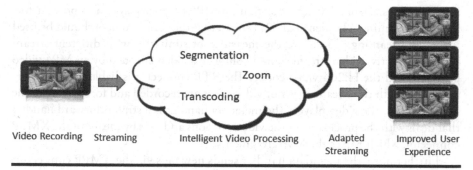

Figure 5.2 Cloud services over video processing.

processing is done for cloud services. Energy efficiency in distributed computing such as mobile technology is one of the greatest challenges. Battery life constraints for advanced smart phones has been the greatest complaint from mobile users. Two primary factors add to the power issue: moderate restrictions due to the limit of batteries and the appeal for energy hungry applications (e.g., video streaming with web-based gaming). To limit the energy effectiveness issue, particularly in mixed media applications, an off-loading strategy is utilized by Xu and Mao [19].

Poor user experience (UX) related to high advancement cost is one of the challenges in video sharing over mobile networks. The fame of portable video use by mobile clients is not tantamount to customary TV or work area video creations. To take care of this issue, Kovachev et al. [20] utilized standard libraries that expand the crude video streams to contain video benefits in cell phones. It is a CPU-intensive task [12], and a few issues influence the client experience for portable video, for example, handling of recordings (concentrating or zooming on specific areas in the video), changes in association speeds, perusing/exploring video on a cell phone and personalization of video streams.

Enhancing UX of mobile video consists of three parts. First, thumbnail cue frames are generated at the transitioning scenes, i.e., events in the video. The thumbnail "seek bar" is placed on the top part. It consists of thumbnails of all the scenes of the video ordered by occurrence. This makes it easy to browse videos. Users can orientate themselves by the thumbnails and do not need to wait until the video is loaded.

In mobile service architecture, for different purposes, different protocols will be utilized for the communication between cloud components and its mobile clients. To upstream and downstream we use RTP, and Egwutuoha et al. and Gonsai et al. [21, 10] stated that the extensible messaging and presence protocol (XMPP) should be used to exchange its metadata information with segment information and its component information used in their devices. Here the protocol Hypertext Transfer Protocol (HTTP) is used to transfer files such as video upload and file upload over cloud networks. By understanding the various responsibilities of model view controller service (MVCS), different handlers are required for its delegation functionalities. Here it makes sense that an MP4 handler plays an important role in video streaming. Hamlen et al. [22] stated that the RTP protocol should be used for video streaming. To ensure the measures of similarity with different stream servers, the active video stream should comprise a video encoded by an MP4 video processor and the H.264 video codec. The RTP connector is liable for the correspondence with the stream server of videos that are recorded and for conveying the video through the video player. The metadata handler is a straightforward handler that deals with the processing of the video portions and tags by means of the XMPP connector, which parses the XML fragments.

Furthermore, the metadata handler sends new tags via the XMPP connector. Additionally, it manages sending the video metadata information like title and description. The LazyList handler is an important part of the mobile UX as it reduces data transfer and memory usage. This handler is utilized by the segment-based "seek bar" and by the browse activities, which include preview thumbnails of the videos. It runs as a fundamental thread with a low need to not influence the interface execution. The versatile feature streams are obliged to hold up a substantial scope of cell phones, with an assortment of feature show resolutions, a unique scope of control framework and inconsequential remote connections like Wi-Fi, 3G and 4G. Also, the available remote connection capacity of a portable device likely will be diverse over positive time and space contingent on sign force, other client activity stack in the same cell and connection state uniqueness. Scalable video coding (SVC), as shown in Figure 5.3, promises great feature streams if the basic layer (BL) is circulated with extra Enhancement Layer (ELs).

Adaptive mobile video services conduct client-based adaptable compact mobile component supervisions, which make distinct authorities for dynamic customers in the convenient cloud, to propose "non-buffering" and "non-ending" flexible element streams to the adaptable customers. The SVC procedure proposes versatile

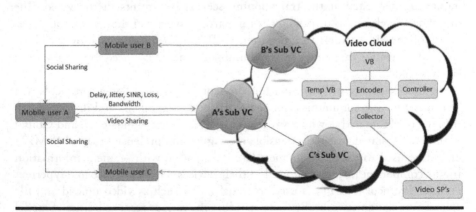

Figure 5.3 Cloud mobile user agent.

and versatile portable feature streams by figuring the blend of feature spilling (layers) in view of the variable relationship circumstance from the portable clients on the premise of client needs and oversees the connection position on the premise of client development.

Conventional video streaming-based systems are for the most part structured with stable Internet connects among servers and clients; consequently, they may perform inadequately in mobile circumstances and video streams can every now and again be upset by bundle packet losses. For a superior quality of service (QoS) experience, the fluctuating connection state must be appropriately taken care of for "stable" video streaming services. Consequently, the video bit rate must be tuned to adapt to the time-fluctuating connection limit. The SVC methodology of the H.264 AVC video norms for compression describes a BL with different ELs. By utilizing SVC, video can be decoded and have the most decreased quality if the BL is passed on, whereas if more ELs are passed on, a better video transfer can be cultivated. Using this strategy, a different class of portable transfers to mobile phones and associated conditions can be created. Each mobile customer autonomously reports the transmission status to the worker, and the worker predicts the open data move limit and passes on genuine video transfers for every client. Presently, the server expects command over the overhead while the amount of customers increases. Now, the server must have the option to manage the cost of a tremendous explosion of simultaneous client requests at peak hours; however, having idle hours makes this practically ineffective.

Cloud computing is ready to deftly provide adaptable resources of its content to its service providers (SPs) by relying upon the present client requests. Cloud servers cannot just effectively give quality-assured progressive video administration to a large amount of Internet clients, yet spare registering and storage of resources are just energy, as stated in Bertino et al. [23, 24], when there are fewer dynamic clients, because of the cloud's auto-scaling capacity. Be that as it may, stretching out the cloud-based administrations to portable conditions requires considering more factors, such as remote connection elements, client mobility, the limited computation of resources and its calculation and storage capacity, as they relate to the confined force supply of cell phones. A significant number of studies on versatile distributed computing methods have proposed virtualizing customized specialists for adjusting dynamic portable clients intelligently, e.g., a cloudlet. In the cloud, different client specialists can be kept up powerfully and productively relying on the time-shifting client requests. So as to decrease the buffering delay, the intelligent services, which pushes a piece of the video record into the cell phone before the client essentially gets to, is profoundly required. In this respect, another pattern to misuse the online Social Network Services (SNSs) for perfecting the intelligent video is becoming progressively popular. By virtue of the sensational ascent in the amount of compact customers who check out the SNSs, e.g., Facebook, Twitter, SinaWeibo, and so forth, a tremendous proportion of video content is shared and spread rapidly and for the most part by using the SNSs.

Most people share interest content through "casual" propagation. A customer may watch a video that his or her friends have recommended. Moreover, they can provide recommendations via Facebook or Twitter account that shares the most forward-thinking famous music recordings, which are likely going to be seen by its fans. Customer associations and interests in SNSs have basic homophily and region properties. Customers are uncommonly packed by geological intrigue and its locale, which can be mishandled for shrewd pushing similar to the ideal task of cloud resources. Assorted mobile clients have different instances of getting to recordings, which are per-customer subordinate on a very basic level due to people's unmistakable lifestyles. The passageway postpone gives us the ability to pre-get before the entrance of customers.

From the above assessments, we researched the probability of prefetching the video totally or to a limited extent to customer devices early, taking into account their online associations in SNSs while considering their passage delays once the customer snaps to watch the video (the video can in a brief moment starting playing without buffering). Thus, prefetching the video can offer chronicles of significant worth with, for the most part, less limit overhead. When a versatile customer viably transfers a video, a cloud administrator will be immediately summarized for that customer. The portable client keeps following estimations, including signal quality, full circle time (RTT) bundle and loss of parcel and information transmission, under a particular commitment cycle.

Furthermore, the customer will intermittently answer to the subVC. The RTP connector is liable for the correspondence with the server full of recordings and for conveying the video to the video player. The metadata handler is an exceptionally straightforward handler. It deals with delivering the video sections and labels by means of the XMPP connector and parses the XML fragments. Furthermore, it sends new tags via the XMPP connector. Additionally, it manages sending the video metadata information such as title and description. The LazyList handler is an important part of the mobile UX as it reduces data transfer and memory usage. This handler is utilized by the segment-based "seek bar" and by the browse activities, which include preview thumbnails of the videos.

5.3 Proposed Methodology

5.3.1 Quantum Error Correction Procedure

Consider an input video that has to be streamed from the servers to a number of users. Suppose the initial state of information $a|0\rangle + b|1\rangle$ has been perfectly encoded as $a|000\rangle + b|111\rangle$. Each of the three encoded qubits is passed through the bit flip channel. Assume that a bit flip occurred on one or more of the qubits, the errors can be recovered using the simple two-stage error-correction procedure, which is described below, to recover the correct quantum state. The Quantum Error Correction Procedure is clearly depicted in Figure 5.4.

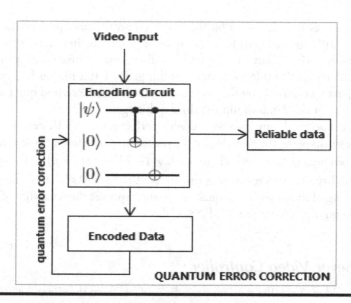

Figure 5.4 Quantum error correction procedure.

5.3.1.1 Stage 1: Error-Detection Procedure

In this process, a measurement is done to know the error that has occurred on the quantum state. This measurement results in error syndrome. The bit flip channel generates four error syndromes that correspond to four projection operators:

If $P_0 = |000\rangle\langle000| + |000\rangle\langle111|$ then the encoded message has no error.
If $P_1 = |000\rangle\langle100| + |011\rangle\langle011|$ then the encoded message has bit flip on qubit one.
If $P_2 = |010\rangle\langle010| + |101\rangle\langle101|$ then the encoded message has bit flip on qubit two.
If $P_1 = |001\rangle\langle001| + |110\rangle\langle110|$ then the encoded message has bit flip on qubit three.

Suppose the bit flip occurred on qubit one, then the corrupted state is $a|100\rangle + b|011\rangle$. Applying unitary operation on P_1 results in $\langle\psi|P_1|\psi\rangle = 1$, which yields a measurement result of certainly 1. Moreover, the syndrome measurement will not cause any change to the state both before and after the measurement. Also, the syndrome measurement does not provide any information about the contents of the message, but it tells that the error occurred in the encoded data. This generic feature of syndrome measurement to perturb a quantum state to get information about that state provides reliability and security on the cloud data.

5.3.1.2 Stage 2: Error Recovery Procedure

Using the value of the error syndrome, the error recovery procedure has to be decided to recover the message to its initial state. For example, if the error measurement result is 1, then a bit flip occurred on the first qubit of the encoded message, $|000\rangle\langle100| + |011\rangle\langle011|$, so that qubit is flipped again to recover to its original state with perfect accuracy. The four possible error syndromes on a three qubit bit flip channel are $P_0 : 0$ (no error), do nothing; $P_1 : 1$ (bit flip on first qubit), flip the first qubit again; P_2: 2 (bit flip on second qubit), flip the second qubit again and P_3: 3 (bit flip on third qubit), flip the third qubit again.

Thus, the original state is recovered with perfect accuracy. This error-correction procedure works perfectly, provided bit flips occur on one or fewer of the three qubits. This method corrects the errors with probability $(1 - p)^3 + 3p(1 - p)^2 = 1 - 3p^2 + 2p^3$. The probability of errors remaining uncorrected is $3p^2 - 2p^3$. Thus, the encoding and decoding of messages in the quantum state improves the reliability of the message in the quantum state provided $p < 1/2$.

5.3.2 Sever Video Controller

The server video controller receives periodic updates from the client, i.e., the mobile device signal strength, battery power, link quality and so forth. After receiving the information, it starts the following process on the service side: (1) predicting the bandwidth of the client device, (2) encoding the video using the three-level encoding process and (3) asymmetric video rendering.

1. First, the server predicts the current bandwidth of the mobile device (the client) using the round trip time (RTT) sent by the mobile device. The Sliding Window Protocol running on the client and server side is used to calculate the RTT. The RTT and current link quality updates are logged periodically to calculate the available bandwidth of the mobile device. This calculation is very important because the mobile device's link capacity may be very scarce and overwhelming.
2. Second, the server performs reliable encoding using a three-level encoding process, which uses FFmpeg, H.264 and quantum error correction (QEC) encoding on the video data to be streamed to achieve reliability. FFmpeg is a multimedia conversion software that is normally available in command line format. It will resize the video according to the size of the mobile device. H.264 is used as an efficient compression technique for compressing the video to be streamed to a ratio of 80%. Our main objective is to achieve reliability of the compressed video, so we use a novel QEC method to stream the video in a reliable manner. The QEC procedure was explained in Section 5.3.1. The reliable encoder calculates the encoding factor, which measures the performance of this process.
3. Third, the server performs the asymmetric video rendering process by analyzing the quality of the video to be streamed. In this process, the video encoding bit rate is significantly reduced for certain video quality, making the video

transmission easier over the wireless network. This process works by setting appropriate video rendering parameters according to the network conditions to achieve high-level user satisfaction. The asymmetric video rendering process calculates the rendering factor and the network factors through which the performance of this process can be measured.

5.3.3 Mobile Device Controller

The mobile device controller consists of different sections like link quality monitor, client buffer and video decoder. Figure 5.5 depicts the Architecture of Video streaming done in mobile cloud. The link quality monitor continuously monitors the mobile device's battery power, available allocated link bandwidth and current signal strength. It periodically sends this information to the mobile device controller. This helps the server to perform adaptive video streaming and to maintain a stable connection between the client and the server. The client buffer helps to store the incoming video and deliver the content to the mobile device without any delay, ensuring continuous video streaming.

The buffer timing is maintained by the Real-Time Message Protocol (RTMP) player, which handles any frame loss due to network connection problems. The mobile device controller also performs synchronization at the mobile device to solve the interruption problem by maintaining a log of video frames received and yet

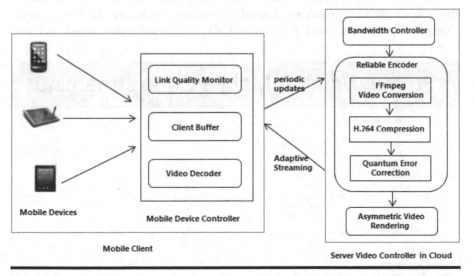

Figure 5.5 Architecture of adaptive and reliable video streaming in mobile cloud.

to be received and so forth. The video decoder receives the video from the mobile device controller and extracts the encoded video by decoding it. The RTMP player has a well-established built-in decoder that decodes the video content to its original format using different bit rates. Thus, any traditional decoding techniques can be used to extract the original video content. To embed the URL of the video content, an HTML embed tag is present in the RTMP player that enables the mobile device to establish a connection with the server.

5.4 Performance Analysis

We used Java programming, which runs on the server side, as a main program to handle all the tasks and on the client side as a subroutine that initializes dynamically by maintaining and terminating Java application instances as private agents for every single dynamic client. We assess the presentation of the system by a model and implementation of the framework and its usages. The video of 230 × 240 goals in the five positions with its resolution is encoded with the H.264 encoder at 23 fps. At this moment, the account is deftly constructing a private operator (subVC) for the dynamic compact customer to offer a "non-finishing" video in real time by changing in accordance with the instability of connection quality subject to SVC strategy, and to provide "non-buffering" video web-based understanding by the establishment of prefetching reliant on the following of the relationship of portable customers in their SNSs. The result of video streaming framework is shown in Figure 5.6.

To process those streams, additionally show the screenshots of the feature streams, which are transmitted through the setting aware and the general interchanges. The mobile client enters the URL of the sub-video cloud and gets

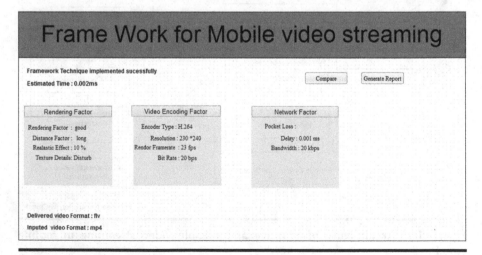

Figure 5.6   Result of video streaming framework.

connected to the AWS instance, which starts the execution process by initially predicting the bandwidth. The bandwidth predictor sends a small file to the mobile client and receives responses for the file sent. The mobile device controller periodically updates the device information that it collected from the link quality monitor, client buffer and video decoder to the bandwidth predictor. The bandwidth predictor now calculates the total RTT, available bandwidth, signal strength, phone type and so forth. The reliable encoder module is executed next, and the FFmpeg execution happens for transcoding the video to a reduced file size based on the link capacity of the client device, which is followed by H.264 compression that is performed to deliver good video quality at a considerably low bit rate. Next, the QEC process is executed, which checks the video for any content or bit loss in each frame to be sent, using a bit flip circuit to achieve reliability. Finally, asymmetric video rendering is performed that analyzes the quality of the video and then streams the video with reduced bit rate based on its quality.

5.5 Conclusion

Cloud computing generally has been perceived as a cutting-edge processing framework that offers clients the foundation (e.g., servers, systems and backup storage files), and administrations such as middleware benefits, working frameworks and programming. There is no doubt about the utilization of databases, such as multimedia in cloud computing, which is improving cloud services. Cloud computing presents the roughly endless registering with computing, scalability with services like on-demand request and different types of administrations. Portable cloud computing is best for clients to utilize rich media applications anytime and at anyplace. An ever-changing way of life is required to get the most up-to-date and quickest innovation to work through personal digital assistance (PDA). It is important to get a handle on a superior strategy for comprehension of the innovation to promote future research.

Security in multimedia has become a significant issue in the mobile registering environment. The exceptional trait of interactive media information bases needs different security strategies [25] that are profoundly benefits subordinate. In versatile distributed computing, secure transmissions are becoming progressively troublesome in an appropriated domain because of the idea of remote channels. To take care of this issue, different security techniques have been discussed that provided progressively compelling and adaptable calculations to address the data storage security issue in distributed networks in MC.

In the future, this model can be improved with extra highlights to empower customized video streams, overlays with extra data layers and intuitive zooming in a solid and secure way. Further work should be done about the proposed approach of using quick prototyping of portable video applications from a designer's point of view. The instructive meetings, live gatherings, social affairs and occasions all have various minimal prerequisites of video quality as information misfortune happens at various degrees in the above fields. Thus, our proposed architecture requires many changes and has had to face many challenges, particularly in terms of bandwidth allocation for rendering live video content from a server cloud and therefore to improve user satisfaction. This proposed method can be deployed in content delivery networks so that video streaming can be faster.

References

1. Yong-Ju Lee, Jin-Hwan Jeong Hag-Young Kim, "Video Block Device For User-Friendly Viewing Patterns in IaaS Clouds," IEEE International Conference on Consumer Electronics (ICCE), IEEE, pp. 455–456, 2012.
2. Han Qi and Abdullah Gani, "Research on Mobile Cloud Computing: Review, Trend and Perspectives," pp. 1–8, 2012, Second International conference on Digital Information and Communication Technology and its applications (DICTAP).
3. Xiaofei Wang, Min Chen, Ted Taekyoung Kwon, Laurence T. Yang, Victor C. M. Leung, "AMES-Cloud: A Framework of Adaptive Mobile Video Streaming and Efficient Social Video Sharing in the Clouds," IEEE Transactions on Multimedia, Vol. 15, No. 4, pp. 811–820, June 2013.
4. D. Kesavaraja, A. Shenbagavalli, "Cloud Video as a Service [VaaS] with Storage, Streaming, Security and Quality of Service Approaches and Directions," International Conference on Circuits, Power and Computing Technologies [ICCPCT-2013], IEEE, pp. 1093–1098, 2013.
5. Amreen Khan, KamalKant Ahirwar, "Mobile Cloud Computing as a Future of Mobile Multimedia Database," International Journal of Computer Science and Communication, Vol. 2, No. 1, pp. 219–221, 2011.
6. Ashutosh Kumar Singh, Ramapati Mishra, Fuzail Ahmad, Raj Kumar Sagar, Anil Kumar Chaudhary, "A Review of Cloud Computing Open Architecture and Its Security Issues," International Journal of Scientific & Technology Research, Vol. 1, No. 6, pp. 67–67, 2012.
7. Mydhili K. Nair, V. Gopalakrishna, ""Cloudcop": Putting Network-Admin on Cloud Nine Towards Cloud Computing for Network Monitoring," 2009 IEEE International Conference on Internet Multimedia Services Architecture and Applications (IMSAA), IEEE, pp. 1–6, 2009.
8. Rakesh Kumar Jha, Upena D. Dalal, "A Performance Comparison with Cost for QoS Application in On-Demand Cloud Computing," 2011 IEEE Recent Advances in Intelligent Computational Systems, IEEE, 2011.
9. Lakshmannaik Ramavathu, Manjula Bairam, Sandanandam Manchala,"A Framework for Mobile Cloud Computing," International Journal of Computer Networking, Wireless and Mobile Communications (IJCNWMC), Vol. 3, No. 1, pp. 1–12, 2013.
10. Atul Gonsai, Rushi Raval, "Mobile Cloud Computing: A Tool for Future," International Journal of Computer Science & Engineering Technology (IJCSET), Vol. 4, No. 7, pp. 1084–1094, 2013.

11. Yong-Ju Lee, Jin-Hwan Jeong, Hag-Young Kim, "Video Block Device for User-friendly Viewing Patterns in IaaS Clouds," IEEE International Conference on Consumer Electronics (ICCE), IEEE, pp. 455–456, 2012.

12. Anand Mohan, "Impact of Multimedia Database and their Issues on Cloud Computing," International Journal of IT, Engineering and Applied Sciences Research (IJIEASR), Vol. 2, No. 6, pp. 8–12, June 2013.

13. Shaoxuan Wang, Sujit Dey, "Adaptive Mobile Cloud Computing to Enable Rich Mobile Multimedia Applications," IEEE Transactions on Multimedia, Vol. 15, No. 4, pp. 870–883, 2013.

14. Deepti Sahu, Shipra Sharma, Vandana Dubey, Alpika Tripathi, "Cloud Computing in Mobile Applications," International Journal of Scientific and Research Publications, Vol. 2, No. 8, pp. 1–9, August 2012.

15. John David N. Dionisio, Alfonso F. Cárdenas, "A Unified Data Model For Representing Multimedia, Timeline, And Simulation Data," IEEE Transactions on Knowledge and Data Engineering, Vol. 10, No. 5, pp. 746–767, Oct 1998.

16. Niroshinie Fernando, Seng W. Loke, Wenny Rahayu, "Mobile Cloud Computing: A Survey," Future Generation Computer Systems, Vol. 29, No. 2013, pp. 84–106, 2012.

17. Nithya Ravi, T. Mala, Madhan Kumar Srinivasan, K. Sarukesi, "Design and Implementation of VOD (Video on Demand) SaaS Framework for Android Platform on Cloud Environment," IEEE 14th International Conference on Mobile Data Management, IEEE, 2013.

18. R Prabhu, K. Gautham, A. Nagajothi, "Adaptive Mobile Video Streaming and Efficient Social Video Sharing in Cloud," International Journal of Computer Trends and Technology (IJCTT), Vol. 9 No. 4, pp. 160–163, March 2014.

19. Yi Xu, Shiwen Mao, "A Survey of Mobile Cloud Computing for Rich Media Applications," IEEE Wireless Communications, Vol. 20, No. 3, pp. 46–53, June 2013.

20. Dejan Kovachev, Yiwei Cao, Ralf Klamma, "Cloud Services for Improved User Experience in Sharing Mobile Videos," IEEE Seventh International Symposium on Service-Oriented System Engineering, IEEE, pp. 298–303, 2013.

21. Ifeanyi P. Egwutuoha, Daniel Schragl, Rafael Calvo, "A Brief Review of Cloud Computing," Challenges and Potential Solutions, Vol. 2, No. 1, pp. 7–14, Jan 2013.

22. Kevin Hamlen, Murat Kantarcioglu, Latifur Khan, "Security Issues for Cloud Computing," International Journal of Information Security and Privacy, Vol. 4, No. 2, pp. 39–51, April-June 2010.

23. Elisa Bertino, Ravi Sandhu, "Database Security—Concepts, Approaches, and Challenges," IEEE Transactions on Dependable and Secure Computing, Vol. 2, No. 1, pp. 2–19, 2005.

24. Bernd Grobauer, Tobias Walloschek, Elmar Stöcker, "Understanding Cloud Computing Vulnerabilities," IEEE Computer and Reliability Societies, Vol. 9, No. 2, pp. 50–57, March/April 2011.

25. Alexandru Iosup, Simon Ostermann, M. NezihYigitbasi, Radu Prodan, Thomas Fahringer, Dick H. J. Epema, "Performance Analysis of Cloud Computing Services for Many-Tasks Scientific Computing," IEEE Transactions on Parallel and Distributed Systems, Vol. 22, No. 6, pp. 931–945, June 2011.

Chapter 6

Reliability and Authenticity of Cloud-Based Technologies in Mobile Grid Environment Using Parameter-Based Malicious Node Detection Method

T. Sasikala, S. Vigneshwari, and G. Nagarajan
Sathyabama Institute of Science and Technology

S. Vimala
Anna University

Contents

6.1 Introduction

Grid computing is an extensive resource-sharing environment in which geologically distributed resources merge together for solving complex compute-intensive and data-intensive tasks. The advantage of a mobile Grid over the wired Grid is that it allows mobility, it is pervasive and it is portable. This effectual performance of the mobile Grid allows it to be employed in medicine, space research and so forth [1, 2].

Technology growth attracts Grid users. With the increase in Grid users, the risk in accessing the data and resources increases. An effectual authenticating and defending service is crucial. The existing security system carried out in the mobile Grid simply concentrates on authentication service. It disregards the malicious users who attempt to disrupt the data and resources during the communication. The proposed work minimizes the total number of keys employed during the communication process and presents an effective authentication service, and the wormhole resistance system (WRS) prevents the malicious wormhole attacks [2].

6.2 Literature Review

This paper [3] explores the security system adopted by the Grid system and the techniques of addressing the issues. In [4], a dual-level key management (DLKM) system is proposed. The Grid system is arranged in a hierarchical form, which employs a hash function for designing the encryption key. This technique presents a shared key for users at the first level. The first-level keys dominate the lower-level nodes. The paper in [5] presents a solution to resource depletion attacks that discharge battery power (the so-called Vampire attack). The proposed scheme in [6] applies Pontryagin's maximum principle to overcome the potential attacks. This paper [7] proposed security for authorization and access control among Grid users. In [8], the paper provides a time-variant authentication service, which uses an automatic variable password to inspect the authenticity of Grid users at equal intervals. The paper in [9] proposes a wormhole-resistant secure routing (WRSR) algorithm to identify wormhole nodes. The identification is done during the route discovery process. The proposed work in [10] identifies wormhole attacks in underwater sensor networks. The attack is identified with the parameters length and the angle the data are transmitted. The paper in [11] proposes a new protocol for detecting malicious nodes and suspicious packet transmissions. The signal strength from the originator's geographical position is used for identifying the attacks. In [12], the wormhole attacks that occur in sensor networks are identified. A method is proposed to find out Guard nodes for identifying wormhole attacks. The proposed algorithm in [13] uses connectivity information for detecting the wormhole attacks. The proposed technique in [14] presents a routing mechanism for multi-hop wireless networks. In this technique, the path is selected to minimize the overall transmission power.

The paper in [15] proposes a prevention system against wormholes attacks. Nodes' locality is used for detecting the wormhole attacks. In [16], a topology method for analyzing wormhole attacks is employed. In the proposed scheme in [17], the wormhole attacks are detected based on time. It measures the overall time taken by the data packet, time taken by the acknowledgement packet and time taken by the control packet, between source and destination. The proposed [18] TIK (Tesla Instant Key) protocol maintains strict timestamp and clock synchronization for preventing wormhole attacks within a specific range. The paper in [19] proposes a node selection method based on probability. In this method, nodes that withstand optimum energy are selected for transmission. The proposed method in [20] presents a formula for calculating the energy spent for packet transmission. The author also proposes a method for measuring the collision caused during the packet flow. In this paper [21], the Battery-Sensing Intrusion Protection System (B-SIPS) is proposed. The system uses the Dynamic Threshold Calculation algorithm. The algorithm detects the diminutive power changes caused by the attacks. The paper in [22] identifies the battery power exhausted during transmission [2].

6.3 Proposed System

The proposed system presents a Group KMS and a WRS. The KMS generates a common key to minimize the number of keys provided for effective authentication, whereas the WRS prevents various types of wormhole attacks. The following paragraphs demonstrate the designed concepts.

6.3.1 Key Management System (KMS)

For users who wish to participate in the Grid register via the Globus Toolkit (GT3) [4], the certificate authority issues a certificate embedded by a private key (K_{id}) to every individual Grid user. In the present cryptographic system, every user uses his private key for encrypting the data. For n user, $n*(n-1)$ number keys are employed. Since the Grid computing is a collaborative group environment, the most exclusive way of transmitting authenticated messages is by employing a common key among Grid users. The proposed work presents an effective key for Grid users. It minimizes the total number of keys employed in the Grid environment. The encryption and decryption process resembles Rivest-Shamir-Adleman (RSA) algorithm. The Group key provides an effective authentication and confidentiality service to the Grid environment [2].

Figure 6.1   Initial secret key generation.

Group key generation process: Let n be the number of Grid users.

STEP 1: The KMS chooses the large prime number M, public key P_{ku0}, and private key P_{kr0}.

STEP 2: The KMS using a hash function generates secret key S_{k0} using its public key P_{ku0}, private key P_{kr0} and a large value M. Figure 6.1 depicts the black box of the secret key generation algorithm.

$$S_{k0} = f(P_{ku0}, P_{kr0}, M) \tag{6.1}$$

STEP 3: When a new user U_1 joins the Grid, the KMS generates a secret key S_{k1} using its private key P_{kr0}, a large value M and the user's U_1 public key P_{Ku1}. The key S_{k1} is then sent to user U_1. Figure 6.2 illustrates the key generation process for user U_1.

STEP 4: User U_1 decrypts secret key S_{k1} using the private key P_{kr1}. The value m is sent to user U_1 by KMS. Using the secret key S_{k1}, user U_1 decrypts the value m.

$$S_{k1} = f(P_{ku1}, P_{kr0}, M) \tag{6.2}$$

$$f(x) = S_{k0} + S_{k1}x \tag{6.3}$$

STEP 5: The KMS constructs a polynomial $f(x)$ using users' secret keys (S_{k0}, S_{k1} ...). The KMS then generates a value K_x using the roots of the polynomial $f(x)$. It then publishes K_x.

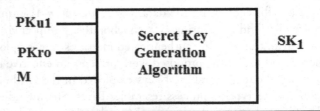

Figure 6.2   Secret key generation for new users.

STEP 6: User U_1 receives K_x. User U_1 computes the Group key (K_g) using Eq. (6.4).

$$K_g = \left(K_x + \left(\frac{S_{kn}}{K_x} m \right) mod m \right) \tag{6.4}$$

Thus, the key K_g is the ultimate Group key designed for the Grid users.

a. **Encryption process (using K_g):** Given a plain text P, cipher text C is calculated as follows

$$C = P^{K_g} mod m \tag{6.5}$$

b. **Decryption process (using K_g):** The decryption key (d_1) is calculated using Eq. (6.6)

$$1 = K_g * d_1 * S_{k1} mod \; \emptyset(m) \tag{6.6}$$

where $\emptyset(m) = (p-1)(q-1)$; q and p are prime numbers and are factors of m. The data are decrypted using user U_1's secret key (S_{k1}) and the decryption key (d_1) as shown in Eq. (6.7).

$$P = C^{d_1 \cdot S_{k1}} mod m \tag{6.7}$$

When user U_2 joins the Grid, the KMS constructs a secret key S_{k2} using its private key P_{kr0}, M and public key P_{Ku2} of user U_2. The KMS generates new secret keys S_{k1} and S_{k2} for users U_1 and U_2, respectively, and sends the keys to the corresponding users. Users U_1 and U_2 decrypt secret keys using their private keys. The KMS sends a new value m to the Users.

The KMS forms a new polynomial $f(x)$ as shown in Eq. (6.8). Using the roots of the constructed polynomial, it generates a new value K_x. It then publishes the value K_x. Users U_1 and U_2 receive K_x and compute the Group key K_g using Eq. (6.4).

$$f(x) = S_{k0} + S_{k1} x + S_{k2} x^2 \tag{6.8}$$

When user U_2 aborts the group, the KMS replaces S_{k2} with a value T_{k2} and forms a new polynomial $f(x)$. The KMS computes a new value K_x and publishes it. The Grid users receive the value K_x and construct the Group key K_g using Eq. (6.4).

$$f(x) = S_{k0} + S_{k1} x + T_{k2} x^2 \tag{6.9}$$

Thus, a Group key is designed for Grid users.

6.3.2 Detection of Wormhole Attack

Figure 6.3 illustrates a mobile Grid environment. It consists of mobile resources and gateway routers. The data between the resources are transferred via the wireless medium. Generally, the wireless medium is more vulnerable to attacks. The most challenging issue in the wireless network is malicious wormhole attacks. The wormhole attackers induce malicious attacks by compromising the valid nodes [2, 12].

During a communication process, a route request beacon signal RREQ (Route Request) is broadcasted. The neighboring nodes receive the RREQ signal. The received nodes validate the next hop addresses present in their routing tables with the route request beacon signal RREQ. An entry is created for the route request in the routing table. Node (I) enters the next hop addresses to the beacon frame and rebroadcasts it. The neighboring nodes receive the rebroadcasted signal. The verification and validation are done at all nodes until the destination. Once a destination receives the beacon signal RREQ, it sends an RREP (Route Reply) signal to the sender. The RREP message specifies the path traced by the RREQ signal. The data packets are sent through the shortest path traced by RREQ to the destination. On

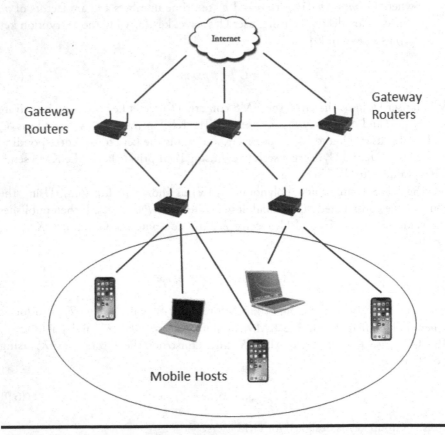

Figure 6.3 Mobile Grid environment.

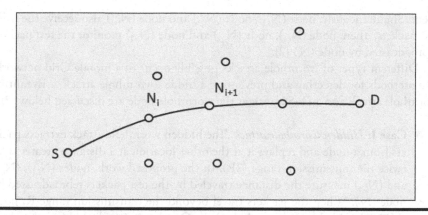

Figure 6.4   Data transmission path.

a reliable path, appropriately the data packets reach the destination. When there is a malicious attack in the routing path, there will be an intolerable packet delay or packet loss at the destination [2, 9]. Figure 6.4 depicts the path traced by the beacon signal RREQ. The proposed system identifies and prevents various wormhole attacks.

6.3.2.1 Wormhole Identification Process

In the proposed work, a significant modification is done to the existing beacon frame and the route discovery process. The route request signal RREQ is broadcasted by the source node initially. The route request signal RREQ is received by the nearest node (N_i). The hop addresses present in the beacon frame are verified and validated with the corresponding addresses present in the routing table. In the proposed work, node (N_i) selects two addresses of nearest neighboring nodes ($N_{i,1}$) and ($N_{i,2}$) from its neighborhood table and adds them to the beacon frame. Node (N_i) rebroadcasts the beacon frame. Subsequently, the two neighboring nodes act as the guard nodes for node (N_i). Further, the RREQ signal traces the shortest path to the destination. The validation and addresses entry process are done at all nodes.

Figure 6.5 depicts the modified beacon frame format. In the proposed work, a wormhole is assumed at node (N_i) in the routing path. When a wormhole exists, there will be an intolerable packet delay or packet loss at the destination. Then the destination node suspects an attack. The destination node sends a suspicious message to the sender. The suspicious message is sent in an alternate path. The sender receives the suspicious message. To find the wormhole node on the path, the sender broadcasts test packets. Node (N_i) receives the hello test packets and rebroadcasts

---	Time	addr₁	addr₂	addr₃	--		$N_{1,1}$	$N_{1,2}$	$N_{2,1}$	$N_{2,2}$	$N_{3,1}$	$N_{3,2}$	--	

Figure 6.5   Modified beacon frame.

them. Simultaneously, node $(N_{i,1})$, node $(N_{i,2})$ and node (N_{i+1}) also receive the hello test packets. Then, node $(N_{i,1})$, node $(N_{i,2})$ and node (N_{i+1}) monitor the test packets rebroadcasted by node (N_i) [2].

Different types of wormhole attacks possibly occur in a mobile Grid network. The methods for detecting and preventing a hidden wormhole attack, a Byzantine wormhole attack and a DoS attack at the wormhole node are discussed below [2].

■ **Case I:** *Hidden wormhole attack*: The hidden wormhole attack extracts packets from a node and replays it at the other location at a distance greater than twice the transmission range (2R). In the proposed work, nodes $(N_{i,1})$, $(N_{i,2})$ and (N_{i+1}) measure the distance traveled by the test packets rebroadcasted by node (N_i). When the packets travel beyond the transmission range R, node (N_i) is identified as the wormhole node. On identifying the hidden wormhole attack, an alert signal is broadcasted by the neighboring nodes; $(N_{i,1})$, $(N_{i,2})$ and (N_{i+1}). Then, node (N_i) is quarantined [2].

■ **Case II:** *Byzantine attack*: During the Byzantine attack, the wormhole node bypasses the packets to an invalid node located at a distance less than the transmission range R.

In the proposed system, the assumed wormhole node (N_i) rebroadcasts the test packets. Nodes $(N_{i,1})$, $(N_{i,2})$ and (N_{i+1}) measure the distance traveled, signal strength expended and the angle of transmission of the test packets rebroadcasted by node (N_i). The measured values are compared with the legitimate values. When a substantial deviation is recognized in the parameter values measured, a hidden wormhole attack is suspected. An alert signal is broadcasted by nodes $(N_{i,1})$, $(N_{i,2})$ and (N_{i+1}). On receiving the suspicious message, node (N_i) is quarantined [2].

The Received Signal Strength can be calculated using Eq. (6.10) [11].

$$P_R = \frac{P_T * G_T * G_R * h_T^2 * h_R^2}{d^4 * L_s} \tag{6.10}$$

where P_R is the Received Signal Strength, h_T and h_R are the heights of the Transmitter and receiver Antenna, respectively; L is the System loss; P_T is the power Transmitted; d is the distance between transmitter and receiver and G_T and G_R are the Gain of Transmitter and Receiver Antenna, respectively [11].

The angle of transmission is calculated by measuring the distance between node (N_i) and the three neighboring nodes $[(N_{i,1})$, $(N_{i,2})$ and $(N_{i+1})]$. The angle can be mathematically calculated using the distance as shown in Figure 6.6. When there is a wormhole to a distance d_1, there will certainly be a change in the angle of transmission. Using the change in the angle (θ), the wormhole can be identified [2, 19].

■ **Case III:** *DoS attack at wormhole node*: The DoS attack bursts packets through the wormhole node.

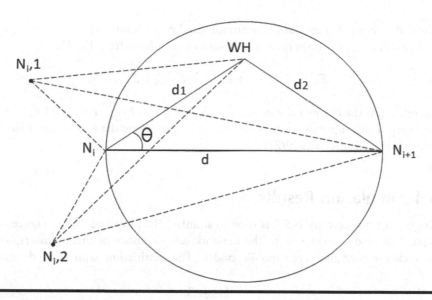

Figure 6.6 Angle of transmission.

The proposed work measures the parameters signal strength and energy consumed to identify the DoS attack. When there is a DoS attack at node (N_i), it rebroadcasts large number of packets along with the test packets. Nodes ($N_{i,1}$), ($N_{i,2}$) and (N_{i+1}) measure both the energy consumed and the signal strength expended by node (N_i). The measured values are compared with legitimate values. If there is a considerable deviation from the legitimate values, a DoS attack is identified at the wormhole node (N_i). On detecting an attack, the authorization of node (N_i) is revoked [2].

The energy consumption at a node can be calculated using Eq. (6.11). The corresponding variation in energy at a receiver node can be calculated using Eq. (6.12) [14].

$$E\left(P_T\right)=\frac{P_T}{B_w * \log_2\left(1+\dfrac{\dfrac{p_T}{D^\gamma}}{\eta * B_w}\right)} \tag{6.11}$$

where P_T = transmit power; B_W = channel bandwidth; γ = attenuation coefficient of the path; D = distance traveled by the packet; η = noise density of the spectrum and N = number of transmissions.

$$P_r = k * \frac{P_T}{D^\gamma} \tag{6.12}$$

where P_r = received energy and k = proportionality constant [14].

Total energy consumption at a node can be calculated from Eq. (6.13).

$$E_{N\_M} = E_{T\_ack} + E_{T\_pck} + E_{R\_ack} + E_{R\_pck} \qquad (6.13)$$

where E_{N_M} is the energy consumed by node and E_{T_pck}, E_{T_ack}, E_{R_ack} and E_{R_pck} are the energy consumptions while transmitting and receiving data and acknowledgement packets, respectively [20].

6.4 Simulation Results

The simulation software NS-2 is used to simulate the proposed WRS. Figure 6.7 depicts the node arrangement. The network setup consists of three clusters, and each cluster contains three mobile nodes. The destination sequenced distance

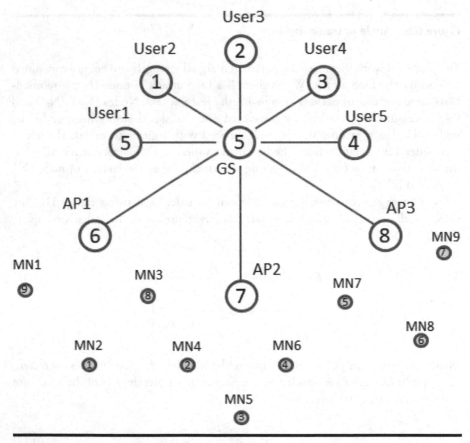

Figure 6.7 Node arrangement.

vector (DSDV) protocol is employed. The transmission range is set to 250 m. The channel data rate is set to 54 Mbps. The packet size of CBR (constant bit rate) traffic is set to 512 bits. Table 6.1 lists parameters and their values. The simulation is done for 30 seconds.

The simulation is done with a wormhole and without wormhole links. In the simulation, two wormholes are set, one at Node 1 and the other at Node 9. The packets are allowed to pass through Node 1 and Node 9 to unauthorized nodes. Various load values are set and the corresponding energy consumption and packet drop are measured at Node 1 and Node 9. The deduced unauthorized node is placed at a variable distance and the signal strength is measured.

The same simulation setup is used without wormhole simulation. Various load values are set and the corresponding energy consumption and packet drop are measured. The measurement is done at nodes 1 and 9. The graphs are drawn for load values versus energy consumption, load values versus packet drop and distance versus signal strength both with and without wormhole conditions. The outcome of the graphs proves that energy consumption and packet drop occur more during

Table 6.1 Parameters and Values

Parameters	Values
Number of users	6
Clusters	3 nos.
Mobile nodes	9 nos.
Mac	802.11
Routing protocol	DSDV
Radio range	250 m
Simulation duration	30 sec
Packet size	512
Traffic source	CBR
Node speed	12 m/sec
Load	500, 1000, 1500, 2000 and 2500 KB
Transmission power (watts)	0.660
Receiving power (watts)	0.395
Idle power (watts)	0.335
Initial energy (joules)	10.1

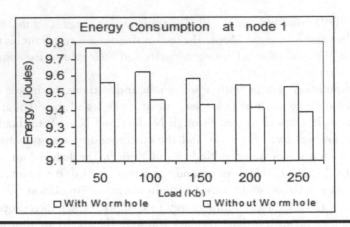

Figure 6.8   Energy consumed by node 1.

a wormhole attack. The results also show that there is considerable change in the signal strength with the link distance.

Figure 6.8 illustrates the energy consumption at node 1 with wormhole and without wormhole versus various load values. The graph shows that node 1 consumes more energy when a wormhole is injected.

The energy consumption at node 9 with and without wormhole for various load scenarios is shown in Figure 6.9. From the graphs, it is concluded that there is substantial energy consumption under the induction of wormholes.

Figure 6.10 illustrates the packet drop measured with and without wormhole at node 1. Figure 6.11 shows the packet drop with and without wormhole at node 9.

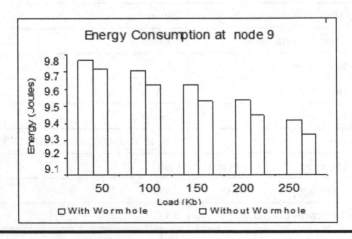

Figure 6.9   Energy consumed by node 9.

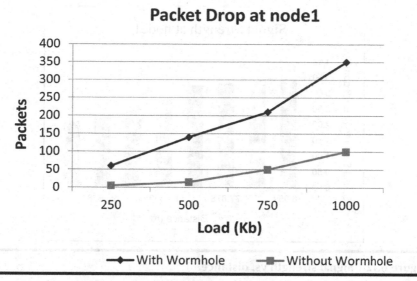

Figure 6.10   Load vs. packet drop at node 1.

The graphs show that the packet drop is more during the wormhole attack compared to without wormhole.

Figure 6.12 illustrates signal strength versus distance at node 1. Figure 6.13 depicts signal strength versus distance at node 9. The simulation proves that there is considerable change in the signal strength when the distance varies.

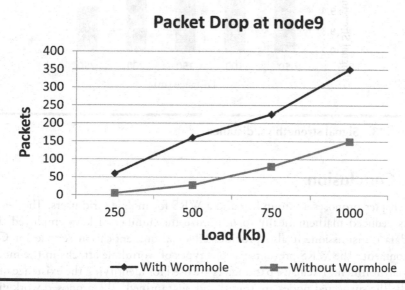

Figure 6.11   Packet drop at node 9.

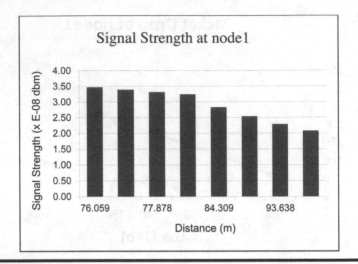

Figure 6.12   Signal strength vs. distance.

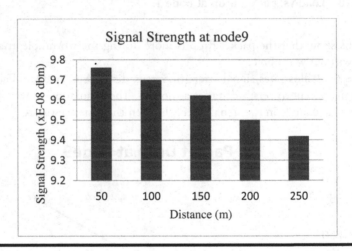

Figure 6.13   Signal strength vs. distance.

6.5 Conclusion

This chapter proposes a Group key and a WRS for mobile Grid users. The Group key is deduced mathematically to minimize the number of keys employed during data transmission. It also provides effectual authentication service for Grid environment. The WRS prevents various types of wormhole attacks in the mobile Grid environment. Exclusive parameters are used for identifying the existence of an attack. The suspected nodes are traced and quarantined. The proposed work gives better solutions compared with the existing techniques.

References

1. Chin SungHo, Taeweon Suh, Yu Heon Chang, "Genetic Algorithm-based Scheduling Method for Efficiency and Reliability in Mobile Grid," Proceedings of the 4th International Conference on Ubiquitous Information Technologies & Applications ICUT '09, Dec 2009.
2. S. Vimala, T. Sasikala, "Secure Mobile Grid Environment Defeating Wormhole Attacks and Scam Users," International Conference on Innovation Information in Computing Technologies, Feb 2015.
3. Erin Cody, Raj Sharman, Raghav H. Rao, Shambhu Upadhyaya, "Security in Grid Computing: A Review and Synthesis," Journal Decision Support Systems, Vol. 44, No. 4, pp. 749–764, March 2008.
4. Xukai Zou, Yuan-Shun Dai, Xiang Ran, "Dual-Level Key Management for Secure Grid Communication in Dynamic and Hierarchical Groups," Journal Future Generation Computer Systems, Vol. 23, No. 6, pp. 776–786, July 2007.
5. Eugene Y. Vasserman, N. Hopper, "Vampire Attacks: Draining Life from Wireless Ad Hoc Sensor Networks," IEEE Transactions on Mobile Computing, Vol. 12, No. 2, pp. 318–332, Feb 2013.
6. M. H. R. Khouzani, Saswati Sarkar, "Maximum Damage Battery Depletion Attack in Mobile Sensor Networks," IEEE Transactions on Automatic Control, Vol. 56, No. 10, pp. 2358–2368, Oct 2011.
7. M. Humphrey, M. R. Thompson, K. R. Jackson, "Security for Grids," Proceedings of the IEEE, Vol. 93, No. 3, pp. 644–652, March 2005.
8. Avijit Bhowmick, Chandan Koner, C. T. Bhunia, "A Novel Time-based Authentication Technique for Enhancing Grid Computing Security," JCA Proceedings on National Conference on Communication Technologies and its impact on Next Generation Computing, Vol. 4, 2012.
9. Rakesh Matam, Somanath Tripathy, "WRSR: Wormhole-resistant Secure Routing for Wireless Mesh Networks," EURASIP Journal on Wireless Communications and Networking, Vol. 2013, pp. 1–12, 2013.
10. Jiejun Kong, Bharat Bhargava, Mario Gerla, "Visualisation of Wormholes in Underwater Sensor Networks: A Distributed Approach," International Journal of Security and Networks, Vol. 3, No. 1, pp. 10–23, Jan. 2008.
11. W. R. Pires, T. H. de Paula Figueiredo, H. C. Wong, A. A. F. Loureiro, "Malicious Node Detection in Wireless Sensor Networks,"18th International Parallel and Distributed Processing Symposium Proceedings, pp. 26–30, April 2004.
12. P. Hemalatha, "Detecting and Preventing Wormhole Attacks in Wireless Sensor Networks," IOSR Journal of Computer Engineering (IOSR-JCE), Vol. 9, No. 6, pp. 19–27, March–April 2013.
13. Tassos Dimitriou, Athanassios Giannetsos, "Wormholes No More? Localized Wormhole Detection and Prevention in Wireless Networks," Lecture Notes in Computer Science, Distributed Computing in Sensor Systems, Vol. 6131, pp. 334–347, 2010.
14. Suman Banerjee, Archan Misra, "Adapting Transmission Power for Optimal Energy Reliable Multi-hop Wireless Communication," Wireless Optimization Workshop (WiOpt'03), Sophia-Antipolis, France, March 2003.
15. Sanjay Kumar Dhurandher, Isaac Woungang, Abhishek Gupta, Bharat K. Bhargava, "E2SIW: An Energy Efficient Scheme Immune to Wormhole Attacks in Wireless Ad Hoc Networks,"26th International Conference on Advanced Information Networking and Applications Workshops, pp. 472–477, 2012.

16. Dezun Dong, MoLi, Yunhao Liu, Xiang-Yang Li, Xiangke Liao, "Topological Detection on Wormholes in Wireless Ad Hoc and Sensor Networks," IEEE/ACM Transactions on Networking, Vol. 19, No. 6, pp. 1787–1796, Dec 2011.
17. Sivaraju Sharmila, G. Umamaheswari, "Transmission Time Based Detection of Wormhole Attack in Wireless Sensor Networks," Special Issue of International Journal of Computer Applications (0975–8887) on Information Processing and Remote Computing–IPRC, Aug 2012.
18. Yih-Chun Hu, A. Perrig, D. B. Johnson, "Wormhole Attacks in Wireless Networks," IEEE Journal on Selected Areas in Communications, Vol. 24, No. 2, pp. 370–380, Feb 2006.
19. Kadir Jailani, Ghazali Osman, Firdhous Mohamed, Hassan Suhaidi, "Node Discovery Based on Energy-Distance Factor in MANET," Internal Journal of Engineering Research and Technology, Vol. 1, No. 7, Consumption in MANET, Sep 2012.
20. Geraud Allard, Pascale Minet, Nguyen Dang-Quan, Nirisha Shrestha, "Evaluation of the Energy Consumption in MANET," Ad-Hoc, Mobile, and Wireless Networks, 5th International Conference, ADHOC-NOW 2006,Vol. 4104, pp. 170–183, 2006.
21. K. Buennemeyer Timothy, Michael Gora, Randy C. Marchany, Joseph G. Tront, "Battery Exhaustion Attack Detection with Small Handheld Mobile Computers," IEEE International Conference on Portable Information Devices (Portable '07), May 2007.
22. Maria Calle, Joseph Kabara, "Measuring Energy Consumption in Wireless Sensor Networks Using GSP," IEEE 17th International Symposium on Personal, Communications Indoor and Mobile Radio, pp. 11–14, Sept 2006.

Chapter 7

Datacenter Reliability Pursuance with Optimized Load Balancers

K. S. Resma

PES University

R.V. College of Engineering (Research Centre Affiliated to VTU-Belagavi)

G. S. Sharvani

R.V. College of Engineering (Research Centre Affiliated to VTU-Belagavi)

Contents

7.1 Introduction

A datacenter conventionally represents server hardware on an organization premises. In a datacenter the data can be stored and accessed through a local network. In
today's era of data explosion, a huge amount of data needs to be processed for business information systems. These analytics requires high computational capabilities;
hence, the storage and processing of these data in a cost-effective way brought about
the idea of cloud datacenters. We can say that cloud data service is a remote version of a datacenter, which is geographically dispersed from the users and is accessible through a network. These datacenters (Figure 7.1) are built on virtualization
technologies and focus on the effective implementation of the cloud computing
paradigm. Load balancing in the cloud is one of the biggest advantages, along with
scaling. It involves the distribution of incoming requests to the back-end servers,
which are capable of serving the request so that the system resources are utilized
efficiently and effectively.

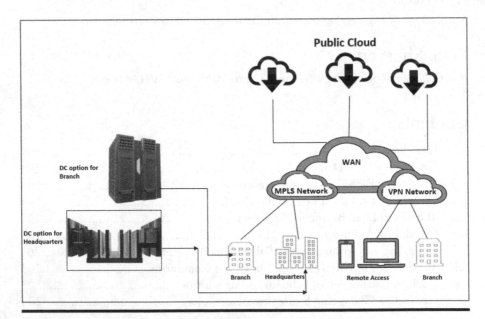

Figure 7.1   A typical datacenter infrastructure.

7.2 Understanding a Datacenter

The architecture of a datacenter [1] can be viewed with respect to the following categories:

- Geographic location of these datacenters
- Internal as well as external security of the datacenter
- Physical infrastructure such as electrical and mechanical components
- Networking infrastructure
- Types of servers
- Storage

1. ***Geographic location of these datacenters:*** The cloud service providers are geographically dispersed [2]. Within those regions they will have a minimum of two to three datacenters separated geographically for providing high availability and resilience.

2. ***Internal as well as external security of the datacenter:*** The internal and external security associated with a datacenter is the physical security of the datacenter. The resources of the cloud datacenters are controlled and maintained by the service providers otherwise known as vendors. Hence, securing the services is solely the responsibility of the service providers. Each of the vendors has his or her own ways of securing the infrastructure.

3. ***Physical infrastructure such as electrical and mechanical components:*** The physical infrastructure includes the generators, power supplies, air conditioners and fire-handling equipment and so forth. They need to be placed at proper locations with proper capacities and configurations to make sure that the datacenter gives a reliable service with good uptime.

4. ***Networking infrastructure:*** This [3] includes the switches, routers and other network middleboxes. They are allotted from the software level; hence, installing a switch or a router cannot be done by the tenant of the cloud. The tenant will be able to implement controls, services and configurations to simulate the physical network functions. There is the possibility of creating virtual networks that can be segmented into Internet Protocol (IP) ranges and can deploy storage, compute and other network middleboxes as per customer requirements. The network connectivity mostly consists of the Multiprotocol Label Switching (MPLS), an encrypted virtual private network (VPN) and wide area networks (WAN).

5. ***Types of servers:*** Servers are usually called virtual machines depending on the cloud service providers. The servers vary depending on the services they provide. Some are web servers, some act as database servers and some servers have high computing capacities to process huge amounts of data. This variance in services provided is the key aspect of the cloud. The service providers can scale the capacity and services provided by these servers on the changing requirement of the users.

6. *Storage:* In a cloud infrastructure the storage is considered unlimited. The cloud datacenter can provide durable and scalable storage services without any limits, depending on the types of data and the type of computing to be performed on this data. The Amazon Web Services (AWS) provides elastic block storage. This elastic block storage can be reconfigured and moved from one instance to other. There are different vendors who can provide a file level as well as object storage capabilities. Storage area networks are also widely in use.

7.3 Challenges Faced by Cloud Datacenters

In spite of the advantages of cloud datacenters in bringing reliability and availability to the services provided by the cloud service provider, there are few challenges faced by these datacenters. The major challenges [4] of these datacenters are caused by improper load balancing. Let us first focus on the following challenges that can pop up because of imbalanced load:

- Energy efficiency
- Monitoring
- Capacity planning
- Performance management

Energy efficiency: Cloud computing provides metered, demand-based services to its customers. The requested services are provided from a centralized pool of resources. These services are largely based on virtualization. The datacenter contains the information as well as services running on the application servers and intelligent storage systems. They contain not only storage and applications but also cables, air conditioners, networks and so forth. Hence, a datacenter requires a great deal of power and releases a huge amount of carbon di oxide. Thus, energy optimization [5] in datacenters is one of the biggest difficulties in cloud computing. This challenge can be faced by an effective distribution of load across the servers, which can be achieved by an optimized load balancing technique. To provide the customers with high reliability, availability and fault tolerance, datacenters are established across the world and each datacenter will be equipped with a huge number of servers. Even if a server is allotted with a small load, the server consumes 50% of the power supply. Since reliability is a primary concern, theservers need to be up and running in spite of having a minimum load. This is the major reason for the need for energy inefficiency. There is a strong coupling between resource utilization and energy consumption. Studies shows that the average resource utilization in most datacenters can range from 20% to 60%; hence, increasing resource utilization is very important. One important effective method to increase resource utilization is task consolidation [6]. Task consolidation can be achieved through an optimized load balancing technique, which is discussed in detail later in the chapter.

1. *Monitoring:* Datacenter monitoring can be defined as a process of keeping track of the operations in conformity with the requirements of a user. It can also be conceived as the use of sophisticated tools to maintain operational reliability to a datacenter. Datacenter monitoring is also known as datacenter management. An effective load balancing technique can make sure that the management or monitoring of a cloud datacenter happens effectively.

2. *Capacity planning:* This [7] can be defined as the confirmation of demand to resources availability. Capacity planning studies the measure of performance of a system, usage pattern of a system and the location of available resources. On demand the resources are provisioned and allotted. The basic requirement of capacity planning is the effective accommodation of workloads. In certain instances, it also helps in optimizing the performance even though performance tuning is not a primary goal of capacity planners. To successfully optimize a system's capacity, understanding and characterizing the workload is very important. Provisioning of resources such as processor, memory, storage and network capacity to satisfy cloud users' demands is the main objective of cloud systems. Each of these resources has a utilization rate, which can be obtained as:

$$\text{Utilization Rate} = \frac{\text{actual output}}{\text{maximum possible output}} \times 100$$

When demand keeps increasing, the resource reaches a ceiling, limiting the performance. For such resources, the capacity planner adds more resources (scale up the resources) and removes the bottleneck to handle the growing demand for resources. From the description of capacity planning, the importance of load balancing is very well understood.

3. *Performance management:* Cloud performance management [8] is about assessing different benchmarks and metrics of cloud system performance. It determines how well a cloud system is functioning and what improvements can be made to the system. The performance metrics include the following:
    a. *System availability:* System availability is the ratio of time a particular system functions well with respect to the expected to work. This can also be defined as the average downtime of a system. Availability can also be defined qualitatively to the extent to which a system can tolerate fault.

Availability of a particular month can be calculated using the following formula:

$$Availability\,(\%) = \left(1 - \left(\frac{d}{u}\right)\right) \times 100$$

where d = total hours the system was not available for service (down time) and u = numbers of available hours during the month (uptime).

This metric is very important, for example, if a system has a downtime of 11 hours in a month. The available time for a month is expected as 24 hours for 30 (assuming a month of 30 days). The availability can be calculated as

$$1 - \left(\frac{11}{(24 \times 30)}\right) \times 100 = 98.47$$

b. ***Reliability:*** Reliability can be defined as the probability a system performs absolutely well for a specific duration of time. During this duration of time, the system will not require any failure handling. Reliability can be defined as the ability of being trustable and consistent. It means that the users can forget the other issues regarding data security and data loss. The phases in the life of a product or device are illustrated using a life cycle curve commonly known as the bathtub curve (Figure 7.2).

There are three phases in a life cycle curve. During the early life or infant stage of a device, failures occur frequently. In the second stage, called the useful life, most devices showcase a constant failure rate. In the last phase, which is the wear-out

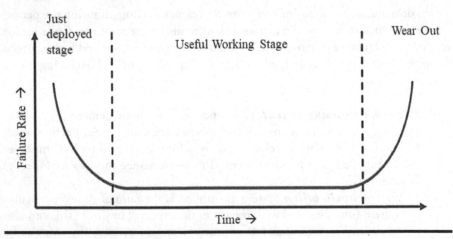

Figure 7.2   Reliability matrix.

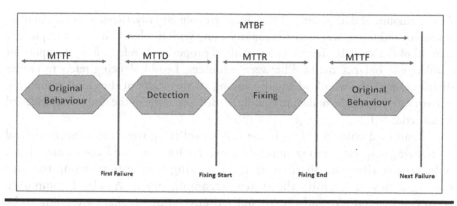

Figure 7.3   Representation of different parameters of reliability.

phase, failure becomes high again and rises rapidly. Mostly the calculation of reliability is made in the useful life phase (phase II). The infant mortality and wear-out phase exhibit too much variation in the failure rate; hence, reliability prediction becomes difficult. These metrics (see Figure 7.3) cannot be observed directly; instead, they are computed through repeated experimentation. Reliability can be calculated with the help of following matrices.

- Mean time between failure (MTBF) = $\frac{\text{Number of hours of operation}}{\text{Number of failures}}$
- Mean time to repair (MTTR)= $\frac{\text{Total time of maintenance}}{\text{Number of repairs}}$ is the average time required to fix a failed component and/or device and return it to production status.

c. ***Response time:*** Response time is an important metric that is defined as the time taken by a virtual environment to respond to a user. The average response time for a cloud datacenter differs with respect to the region of the user and the datacenter. When a user and datacenter are geographically dispersed, the response time increases. There are still more metrics that determine the performance of a cloud datacenter including throughput, capacity, scalability, cost per customer and so forth. The implementation of a proper load balancing technique can help in achieving these reliability and performance metrics to a great extent. The remaining part of this chapter will be focusing on various Load balancing techniques to achieve better performance for a virtualized cloud infrastructure.

7.4 Closer Look at Cloud Load Balancing

Cloud computing has confronted numerous difficulties, including security, scaling, efficient load balancing, resource scheduling, performance monitoring, energy consumption, service availability and quality of service (QoS) management [9].

As the amount of data generated is increasing exponentially, the demand for sharing resources and usage also increases rapidly along with it. Hence, it is very important that all of the available resources are utilized properly; therefore, it is an important challenge to balance the load between resources. Load balancing refers to proper distribution of the workload equally among all the nodes of the cloud computing network so that all the nodes are equally loaded and none of the nodes is overloaded or underloaded.

Cloud load balancing [10] is the task of splitting the users' workloads and computing requests among multiple servers within a cloud datacenter. Load balancing is all about distributing the incoming load evenly among the processing nodes to intensify the system accomplishment. As cloud computing is an on-demand pay and use virtualized environment, there are going to be a many variations in the number of users and amount of resources getting consumed with respect to time. This scenario can lead to situations such as underutilization as well as overloading of servers. There has to be proper balance within the system, which means load needs to be distributed in such a way that no servers are either underutilized or overloaded. From the previous sections it is very clear that for performance and reliability a noble approach to load balancing is very important. The cloud service providers need to manage the workloads by implementing mechanisms capable of provisioning efficient usage of on-demand computing resources. The efficient resource management is a very important component that can bring reliability and reduce operational cost.

7.5 The Cloud Load Balancing Architecture

Previously we discussed the major challenges faced by a load balancer. We also stated that an effective solution to those challenges is an efficient load balancing technique. To understand effective load balancing techniques, we need to understand a load balancer. Figure 7.4 shows the architecture and Figure 7.5 shows the data flow in a typical load balancer. A load balancer distributes incoming network traffic. Load balancers [11] help to increase the capacity of the datacenter, which is the number of concurrent users, and improve the reliability of applications. They help the servers perform well when managing applications, network sessions and application-specific tasks.

Load balancers are broadly categorized as layer 4 and layer 7. The Layer 4 load balancers take care of the network and transport layer load, whereas layer 7 load balancers distribute requests found in application layer protocols such as Hypertext Transfer Protocol (HTTP).

There are various methods and algorithms that can help to balance the client access requests across the pool of servers. The choice of method depends on

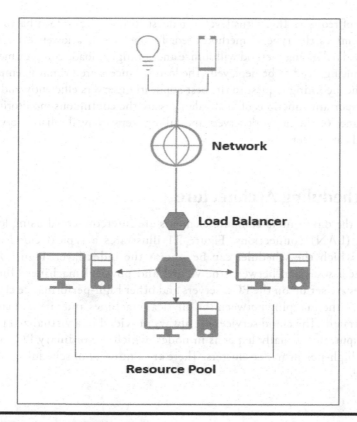

Figure 7.4   Typical load balancer.

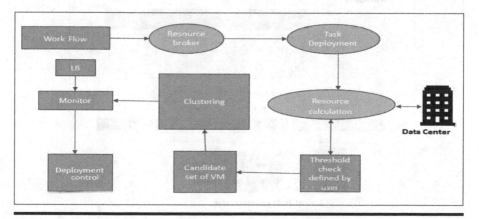

Figure 7.5   Data flow in a typical load balanced cloud environment. LB, load balancer; VM, virtual machine.

the type of request. The status level of request to the type of load balancers usually determines the type of method used. In the case of a lower level of load, a simple load balancing method will suffice and for higher loads complex methods of load balancing need to be deployed. The load balancers are primarily employed to deliver the incoming request to the best application servers efficiently and quickly. Other important functions of load balancers are the continuous monitoring of the performance of the network servers and taking steps to avail reliable service from the cloud datacenter.

7.6 Scheduling Architecture

Most of the datacenters compute elements are interconnected using local area network (LAN) connections. Figure 7.1 illustrates a typical cloud architecture, in which the scheduler can be seen at the index layer. Figure 7.6 illustrates the association between the virtual and physical machines. The virtual machines are set up on the PCs, servers and other high-performance clusters. In Figure 7.7, the mapping between the physical machines and virtual machines is demonstrated. The cloud services are always provided in a virtualized platform. The computation usually happens in nodes, which are ordinary PCs or servers or some high-performance clusters. There are a number of scheduling strategies available.

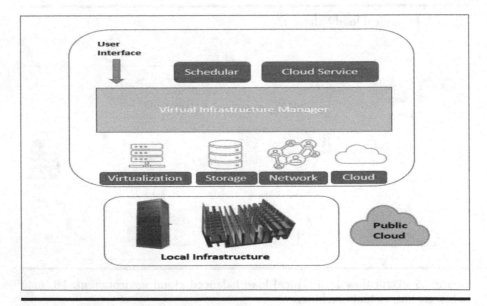

Figure 7.6   Cloud infrastructure manager.

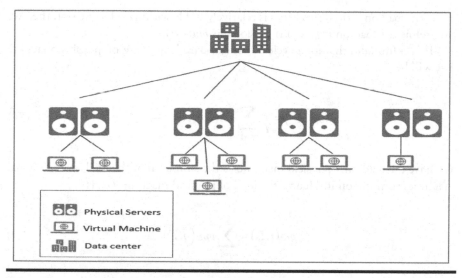

Figure 7.7   Architecture of load scheduling.

7.7 Designing an Optimal and Reliable Load Balancer

1. **Virtual machine model:** Figure 7.7 represents the association of virtual machines to physical machines. Hence, we can have the following conclusions from Figure 7.7: pm represents a physical machine, where $pm = \{pm_1, pm_2, \ldots pm_n\}$ represents the set of all physical machines, n is the number of physical machines and vm represents the virtual machines. For each physical machine pm_i there is a set of virtual machines that pm_i will be associated with, $vm_i = \{vm_{i1}, vm_{i2}, \ldots vm_{ir}\}$; r represents the number of virtual machines associated with each pm_i. The association between the physical machine pm_i to the set of virtual machines vm_i is represented as a_i, where a_i is an element of the set of associations $a = \{a_1, a_{i2}, \ldots a_{in}\}$ for each physical machine to its set of virtual machines.

2. **Derive the load:** The load on a particular physical machine is the summation of loads of all the virtual machines associated with that physical machine. Let T be the time span monitored for the past data, as monitoring of past data is important for the analysis of current load is important. Hence, T is the time zone to be monitored for past data, which starts from the current time zone.

T is the time zone from live to prior date. The physical machine load time T is highly fluctuating and can be further divided into n time slots as $T = \left[(t_1 - t_0), (t_2 - t_1), \ldots, (t_n - t_{n-1}) \right]$.

Hence from definition, to represent time slot k, we will have $(t_k - t_{k-1})$.

If the load on virtual machines is relatively stable within each time slot, then we can define the load on vm_i for a time slot k as $vm(i,k)$.

This culminates that for a cycle T, the standard load of vm_i on physical machine pm_i will be

$$\overline{vm_i(i,T)} = \frac{1}{T} \sum_{k=1}^{n} vm(i,k) \times (t_k - t_{k-1}) \tag{7.1}$$

We have the load on a physical machine as the sum total of the load on the virtual machines running on it. Hence, the load of physical machine pm_i is

$$pm(i,T) = \sum_{j=1}^{m_i} \overline{vm_i(j,T)} \tag{7.2}$$

To establish a *vm*, the resource information for the latest virtual machine is already enumerated. Using that enumeration estimation of the load on the new virtual machine as *vm* can be obtained. Hence, the load on the individual physical machine can be calculated as:

$$pm(i,T) = \begin{cases} pm(i,T) + vm' \; including \; new \; vm \\ pm(i,T) \; otherwise \end{cases} \tag{7.3}$$

Once a new virtual machine is deployed to a physical machine, there should be some changes in the existing loads; hence, the loads need to be balanced once a new virtual machine is included. The load, after considering the association factor a_i, for the period T, after including virtual machine *vm*, is arranged to physical machine *pm*, which will be

$$\sigma_i(T) = \sqrt{\frac{1}{n} \sum_{i=1}^{n} \left(\overline{pm(T)' - pm(i,T)'} \right)^2} \tag{7.4}$$

where

$$\overline{pm(T)'} \frac{1}{n} \sum_{i=1}^{n} p_m(i,T)' \tag{7.5}$$

3. ***Mathematical model of a typical load balancer:*** A mathematical model can be derived [12] from the previous analysis.

Derivation 1: Under system association solution a_i, the total load on an individual physical machine, $pm(i,T)'$, and the total load deviation, which is the total mean deviation of the average load for a time slot T, can be defined as

$$\sigma_i\left(a_i,T\right)=\sqrt{\frac{1}{n}\sum_{i=1}^{n}\overline{\left(pm(T)'-pm\left(i,T\right)'\right)^2}} \qquad (7.6)$$

$$where\ \ \overline{pm(T)}'\ \frac{1}{n}\sum_{i=1}^{n}p_m\left(i,T\right)' \qquad (7.7)$$

Derivation 2: The association between the virtual machine and the physical machine can be balanced as a balanced association, which becomes a_i' from a_i. Then the set of association is

$$a'=\left\{a_{i1}',a_{i2}',\dots\dots\dots a_{in}'\right\}$$

Hence, we can say that a_i' is the appropriate association for $\sigma_i\left(a_i,T\right)$ to match the predefined load constraint.

Derivation 3: If the number of virtual machines to be migrated for balancing the load is designated as M' and M designates number of virtual machines, then for every association a_i, the cost devisor $\rho\left(a_i\right)$ to reach an optimum load balancing state can be defined as

$$\rho\left(a_i\right)=\frac{M'}{M} \qquad (7.8)$$

While designing a load balancer, the focus has to always be in achieving the best association solution and in achieving the best cost devisor. This defines the important requirement in the design of a reliable and high-performance load balancer.

7.8 The Scheduling Strategies Used in Cloud Computing

Scheduling strategies are basically the algorithms [13] used in the load balancers. The load balancing algorithms can be broadly classified as static and dynamic load balancing algorithms.

7.8.1 Classification of Scheduling Algorithms

a. **Static load balancing algorithms:** In case of static algorithms [14], the load distribution is based on the load, during the node selection. Foregoing information on the system is a prerequisite for this type of load balancing. The node performance is determined when the execution commences. Once the workload is allotted to the node, the node calculates the result and submits it to the remote node. In static algorithms the workload is calculated at the beginning of the allotment. It does not take care of the changing loads. The static load balancing algorithm works with a non–pre-emptive strategy. These algorithms will not consider the current load status on a system while allocating the load.

b. ***Dynamic load balancing algorithms:*** The workload of the system here is monitored, and the work is redistributed accordingly. At runtime, the distribution of the workload takes place, and this is how it differs the most from static algorithms. Based on the new information collected, the slaves are assigned new process by the master. Unlike static algorithms, when underloading takes place at one of the processors, process allocation is done by the dynamic algorithm. Also, on the main host, buffering takes place in the queue and when the remote requests are received, allocation is done dynamically. The algorithms used here are based on three strategies: location strategy, transfer strategy and information strategy (e.g., least connection algorithm).

In this study, few load balancing algorithms are selected and they have been analyzed to understand their uniqueness in improving the load balancing issue and to put forth a new strategy for load balancing to address this issue in cloud computing.

Next, a few of the algorithms used as strategies for load balancers will be discussed with the advantages and disadvantages of each of them.

7.8.2 Load Balancing Strategies: Algorithms

a. ***Round robin algorithm:*** Round robin is an elementary method of load balancing strategy. The incoming requests are forwarded to each client in turns. When the end of the list is reached, a looping back happens to the end of the list; hence, sending the next request to the server listed first, the one after that to the next server and continuing in the same manner. Due to the assumption that all servers are identical with respect to load, storage and computation capacity, this algorithm sometimes gives an inefficient load distribution. Figure 7.8 represents the resource allocation for round robin algorithm. There are two more variations of the round robin that take into account certain additional features and give a better result of load balancing (weighted round robin and dynamic round robin).

In the weighted round robin, a weight is assigned to each server based on the user requirement. The servers with maximum weights receive the highest portion of the client request. For example, assume that an enterprise has three servers:

■ Server X can handle 15 requests per second, on average.
■ Server Y can handle 10 requests per second, on average.
■ Server Z can handle 5 requests per second, on average.

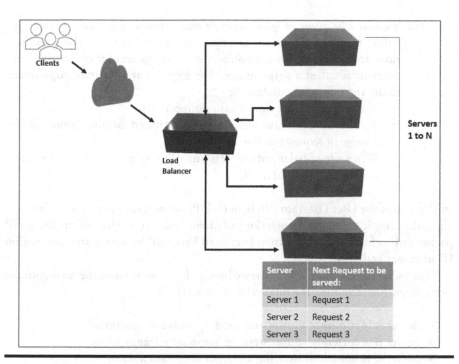

Figure 7.8   Round robin technology.

Next, assume that the load balancer received six requests. Then the load will be distributed in the following way:

- Three requests are sent to Server X.
- Two requests are sent to Server Y.
- One request is sent to Server Z.

Hence, we say that the weighted round robin algorithm distributes the load based on the server capacity. In the case of dynamic round robin, weights are assigned dynamically to each server. This weight assigned is positioned conferring to real-time status of the servers, which interpolates the load as well, and is called the idle capacity of the server.

  b. *Least connections algorithm:* In a cloud datacenter, when we use the least connections algorithm for load balancing a service bearing a minimum number of active connections is selected. This is the default behavior, which can provide an optimized performance.

  Connections active to a server: The requests sent from the client to the virtual servers are in turn forwarded to the service by the virtual servers. These connections are termed as active connections.

Surge queue (the queue of connections in wait): This is when the connections before reaching the virtual servers enters a waiting state. These connections are called the waiting connections. The queue of these waiting connections is called a surge queue. The requests are put into surge queue under the following conditions:

- The services have a limit to the connections.
- There is a configuration enabled and activated for surge protection by a surge in requests to the virtual server.
- When a load-balanced server is unable to open a new connection as it reaches the internal limit.

In the case of the User Diagram Protocol (UDP) connections, the least connection algorithm considers all the associations of client and server. First, when the UDP packet arrives for a session, a session is created between the source and destination IP addresses and ports.

The following example will illustrate how a virtual server uses the least connections algorithm. Examine the following three services:

- Server A is currently administrating 3 operative transactions.
- Server B is currently administrating 5 operative transactions.
- Server C is not administrating any operative transactions.

As in Figure 7.9, for each incoming request, services with minimum operative transactions are allotted by the virtual server. The client requests are forwarded in the following sequence:

- The first request goes to Server C, because the number of 3 operative transactions of C was null. That means the service with nil active transaction will be selected first.
- The second request also goes to Server C (next least number of 3 operative transactions of 1).
- The third request also goes to Server C as the service has the next least number of 3 operative transactions of 2.
- Now Server A and Server C have the same number of 3 operative transactions. The decision of allocation needs to be taken between both of these services. This decision can be taken based on the weights, priority or in a round robin fashion. Here the fourth request will go to Server A, if the virtual server uses the round robin method to choose between them.
- Server C will be receiving the fifth request.
- Server A will be receiving the next request, and so on. If we continue with the allotment in this way, the ninth request will go to Server B. Note that If any connections to Server B close, then it could accept new connections prior to the other two services accumulating five active transactions.

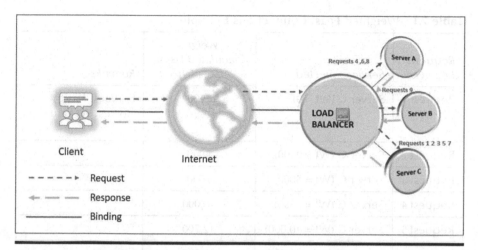

Figure 7.9   Least connections strategy of load balancing.

Figure 7.9 illustrates the above scenario, where a particular load balancer allocates the incoming requests using the least connection method. Server B will be selected for load balancing under the following three conditions: when the active transactions assigned are completed; the current connections are closed or when the other two services, Server A and Server C, have five or more connections each.

   c. ***Weighted least connections:*** The load balancer can also use the least connection method with weights associated. The servers can be selected based on a weight (Wt) calculated using the following expression:

$$\text{Wt} = (\text{Number of transactions in active state}) \times (10000/\text{weight}) \qquad (7.9)$$

Consider the following example scenario (Table 7.1) demonstrating the least connection method when the requests are assigned with weights. For the analysis we take that Server A, Server B and Server C are assigned weights 2, 3 and 4, respectively. Here the allocations will be done as follows.

Server C receives the first request, because the service is not handling any active transactions. But If services are not handling any active transactions, irrespective of the weights assigned to each of the services, the load balancer uses the round robin method for load distribution. Because of the lowest Wt value, Server C receives the second, third, fourth, fifth, sixth and seventh requests; Server A receives the eighth request and Server C receives the ninth request.

   The advantages and disadvantages of least connection algorithm: The advantage of the least connections algorithm is that it prevents a server from being overloaded by checking the number of connections the server is already

Table 7.1 Weighted Least Connections Example

Requests Received	Service Selected	Weight Calculated Using Eq. (7.9)	Remarks
Request 1	Server C (Wt = 0)	2500	Server C has the lowest Wt value
Request 2	Server C (Wt = 2500)	5000	
Request 3	Server C (Wt = 5000)	7500	
Request 4	Server C (Wt = 7500)	10,000	
Request 5	Server C (Wt = 10,000)	12,500	
Request 6	Server C (Wt = 12,500)	15,000	
Request 7	Server A (Wt = 15,000)	20,000	Server A and Server C have the same Wt values
Request 8	Server C (Wt = 15,000)	17,500	

having. The disadvantage of this algorithm is that this algorithm is not considering the server capacity while considering the number of current connections. This can be explained as if Server X has 15 connections and Server
Y has 25. The next incoming request will be sent to Server X because it has
a smaller number of connections; however, Server X may have a capacity of
18 connections, whereas Server Y has 50, making Server X more likely to
become overloaded. Weighted least connections take into consideration the
capability of the server and the number of current connections to prevent
overloading and crashing.

   d. ***Hashing algorithms:*** There are load balancing methods based on the hashing algorithm, involving the hashing of header information or the connection
   information. The hashes are easier to use and are shorter than the original
   information, and hashing retains enough information to avoid collision.
   There are different types of hashing methods, depending on how the hash
   values are calculated. When new services are added, these algorithms ensure
   a minimum amount of disruption. Hashing algorithms mostly calculate hash
   values in the following way:
   - Hashing the server IP address and port
   - Hashing the incoming URL, the domain name, the source or destination IP address or both, depending on the configured hash calculation
   method

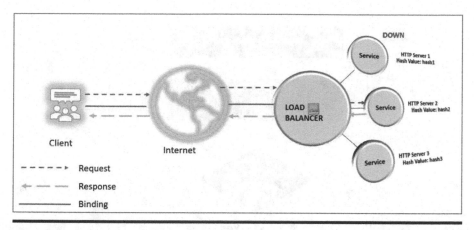

Figure 7.10   Hash algorithm data flow.

The service request is forwarded to the server with the highest hash value. A cache is populated every time a request is allotted to a server bas ed on the hash value. As a result, a new request, which gives a hash value the same as the one created before, is given to the same server. The data flow of the hash algorithm is illustrated in Figure 7.10.

Consider the three servers A, B and C. These three servers are associated with a virtual server. If the hash function creates a value "hash 1" then the request is allocated to server1. If the server is not up, then the request is forwarded to Server B. This scenario is represented in Figure 7.10.

> *Calculation of hash value:* To calculate the hash value, the load balancer uses a specific algorithm. In the case of the **URL hash method**, it scrutinizes a portion of the URL. In most cases the portion is the starting 80 bytes, but the length of the URL to be hashed can be customized. A longer URL for hashing brings in a lower number of collisions, which is a good characteristic of a good hashing calculation. Figure 7.11 represents the flowchart of hash algorithm.

In the case of a load balancer configured with the **domain hash method**, the hashed value of the domain name in the HTTP request is used to select a service. In the case of the domain name being present in both the URL and header, the URL domain name will be given preference. In case the incoming request does not carry a domain name, the load balancer will switch to some other type of load balancing strategy, such as the round robin.

A load balancer configured for *source IP destination IP hash method* makes use of the source and destination of the IP address for hash value calculation. It can be either IPv4 or IPv6.

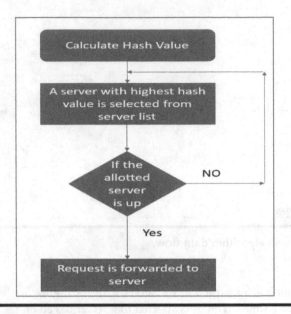

Figure 7.11   Hash algorithm flowchart.

A load balancing virtual server that is configured for the *call ID hash method* uses the call ID in the SIP header for hash value calculation. Similarly, there are different methods of calculating the hash value. As per the description of the hashing algorithm, for the perfect design of a load balancer the hash calculation needs to be prioritized. Usually hash functions make use of modulus arithmetic on some prime values.

For any prime number p such that $p > m$, and for any $1 \leq a \leq p$ and $0 \leq b \leq n$ $(ax + b \bmod p) \bmod m$ can be defined. Let $H = \{h_{a,b} \mid 0 \leq b < p, 1 \leq a < p\}$

For every $x \neq y \in \{0, \ldots \ldots, p\}$,

$$Pr_{h \in H}\left[h_{a,b}(x) = h(y)\right] \leq \frac{1}{p}$$

If we say $h(x) = h(y)$ we need to say that $ax + b = ay + b + i.m \bmod p$ for any integer i. Hence, there will be two remainders of $ax + b$ and $ay + b$ equivalent to *mod*. The b's will get canceled and the equation can be solved for a:

$$a = im(x - y)^{-1} \bmod p \qquad (7.10)$$

There are $(p - 1)$ possible choices for the value of a because $a \neq 0$. Also, picking a value of i greater than $\left(\frac{p}{m}\right)$ will not make much sense as we are working with modulo. So, there are $\left\lceil \frac{(p-1)}{m} \right\rceil$ possible values for the right-hand side (RHS) of

Eq. (7.10). So, if chosen randomly, [remember, $(x - y)$ is fixed ahead of time, so the only choice is, i], then there is a $\left(\left(p-1\right)\big/_m\right)$ in $(p-1)$ chance that the equality holds, which is at most $\frac{1}{m}$. To be exact you should account for taking a floor of $\left(\left(p-1\right)\big/_m\right)$ when m does not evenly divide $(p-1)$, but that will reduce the overall probability. The reason hashing finds its application in load balancing is because the input data is random.

e. ***Genetic algorithm:*** In the cloud datacenter, resource allocation is on demand for the subscribers. This allocation needs to be on par with the Service-Level Agreement (SLA). Virtualization [15] is an effective solution to manage dynamic resources for the datacenter. The virtualization also solves the heterogeneity of users and platform dependency. Genetic algorithm is based on the rule of evolution—survival of the fittest. It provides an upgraded constant parallelism and optimization.

The concept of the genetic algorithm [16] is based on three basic operations: selection, genetic operation and replacement. The concept of the genetic algorithm can be used as an optimized load balancing technique.

Consider J_n is the number of jobs submitted and P is the number of processing units. The individual processing unit has its own utilization with respect to time. The changing utilization status of each P can be represented as a unit vector (Pv). This vector is a function of the number of instructions processed per second (IPS) by the machine and c represents the cost of instruction execution and lag cost (d), where d is the penalty paid by the service provider to the user in case of a deadline extension in process completion. Hence, we have

$$Pv = f\left(IPS, c, d\right) \tag{7.11}$$

Each job coming to the cloud system can be represented by a unit vector (Jv). The vector is a combination of different attributes of a submitted job. The attributes of the submitted job include service provided such as SaaS, IaaS and PaaS represented as St. Each job consists of a number of instructions (I), arrival time (At) of the job and worst-case completion time (ct_w) for a job taken by the processing unit. The job unit vector can be represented as a function of the above components as

$$Jv = f\ \left(I,\ At, ct_w, St\right) \tag{7.12}$$

The number of jobs, J_n, needs to be distributed among the processing units, P. This distribution needs to happen with minimum cost with high reliability. This can be achieved with minimized cost (cost function) J as follows:

$$J = w_0 \times \alpha\left(I \div IPS\right) + w_1 \times d \tag{7.13}$$

where w_0 and w_1 are predefined weights. The weights are mostly decided based on the user's preference. The genetic algorithm is a widely accepted artificial intelligence–based searching and optimization technique. It is primarily based on natural selection and genetics. In vast search space the genetic algorithms have proved to be very stable in giving out optimal solutions.

> **Algorithm working:** The algorithm works in three major steps: selection, genetic operation and replacement. As discussed earlier, this method has the advantage of handling vast search space, applicability to complex objective functions and it never gets trapped into the local optimal solution. The genetic algorithm can be described as follows:
>
> 1. ***Initial population propagation:*** The genetic algorithm is based on individual solutions of fixed bit string representation. Hence, a binary string is obtained as an encoding of all possible solutions spaces. From the binary string of possible solutions, random chromosome values are selected.
> 2. ***Crossover:*** During this step, the best pair of individuals is selected for the crossover. The fitness values of individual chromosomes are calculated using the fitness function, Eq. (7.3). The set of chromosomes undergoes random crossover and, depending on the point of crossover, the portions lying on either side of the crossover point are exchanged, resulting a new combo of entity.
> 3. ***Mutation:*** A value called a mutation probability is selected. It will be small like 0.05. Toggling (0-1/1-0) of the chromosome's bits are done based on the mutation values. The final outcome of this step results in a new mating pool ready for crossover.

These steps are looped until the fittest chromosome (optimal solution) is found or the termination condition (maximum number of iteration) is exceeded. There are many more load balancing algorithms used in load balancers, such as agent-based adaptive load balancing, chained failover or fixed weighted, weighted response time, nature inspired algorithms and so forth. But we are limiting our discussion to a few of the previously discussed algorithms that have found a wide range of use in the current scenario.

7.9 Case Study on Elastic Load Balancers: Classic Load Balancers

Elastic load balancing is the distribution of the incoming traffic within the targets, providing optimized availability and fault tolerance to the application. The targets can be within or not within an availability zone. For an elastic load balancer (ELB), the addition or removal of compute resources can take place without disrupting an incoming request. This quality makes sure that the system works with high availability. The configuration of health checks for the load balancer makes sure that the incoming requests are forwarded to the healthy instances only. The ELB provides security by providing encryption and decryption. The incoming requests are accepted by the listeners. Listeners are system processes that are continuously checking for any incoming request to the system. There are ports and protocols of listeners. These ports and the protocol configuration help in the communication between load balancer, clients and targets.

The internal load balancers are configured with private IP addresses, and thus their domain name server (DNS) names are resolvable publicly only to the network nodes' private IP addresses. These can route incoming requests from the users who have access to the Virtual Private Cloud (VPC). However, Internet-facing load balancers are configured with public IP addresses, so their DNS names are resolvable publicly to the network nodes' public IP addresses. These can route incoming requests from the users over the Internet. These load balancers help in spreading the load across various instances downstream. The ELBs exposed the applications to single DNSs. The ELB provides regular health checks and better failure handling for downstream servers. They also help in providing Secure Sockets Layer (SSL) termination or Hypertext Transfer Protocol Secure (HTTPS) to the application websites at load balancer levels. An ELB enforces the stickiness of users, which means the same user is repeatedly going to the same instance with the help of cookies. It also segregates public and private traffic. There are three different kinds of elastic ELBs in AWS: classic, application and network. These are discussed in detail below. In this section we will focus on the classic load balancers in AWS as a case study. The entire implementation and configuration details are also included.

7.9.1 Classic Load Balancers

A classic load balancer is the old generation load balancer; it is the v1 load balancer that was used in 2009. The decisions on routing are taken at the transport layer (Transmission Control Protocol (TCP)/SSL) or the application layer (HTTP/HTTPS). There is a relationship predefined and established between the instance port and the port of the classic load balancer. The classic load balancer takes care that the load request is equally shared among the registered set of instances belonging to a particular availability zone. The distribution of load is evenly distributed among the availability zones also, for example, if an availability zone has 20 instances and another availability zone has 10 instances. But the total incoming requests are equally distributed to both of the availability zones irrespective of the number of instances in each zone. This imbalance is solved with the cross-zone load balancing technique. The major advantages of using the classic load balancer is the ease of registering the EC2 instances, the ease of registering the EC2 instances, EC2-Classic instances support, use of TCP/SSL listeners and support for sticky sessions. The limitations include the absence of different routing mechanisms, custom HTTP responses and very minimal logs.

7.9.2 Health Checks on Classic Load Balancers

Health checks helps the classic load balancers to know whether the instance to which the load is forwarded is healthy, which means it is available to provide the required service. A port and a route are used to do a health check; hence, the health check is configured in a classic load balancer so the load requests are forwarded to the healthy instances only. Figure 7.13 represents the health checks for a classic load balancer. If the instance is found to be healthy, the status is displayed as "In Service", so the incoming network load will be forwarded to that healthy instance. An application that passes the health check shows the status as a healthy application. The health checks can vary the thresholds, targets and timeouts; hence, we can says that these health checks can give a better availability and better response to the incoming network load.

7.9.3 Deployment Steps: Creating an EC2 Account

Created Five Instances: Four Server and One Load Balancer

Step 1: Machine Image – Deployed A Machine Image
   Amazon Linux Ami – Red Hat Distribution
Step 2: The selection of Instance type
   T2 Micro Free Tier
      1 GB RAM
      1 Virtual central processing unit (CPU)
      Elastic Block Storage Volumes
      8 GB Storage
Step 3: Configuration of Instances
Step 4: Select a Security Group
   – Type SSH (Secure Socket Shell)
   – HTTP and HTTPS
   – Source open for all secured by a private key
Step 5: Create a Key
   – 2 keys: Public key, with the instance; private key – with user

- Download and configure super putty and putty.
- Using putty establish an SSH connection on windows.
- Use putty key gen to link the private key and store it in EC2 user.
- Use the IP address of each instance as the putty host name.
- Repeat these steps for each instance.

Figures 7.12 through 7.23 illustrate [17] the steps in creation of a classic load balancer, the health check configuration and implementation in the AWS environment.

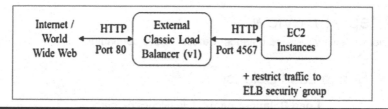

Figure.7.12 **Classic load balancer ports and protocols.**

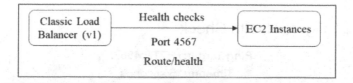

Figure 7.13 **Classic load balancer health checks.**

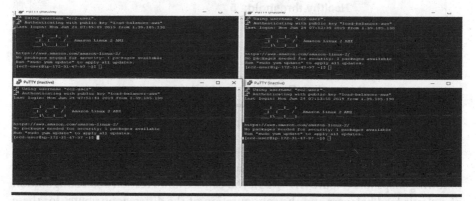

Figure 7.14 **Instances connection snapshot using putty.**

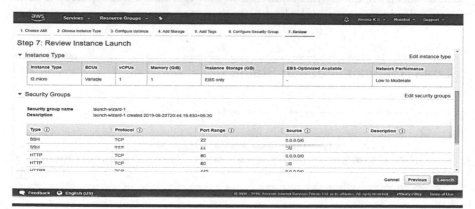

Figure 7.15 **Launching an instance.**

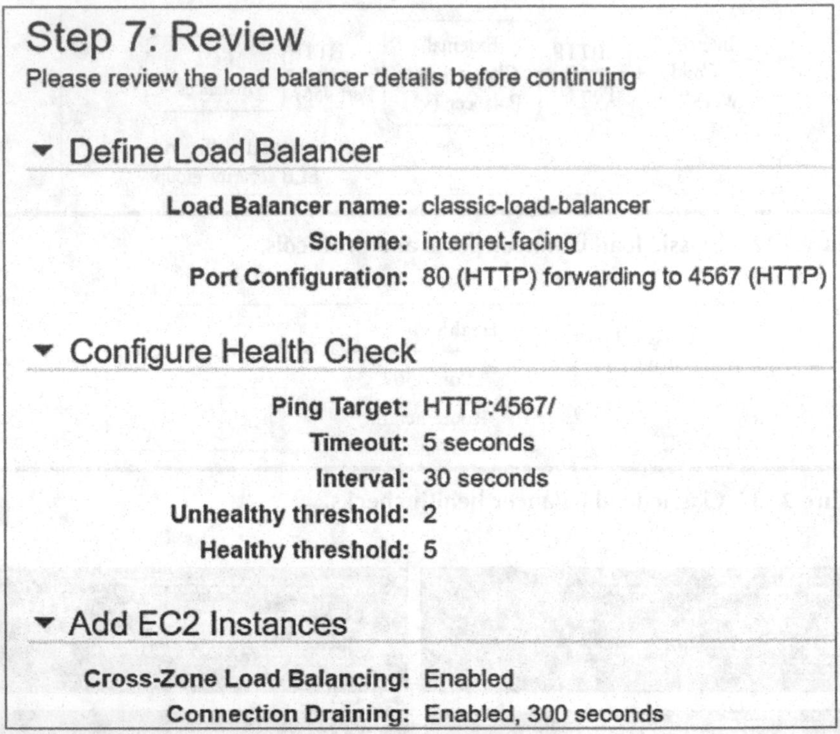

Step 7: Review
Please review the load balancer details before continuing

▼ Define Load Balancer

Load Balancer name: classic-load-balancer
Scheme: internet-facing
Port Configuration: 80 (HTTP) forwarding to 4567 (HTTP)

▼ Configure Health Check

Ping Target: HTTP:4567/
Timeout: 5 seconds
Interval: 30 seconds
Unhealthy threshold: 2
Healthy threshold: 5

▼ Add EC2 Instances

Cross-Zone Load Balancing: Enabled
Connection Draining: Enabled, 300 seconds

Figure 7.16   Load balancer attributes before creation.

Steps 1 to 5 of the AWS EC2 workstation are about creating an instance. In the following snapshots (Figure 7.17–7.23), you can see how creation and configuration of a classic load balancer and the configuration of the different attributes for these load balancers are done. The snapshots also showcase how a security setup is done for these load balancers and the health check configurations.

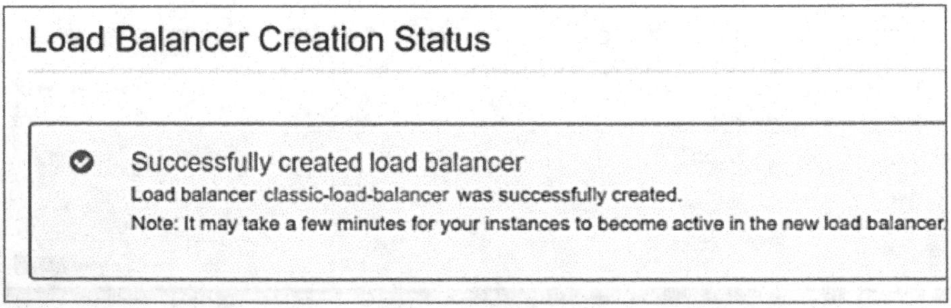

Load Balancer Creation Status

⊘   Successfully created load balancer
Load balancer classic-load-balancer was successfully created.
Note: It may take a few minutes for your instances to become active in the new load balancer.

Figure 7.17   Load balancer creation status.

Figure 7.18 Configuration of classic load balancer.

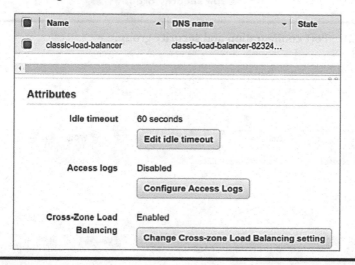

Figure 7.19 Classic load balancer attributes.

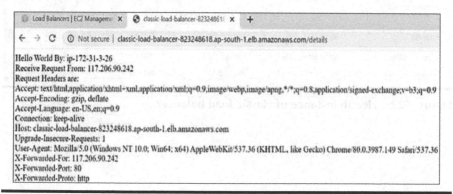

Figure 7.20 View of created load balancer from browser.

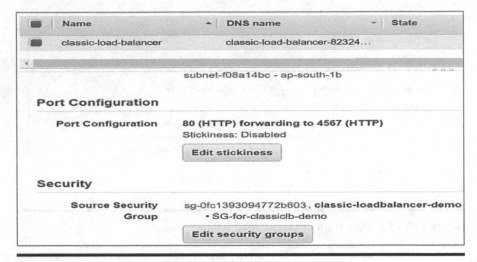

▣	Name	▲	DNS name	▾	State
▣	classic-load-balancer		classic-load-balancer-82324...		

subnet-f08a14bc – ap-south-1b

Port Configuration

Port Configuration	80 (HTTP) forwarding to 4567 (HTTP)
	Stickiness: Disabled

    Edit stickiness

Security

Source Security Group	sg-0fc1393094772b603 , **classic-loadbalancer-demo**
	• SG-for-classiclb-demo

    Edit security groups

Figure 7.21   Port configuration and security group.

▣	Name	▲	DNS name	▾	State	▾	VPC ID	▾	Availability
▣	classic-load-balancer		classic-load-balancer-82324...				vpc-a59494cd		ap-south-1a,

Connection Draining: Enabled, 300 seconds (Edit)

    Edit Instances

Instance ID	Name	Availability Zone	Status	Actions
i-0cb66edb207aa7636	Application machine 2	ap-south-1a	InService ⓘ	Remove from Load Balancer
i-02d94b01bbcba3985	Application Machine 1	ap-south-1b	InService ⓘ	Remove from Load Balancer

Figure 7.22   Health instance of classic load balancer.

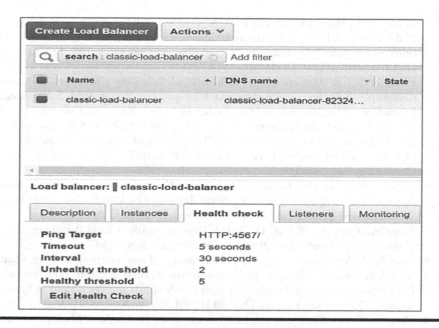

Figure 7.23 Health check criteria of classic load balancer.

7.10 Conclusion

This chapter highlighted the structure of a cloud datacenter and hurdles associated with datacenters in achieving high performance. To achieve good performance and reliability in the cloud environment one of the proposed solutions is to have an optimized load balancer. This chapter explains in detail the design architecture of a good load balancer and different strategies used in load balancing to achieve high reliability with less energy consumption. The mathematical model of a load balancer is derived and the algorithms that can provide an efficient system performance are discussed. The implementation details for creating a real-time load balancer are also discussed with detailed steps and snapshots. Hence, it can be concluded that an optimized load balancer can bring a great deal of performance appraisal to a system. In an energy-efficient datacenter performance appraisal, reliability and availability can be achieved using the discussed load balancing techniques.

References

1. Bilal, K., Rehman Malik, S. U., & Khan, S.U. (2014). Trends and Challenges in Cloud Datacenters. IEEE Cloud Computing, 1(1), 10–20.
2. Gutierrez, J. (2017). Collaborative Agents for Distributed Load Management in Cloud Data Centers Using Live Migration of Virtual Machines. IEEE Transactions on Services Computing, 8(6), 916–929.

3. Resma, K. S., Sharvani, G. S., & Paul, A. T. (2019). A Closer Look at the Network Middleboxes, 2019 1st International Conference on Advanced Technologies in Intelligent Control, Environment, Computing & Communication Engineering, DOI 10.1109/ICATIECE45860.2019.9063794.

4. Khan, R. Z., & Ahmad, M. O. (2016). Load Balancing Challenges on Cloud Computing: A Survey, D. K. Lobiyal, D. Mohapatra, A. Nagar, & M. Sahoo (eds.), Proceedings of the International Conference on Signal, Networks, Computing, and Systems, Lecture Notes in Electrical Engineering, Vol. 396. New Delhi: Springer.

5. Luo, J., Rao, L., & Liu, X. (2017). Spatio-Temporal Load Balancing for Energy Cost Optimization in Distributed Internet Data Centers. IEEE Transactions on Cloud Computing, 3(3), 387–397.

6. Ding, Y., Hu, L., & Xu, G. (2016). A Heuristic Clustering-based Task Deployment Approach for Load Balancing Using Bayes Theorem in Cloud Environment. IEEE Transactions on Parallel and Distributed Systems, 27(2), 305–316.

7. Nahir, A., Orda, A., & Raz, D. (2016). Replication Based Load Balancing. IEEE Transactions on Parallel and Distributed Systems, 27(2), 494–507.

8. Özer, A. H., & Özturan, C. (2009). An auction based mathematical model and heuristics for resource co-allocation problem in grids and clouds, 2009 Fifth International Conference on Soft Computing, Computing with Words and Perceptions in System Analysis, Decision and Control, DOI 10.1109/ICSCCW.2009.5379493.

9. Deng, X., Wu, D., Shen, J., & He, J. (2016). Eco-aware Online Power Management and Load Scheduling For Green Cloud Datacenters. IEEE Systems Journal, 10(1), 78–87.

10. Mishra, S. K., Sahoo, B., & Parida, P. P. (2020). Load Balancing in Cloud Computing: A Big Picture. Journal of King Saud University–Computer and Information Sciences, 32(2), 149–158.

11. Belkhouraf, M., Kartit, A., Ouahmane, H., Kamal Idrissi, H., Kartit, Z., & El Marraki, M. (2015). Secured Load Balancing Architecture for Cloud Computing Based on Multiple Clusters, 2015 International Conference on Cloud Technologies and Applications, DOI 10.1109/CloudTech.2015.7336978.

12. Gu, J., Hu, J., & Zhao, T. (2012). A New Resource Scheduling Strategy Based on Genetic Algorithm in Cloud Computing Environment. Journal of Computers, 7(1), 42–52.

13. Chen, S.-L., Chen, Y.-Y., & Kuo, S.-H. (2017). CLB: A Novel Load Balancing Architecture and Algorithm for Cloud Service. Computers & Electrical Engineering, 58, 154–160.

14. Damanal, S. G., & Reddy, G. R. M. (2014). Optimal Load Balancing in Cloud Computing by Efficient Utilization of Virtual Machines, 2014 Sixth International Conference on Communication Systems and Networks, DOI 10.1109/COMSNETS.2014.6734930.

15. Resma K. S., & Sharvani, G. S. (2019). Edge Distributed Cloud Middleboxes. International Journal of Advance Research, Ideas and Innovations in Technology, 5(3), 988–995.

16. Dasguptaa, K., Mandalb, B., Duttac, P., Mondald, J. K., & Dame, S. (2013). A Genetic Algorithm (GA)-based Load Balancing Strategy for Cloud Computing. Procedia Technology, 10, 340–347.

17. Resma, K. S., Hegde, A., & Sharvani, G. S. (2020). Elastic Load Balancing in Real-time Cloud Environment. International Journal of Advanced Science and Technology, 29(12), 269–283.

Chapter 8

Dynamic Load Balancing by Employing Genetic Algorithm

S. Sandhya and N. K. Cauvery

R.V. College of Engineering

Contents

8.1 Introduction

One of the most sought after technologies in recent times is cloud computing. It provides a reliable virtual environment for storage and computation to people of all domains. The increasing prominence of a digital presence and its use by various firms to promote their products have further given impetus to the use of cloud for storage, which overcomes the geographical limitations of users worldwide. It is a natural choice to adopt the latest technologies and techniques to make the processing and user experience a pleasurable one. In regard to this, the problem to balance load becomes important and crucial to make the cloud more reliable, which also facilitates the availability of cloud services.

A prominent area of research in the field of networking, distributed systems and cloud computing is load balancing, which has gained attention recently. Research in load balancing has observed a raise in interest with the increasing advancements in computer networking technologies. Any load balancing algorithm needs to guarantee improved and relatively better overall performance by spreading the load to lightly loaded/normal nodes from the heavy ones. This scheme should balance load transparently, and results needs to be comparable to a given metric that determines the performance of the system. The algorithms employed to balance the load are desired to meet a set of goals such as minimizing the communication delays, overheads and execution times and maximizing the throughput and overall resource utilization. Determining a suitable node that is lightly loaded and that can accept the migrated process from any heavily loaded node is one of the major challenges since the time spent in identifying suitable node is mere overhead. The process of determining a lightly loaded node includes the exchange of multiple request-response messages among the participating nodes in the system. These exchanges are an overhead adding to the task processing time resulting in congestion, thus reducing the processor utilization and system throughput. Hence a genetic algorithm (GA) [1] could be used for selecting the destination node that accepts the migrated task. GAs are a form of computation inspired by evolution and are employed widely as a constrained optimization technique. This is a search-based algorithm that employs natural genetics and natural selection. Load balancing is observed to be more efficient when a GA is used as compared to the other conventional methods.

8.1.1 Load Balancing

Load balancing is an approach of distributing load fairly across multiple systems, central processing units (CPUs), network links and hard drives to achieve better response times, optimal resource utilization and increased throughput to avoid overload of any node/system. There is a delay between the cloud service providers and users, as the cloud users increase, which in turn implicitly decreases the existing resources, raising the need for load balancing. Load balancing can avoid the situations where one system remains idle while the other systems get overloaded. Load balancing is said to be achieved when all the nodes in the system have approximately equal load and a set of nodes is not overloaded [3].

In view of this, the various techniques for balancing load in the cloud have been analyzed and a comparative summary of the latest research work is tabulated as in Table 8.1. A comparative analysis with respect to different performance

Table 8.1 Comparision of Existing Load Balancing Techniques

Metrics/Techniques	Throughput	Overhead	Fault Tolerance	Migration Time	Response Time	Resource Utilization	Scalability	Performance
Round robin (RR)	Yes	Yes	No	No	Yes	Yes	Yes	Yes
Dynamic RR	Yes	Yes	Yes	Yes	No	Yes	No	No
Active monitoring	Yes	Yes	No	Yes	Yes	Yes	Yes	No
Min-min	Yes	Yes	No	No	Yes	Yes	No	Yes
Max-min	Yes	Yes	No	No	Yes	Yes	No	Yes
Throttled	No	No	Yes	Yes	Yes	Yes	Yes	Yes
Active clustering	No	Yes	No	Yes	Yes	Yes	No	No
Biased random sampling	No	Yes	No	No	Yes	Yes	No	Yes

Source: Raghava and Singh, 2014 [2].

parameters/matrices like throughput, time indicators including migration time and response time, fault tolerance, utilization of resources and other overheads for various techniques is presented.

8.1.2 Challenges in Load Balancing

The potentially unpredictable nature of the arrival and departure of tasks in the cloud computing scenario makes dynamic load balancing strategy a challenging research topic that needs to be given the utmost priority. Compared with balancing load on a distributed system, the cloud puts forth additional challenges like migrating virtual machines(VMs), security for VM migration, satisfaction of quality of service (QoS) and so forth, A few of these challenges are listed below:

1. ***Nodes are distributed geographically:*** For the purpose of computing, the datacenters are distributed geographically and treated as a single system for processing user tasks. Unlike the distributed system, the cloud poses additional challenge of considering various aspects like delays encountered due to networks, communication between nodes, distance between nodes and so forth, for balancing loads.

2. ***One point failures:*** It is a usual practice to assign a single node that takes centralized decisions for balancing load in distributed system. In contrast, a distributed approach is employed for the cloud.

3. ***Migration of VMs:*** Cloud computing creates VMs that vary in configuration and are independent. Hence, load balancing needs to additionally consider the configuration while distributing the load.

4. ***Node heterogeneity:*** Balancing load among homogeneous systems is researched highly and proposed. Considering heterogeneity of the nodes, the load balancing algorithms might have to be designed to consider the varying architecture, a configuration that imposes constraints on achieving effective response times and resource utilization. Therefore, an approach is needed that dynamically balances load considering these factors for the cloud.

5. ***Scalability of load balancing:*** In cloud computing, users are allowed to access the services any time and from anywhere; hence cloud services are ensured for high availability and need to scale asper the growing demand. These factors impose another challenge for load balancing, which are required to consider these on-demand requests and process effectively.

6. ***Managing storage/resources:*** The cloud provides storage and resources as services to users. The requirements are increasing on a day-to-day basis, thus managing these services along with the application and data becomes crucial. Hence, the load balancing approach should effectively handle distribution of data by employing an efficient management system.

8.1.3 Types of Load Balancing

Based on the instant at which the load balancing decision is made, two types of load balancing [2, 4] are listed:

- **Static load balancing:** This scheme focuses on distributing the load by considering the information influencing the balancing decision in advance before the process starts its execution. It distributes the load/processes based on the previous system state before the process is initiated. Static load balancing does not consider the current load, and the decisions are made based on general machine statistics and the performance history of the network. These rules are either deterministic or probabilistic in nature.
- **Dynamic load balancing:** This strategy carefully considers the current state of loads on the node to make decisions regarding load balancing. Even though this strategy may involve some overhead, the resource utilization of the cluster is maximized in an efficient manner.

Dynamic load balancing can further be characterized into *centralized* and *distributed approaches (decentralized)* depending on how it is implemented. The centralized approach mainly uses a centralized entity such as centralized server/master/scheduler to distribute load based on the information policy. In contrast, the distributed approach balances load by having all the nodes participate in the process of load distribution. The load in the distributed approach will be balanced based on the state information shared among the nodes.

The different axes under which the load balancing schemes are categorized are given below:

- **Local scheme versus global scheme:** The global information of the entire system is used by the global scheme to manage and schedule processes onto the available processors for achieving optimized system performance. In contrast, the local state of a single CPU forms the base for the scheduling method in the local scheme that schedules and executes processes on that particular CPU.
- **Static versus dynamic:** The static approach bases its load balancing decision on prior information about the system, considering average behavior of the input traffic; whereas the dynamic approach distributes load by monitoring the changes of the system workload.
- **Distributed versus centralized:** The distributed approach relies on the state information collected from each of the participating nodes in the system for load balancing. Receiver-initiated, sender-initiated, random and symmetric are some of the well-known categories of distributed scheduling policies. Scheduling in the centralized approach is the responsibility of a single node in the system; hence, if this single node fails the load distribution ceases for the entire system, resulting in dependability issues.

- **Deterministic versus probabilistic:** The state information of the node and the process attributes at a given instant are used to schedule processes in the deterministic approach, whereas the static attributes of the system such as the number of nodes, topology and so forth are used to schedule and distribute processes between nodes in the probabilistic approach.
- **Cooperative versus non-cooperative:** The nodes that form the computing entities of the system collaborate with one another in cooperative algorithms, whereas in the non-cooperative algorithms, computing entities make decisions for scheduling independently. Irrespective of the type of load balancing algorithm used, the performance of all hosts, even those with light loads, are generally improved by load balancing. Load balancing provides benefits such as reliability, fault tolerance, efficiency and high performance.

8.2 Dynamic Load Balancing Overview

Dynamic load balancing strategy is a challenging research area due to the potentially unpredictable nature of load in the cloud. The policies that characterize dynamic load balancing include initiation policy, transfer policy, selection policy, profitability policy, location and information policy [5].

- **Initiation policy** is mainly concerned about which node invokes the activity for load balancing.
- **Transfer policy** determines if the state of the node is eligible to participate in transferring load.
- **Selection policy** is concerned with choosing the most appropriate process for migration on an overloaded node.
- **Profitability policy** makes a decision based on the load imbalance factor when balancing the load at a given instant.
- **Location policy** is concerned with choosing the destination nodes that are most suitable to accept the transmitted load.
- **Information policy** comprises the states of the system, including the load, which is communicated and shared among other nodes.

The control law, employed in load balancing, includes initiation, transfer, selection, profitability and location policies while the information policy disseminates the load information of each node to make the migration decision. The interaction among the various components of the load balancing approach is represented in Figure 8.1.

The load balancing problem could be optimized since it has an exponential solution space that includes all possible solutions derived for the said problem. The algorithms for optimization are search algorithms that work on the

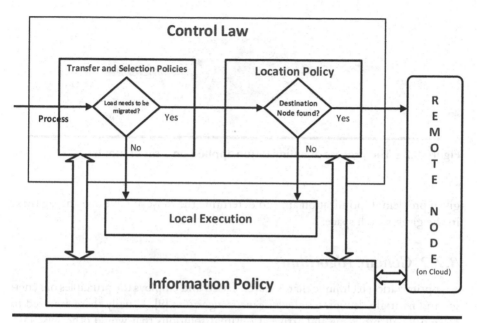

Figure 8.1 Components of dynamic load balancing approach.

available search space from which they determine the optimal solution. The task of distributing load is NP-hard. The approach to balancing load has been researched over the past 30 years, and extensive methodologies that deal with homogeneous and heterogeneous systems [6] for different workloads have been developed. In general, any design of load balancing algorithms considers job arrival rate, bandwidth of the communication network and topology of the network.

The other nine quantifiable parameters for design [7] suggested for load balancing algorithms are system size, system load, system traffic intensity, migration threshold, task size, overhead cost, response time, system horizon and resource demand. A GA is employed more frequently to solve and optimize solution in various research domains; hence, GA can be employed effectively to optimize the solution of load balancing [8] for cloud environments.

8.2.1 Problem of Optimization Employing Genetic Algorithms

The essence of optimization is determining better and improved results for any given problem. Any process could be generalized to accept a set of inputs, process them through various steps described in the program and produce results as indicated in Figure 8.2. In GA, all combinations of values and every possible solution for a given problem that forms the input set are included in the search space. This search space includes the optimal solution or set of these identified for the

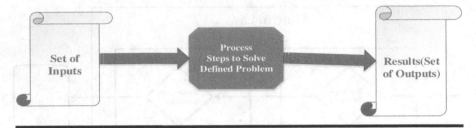

Figure 8.2   The process of optimization applied on a set of inputs.

given problem. Optimization aims to determine the most suitable one among these in the given search space.

8.2.2 Genetic Algorithm

An optimization technique that is search-based and employs the principles of genetics and natural selection is called a *genetic algorithm* [9]. Usually these are used to solve difficult problems and arrive at optimal solutions that would otherwise take an arbitrarily long time to resolve. GAs are employed more frequently to solve and optimize solutions in various research domains.

8.2.2.1 Basic Structure of a Genetic Algorithm

GA, as illustrated in Figure 8.3, starts with initial strings referred to as the initial population/initial string, which are randomly generated or aided by heuristics. These strings are evaluated for the fitness to determine their feasibility to apply them to the solution. They further undergo basic genetic operations, namely crossover and mutation on the selected parent strings, to create new offspring. This process repeats until fitter strings are determined and the terminating condition is met or a fitter solution is derived. Hence, the process attempts to mimic the evolution of human to a given extent.

8.2.3 Load Balancing Employing Genetic Algorithms

The approach to balance load dynamically on each node in cloud environment [10] monitors the load that it is handling and employs a transfer policy to check if the load is seen to exceed beyond the node's capacity. The transfer policy could be any strategy such as presetting maximum load for the given node by the administration. As the node is seen to exceed this load, the node employs other aspects of load balancing to migrate the load. The other aspects include *the selection policy*, which mainly identifies the process/VM that will be migrated, and *the location policy*, which mainly identifies the destination node on to which the process/VM

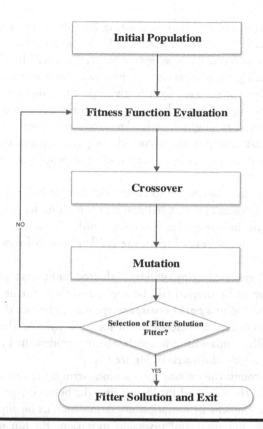

Figure 8.3 Function of a genetic algorithm.

is migrated. Based on the information shared by other peers in the cloud environment, the load is either migrated or carried on the same node.

The approach discussed here focuses on the location policy, which is responsible for identifying the destination node. Each node monitors the load experienced by itself, and based on its state it either continues or decides to initiate migration. Once the node initiates migration, the usual approach to determine destination node is the exchange of load information among the peers to decide on the destination; hence, the node sends request messages to the rest of the nodes to determine whether they could handle additional load. The peer nodes then respond back with their state/consent. This is truly an overhead that needs to be handled in a more optimal way. It is here that the GA [11] comes to the rescue in minimizing this overhead. Rather than sending messages to all other nodes, the GA sends messages to the probable nodes, which are capable of accepting additional load. The process employed by the GA to come up with these probable nodes is discussed below.

The *initial population* represents the solution space that can be encoded by employing any approach such as binary encoding, real valued encoding and so forth. This section discusses binary encoding for generating the initial strings. The strings are made up of '0's or '1's, which can be employed to represent the subset of available solutions. These generated strings will be further modified by applying various genetic operators to produce the fittest or best string that results in the optimized solution for the given problem domain. Since load balancing is done among nodes in the cloud, '1' represents a node that is heavily loaded and '0' represents a lighter node. Any node represented as '1' or '0' incorporates various load computations considering the aspects such as processor load, number of arrived processes to the number of processes served, bandwidth and so forth.

For instance, if four nodes are to be considered for balancing the load then the string '1001' represents overloaded first and fourth nodes, whereas the second and third nodes are lighter nodes. Therefore, only the second and third nodes will be sent request messages reducing the total number of messages exchanged among peers.

These initially generated strings will be evaluated for fitness and then the genetic operator's crossover and mutation will be applied to them further to choose/select the fitter solutions. The *one point crossover* approach chooses the crossover point randomly, which acts as the reference point for both strings. These strings would then swap the trailing ends with one another from the identified reference point to form better offspring, as illustrated in Figure 8.4.

After going through the crossover operation, strings are mutated. Mutation is another operator in the GA used for identifying the better offspring strings. There are several ways to implement mutation operation such as bit flip mutation, swap mutation, scramble mutation and inversion mutation. Bit flip mutation is illustrated in Figure 8.5.

Bit flip mutation chooses a bit randomly and then flips the chosen bit. This is specially employed for binary encoded strings in GA. This operation can be applied to a single bit or randomly multiple bits as needed.

The offspring are evaluated for their suitability or fitness by employing the objective function (OF). This is taken as the fitness function of the GA. The load of any node can be estimated by employing Eq. (8.1).

$$L_i = n^p + n^q + n^r \tag{8.1}$$

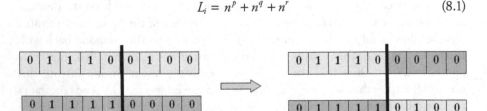

Figure 8.4 Implementation of one point crossover.

Figure 8.5   Implementation of bit flip mutation.

where p, q and r are the number of pending, queued and running jobs. Load deviation from the mean load is factored as the fitness function. The total load is given by Eq. (8.2).

$$L_{total} = \sum_{i=1}^{m} L_i \qquad (8.2)$$

where L_i is the load of node i.

Mean load of a node is obtained as in Eq. (8.3):

$$L_{mean} = \frac{L_{total}}{m} \qquad (8.3)$$

Thus *OF* for the load deviation of a node is given as in Eq. (8.4):

$$OF = \frac{1}{m} \sum_{j=1}^{m} (L_j - L_{mean})^2 \qquad (8.4)$$

Therefore, the fitness function

$$f = \frac{1}{OF} \qquad (8.5)$$

This objective is to be minimized as the evaluation criterion for the fitness function as given in Eq. (8.5). The strings are evaluated for fitness by employing the approach as discussed above, which would result in fitter offspring. These strings indicate whether the nodes are lightly/heavily loaded. The lightly loaded nodes identified by the fitter strings have a better probability of accepting the migrated load coming from the overloaded nodes. Since the probability of accepting the migrated load is greater, the overhead to identify the destination node for migration is reduced, which reduces the overall migration time; thus optimizing the approach to balance the load.

After the fitter strings are evaluated by the GA, the request messages are sent out only to those nodes whose probability of load acceptance is guaranteed. In other words, request messages are sent to nodes 'i' only if the evaluated string has '0' for the corresponding ith bit. There can be three cases of strings evaluated after applying the GA operators and fitness evaluation to the initial strings (the example discussed in the previous sections with four nodes is considered):

■ ***Case 1:*** *The evaluated string contains all '1's.* In this case, the string evaluated would be '**1111**', where all nodes are overloaded. Since all the nodes are overloaded, there is no node capable of taking up the additional load, so there is no migration of the load. In the usual approach (without the GA), each node would send out 3 request messages to their peer nodes resulting in a total of at least 12 request messages. Further, the responses from each node rejecting these requests are sent back to the senders, adding to 12 more response messages. These exchanged messages add to the congestion of the network, which exhausts resources, and time spent in these exchanges is an overhead. In contrast to this usual approach, the GA-based load balancing initiation policy will not initiate migration from any node. Hence, there will be no request/response messages exchanged, reducing the overhead and unnecessary traffic.

■ ***Case 2:*** *The evaluated string contains all '0's.* In this case, the string evaluated would be '**0000**', where all nodes are underloaded. Since all nodes are underloaded, there is no need for any node to off-load any tasks, hence, there will be no request/response messages exchanged.

■ ***Case 3:*** *The evaluated string contains a combination of '0's and '1's.* In this case, the string evaluated would contain any combination of **1's and 0's viz 0100**. This is a case where few nodes are overloaded (represented by '1' in the evaluated string), while others are underloaded (represented by '0' in the evaluated string). The combination of bits in the string is based on various load factors and evaluated by a proposed fitness function employed by the GA. This scenario requires load balancing among the nodes in the system, and the usual approach follows the same steps as discussed in case1. In contrast, the request messages are sent out only to the processors, which are represented by '0' in the evaluated string. Although the usual approach exchanges up to n^2 messages among peers, the GA-based load balancing exchanges fewer than n^2 messages depending on the number of zeros in the evaluated string.

It is obvious from the cases discussed above that compared to the common approach employed, fewer request messages are sent out to and fro, thereby reducing the congestion, migration preparation time and increasing the performance and reliability of nodes in the system.

8.3 Conclusion

The discussed GA-based load balancing is distributed as each node monitors the load it handles and initiates the process of off-loading as and when required. The GA employed in this approach is responsible for optimizing the overhead experienced by the conventional load balancing approach. Whenever each node in the system becomes overloaded, this approach can be employed to overcome single point failures; thus achieving better availability. Once the destination node is identified, the cloud can employ any migration strategy to off-load the tasks/VMs. Therefore, using the proposed approach facilitates to improve availability and reliability.

References

1. A. Y. Zomaya, Y.-H. Teh, *"Observations on Using Genetic Algorithms for Dynamic Load-Balancing,"* IEEE Transactions on Parallel and Distributed Systems, Vol. 12, No. 9, September 2001, pp. 899–911.
2. N. S. Raghava, D. Singh, *"Comparative Study on Load Balancing Techniques in Cloud Computing,"* Open Journal of Mobile Computing and Cloud Computing, Vol. 1, No. 1, August 2014, pp. 18–25.
3. W. Wang, X. Geng, Q. Wang, "Design of a Dynamic Load Balancing Model for Multiprocessor Systems," 3rd International Conference on Communication Software and Networks (ICCSN), 2011, pp. 641–643.
4. P. A. Tijare, P. R. Deshmukh, *"Schemes for Dynamic Load Balancing – A Review,"* International Journal of Advanced Research in Computer Science and Software Engineering, Vol. 3, No. 6, June 2013, pp. 688–696.
5. B. Gerofi, H. Fujita,Y. Ishikawa, "An Efficient Process Live Migration Mechanism for Load Balanced Distributed Virtual Environments," IEEE International Conference on Cluster Computing, 2010, pp. 197–206.
6. P. Kanungo, *"Load Measurement Issues in Dynamic Load Balancing in Distributed Computing Environment,"* International Journal of Advanced Research in Computer Science and Software Engineering, Vol. 3, No. 10, October 2013, pp. 547–554.
7. R. Shah, B. Veeravalli, *"On the Design of Adaptive and Decentralized Load-Balancing Algorithms with Load Estimation for Computational Grid Environments,"* IEEE Transactions on Parallel and Distributed Systems, Vol. 18, No. 12, December 2007, pp. 1675–1686.
8. S. Sandhya, K. N. Ranjitha, N. K. Cauvery, *"A Survey On: Pre-emptive Migration of a Video Process using Genetic Algorithm on Virtual Machine,"* International Journal of Engineering and Computer Science, Vol. 3, No. 5, May 2014, pp. 5897–5900.
9. D. Devi, Y. J. Singh, *"A Modified Genetic Algorithm Based Load Distribution Approach Towards Web Hotspot Rescue,"* Proceedings of the Third International Conference on Computational Intelligence and Information Technology, 2013, pp. 9–19.
10. S. Sandhya, N.K. Cauvery, *"Dynamic load balancing for video processing system in cloud,"* Advances in Intelligent Systems and Computing, Springer, Vol. 332, 2015, 189 –197.
11. S. Sandhya, N. K. Cauvery, *"Dynamic Load Balancing Based on Genetic Algorithm,"* International Journal of Innovative Technology and Exploring Engineering, Vol. 8, No. 11, September 2019, pp. 176 –179.

Further Readings

A. Zarrabi, *"A Generic Process Migration Algorithm,"* International Journal of Distributed and Parallel Systems, Vol.3, No.5, September 2012, pp. 29–37.

M. Mishra, A. Das, P. Kulkarni, A. Sahoo, *"Dynamic Resource Management Using Virtual Machine Migrations,"* IEEE Communications Magazine, Vol. 50, No. 9, September 2012, pp. 34–40.

S.-H. Lee, C.-S. Hwang, "Dynamic Load Balancing Approach Using Genetic Algorithm in Distributed Systems," 1998 IEEE International Conference on Evolutionary Computation Proceedings. IEEE World Congress on Computational Intelligence (Cat. No.98TH8360), Anchorage, AK, 1998, pp. 639–644. DOI: 10.1109/ICEC.1998.700103.

K. Singh, C. Kukreja, "A Sender-Initiated Load Balancing Approach with Genetic Algorithm," International Journal of Software and Web Sciences, 2012, pp. 1–3, ISSN (Online): 2279-0071.

P. Shah, S. M. Shah, *"Load Balancing in Distributed System Using Genetic Algorithm,"* IP Multimedia Communications, A Special Issue from IJCA, 2011, pp. 139–142.

W. A. Greene, *"Dynamic Load-Balancing via a Genetic Algorithm,"* Proceedings of the Thirteenth IEEE International Conference on Tools with Artificial Intelligence, 2001, pp. 121–128.

M. Nejadkheirallah, K. Darvish, R. Sookhtsaraei, M. Shahnazi, "A New Genetic-based Algorithm for Reliable Distributed Resources," IEEE 3rd International Conference on Communication Software and Networks (ICCSN), 2011, pp. 511–515.

T. Maoz, A. Barak, L. Amar, "Combining Virtual Machine Migration with Process Migration for HPC on Multi-clusters and Grids," IEEE International Conference on Cluster Computing, 2008, pp. 89–98. DOI: 10.1109/CLUSTR.2008.4663759.

C.-C. Lin, H.-H. Chin, D.-J. Deng, *"Dynamic Multi-service Load Balancing in Cloud-based Multimedia System,"* Systems Journal, Vol. 8, No. 1, March 2013, pp. 225–234.

Chapter 9

Predicting Reliability and Risk

S. Sharanya and E. Sasikala
SRM Institute of Science and Technology

S. Karthikeyan
BSACIST

Contents

9.1 Introduction to Reliability and Risk

Reliability and risk are two tightly coupled non-functional requirements of any type of software or services. The inherent meaning of these terms is well established by the International Organization for Standardization (ISO). According to ISO/IEC 25000 standards "Reliability is the degree to which a system performs specified functions under specified conditions for a specified period". On the other hand, ISO 31000 has standardized the notion of risk as "the effect of uncertainty on objectives". Understanding these terms is very important when building fault-tolerant complex cloud computing systems, as failures are always an inherent part of any system or component. A cloud system is said to encounter failure when one of the following conditions are met:

- Increased service response time
- Failure of service requests
- Service unavailability due to hardware failures
- Impaired services

Predicting the forge in reliability is an important trait of any service-oriented architecture. Reliability prediction is the estimated probability of a failure-free operation of a system based on historical data [1]. Numerous failure prediction models are in place that operate on accumulated data over a period of time. Some of the models that deserve attention are Putnam's model [2], Musa's model [3], the laboratory model of Rome [4] and so on. Any part of the software or system must undergo stringent reliability testing before being deployed at the client's site. In case of cloud computing tools, additional tests are done to ensure their promised operation adhering to the client's characteristics and environment. Service unavailability is the highest level of reliability failure that evolves through the phases of occurrence of failure, inconsistent operation, service degradation and finally service unavailability. The measures taken by service providers after reaching the final phase of service unavailability is too costly; hence, predicting the reliability of the service is the most optimal solution.

Cloud services and tools are prone to a variety of risks such as cyberattacks, breaches in physical and logical controls, hijacking user credentials, diverse regulatory compliance across countries, disaster recovery procedures, malware, customer contract breaches, unauthorized data and service access, availability risks and so forth. The effect of the given exhaustive list of risks can be mitigated by implementing proper access control policies and prognostic recovery actions.

9.2 Reliability Metrics

Reliability is measured in terms of correct delivery of services within the stipulated time. There are a variety of metrics to quantify reliability. Measuring reliability with a single metric is not encouraged. Some of the popularly used metrics are discussed here:

1. **Mean time to failure (MTTF):** This is the time duration between the occurrences of two failures. This is measured in time units.
2. **Mean time to repair (MTTR):** This is the restoration of the service to its normal operating condition. This duration is the summation of time taken to repair, test and restore the system and is expressed as Eq. (9.1).

$$MTTR = \frac{Total\_ma\operatorname{int}enance\_time}{number\_of\_repairs} \qquad (9.1)$$

3. **Mean time between failures (MTBF):** This is a direct metric of reliability and availability. It is the duration between the first occurrence of failure and its next occurrence. To be more precise, it is the interval between the first recovery and next failure as given in Eq. (9.2).

$$MTBF = \frac{Total\_operational\_time}{number\_of\_repairs} \qquad (9.2)$$

4. **Rate of occurrence of failure (ROCOF):** It is the count of failures that occurred during a specified time interval. This measure directly corresponds to the frequency of failure occurrence.
5. **Service reliability:** This is expressed as a ratio of successful responses within a specified timeline against total request made to the service as given in Eq. (9.3).

$$Service\,Re\,liability = \frac{Successful\_responses}{Number\_of\_Re\,quests} \qquad (9.3)$$

The reliability timeline is shown in Figure 9.1. The reliability handbook released by the U.S. Federal Aviation Administration has classified the reliability of services as:

■ **Critical:** The service availability should be 99.999%, any decrease in this will be seen as a risk. The lower availability value means that the system can no longer render efficient and safe operations.

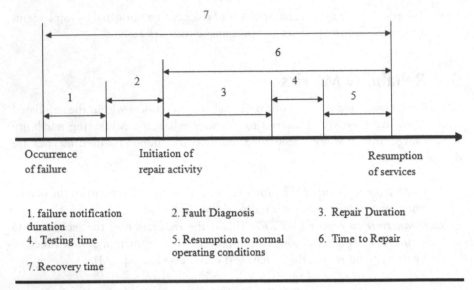

Figure 9.1 Various timelines for achieving reliability.

■ *Essential:* The service availability should be 99.9%. Any loss is a threat to the system's safety and efficiency.
■ *Routine:* The service availability rating would be 99%. The loss in this will have little impact on risk.

9.3 Failure Modes in Cloud Computing

Software, hardware, communication links and storage point faults may sometimes induce errors apart from design flaws. These failures, when not attended, may escalate and propagate hindering the normal working conditions. These primary failures may become a vital cause for cascade of a secondary failure. Failures in the cloud environment are generally classified into six types: software, hardware, security, management, human errors and environmental failures [5] (Figure 9.2).

9.3.1 Software Failure Modes

This can be further broken down into:

■ *Failures in system/application software:* These include bugs, errors, software faults at cloud tasks and hypervisors running at different cloud computing nodes.
■ *Failures in the database:* These include data loss due to hardware and software failures at the datacenter.

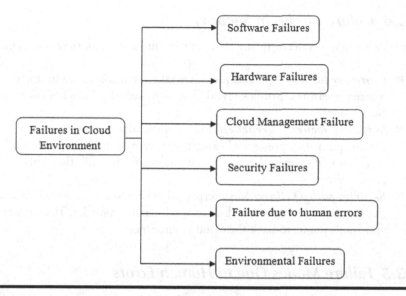

Figure 9.2   Classification of cloud failure modes.

9.3.2 Hardware Failure Modes

Some of the very common hardware failures encountered include:

- *Failure of the hardware component:* These include failure of storage devices, nodes, processors, memory elements and so forth.
- *Failures in communication links:* Disrupted communication channels, faults in interconnecting devices and communication links are common network failures. They become more prominent when accessing and transferring a large amount of remote resources.

9.3.3 Management System Failure Modes

This is the most crucial category of failure modes in the cloud. They may occur at the architectural level or at the interfaces. The common pitfalls include:

- *Overflow failure:* Inappropriate upper limit to the request queue may sometimes overwhelm the queue and may lead to dropping of new requests.
- *Timeout failure:* The duration for which the request is allowed to wait in the queue. After the stipulated time the request cannot be processed.
- *Missing data resource:* The data resource manager will not be able to fetch the requested data because the data resource may have been removed, but the logs are not updated.
- *Missing computing resource:* The hardware may be in an inactive state, so it cannot service any requests.

9.3.4 Failure Modes in Security

Security is a major concern in any cloud environment. The common faults include:

- *Customer faults:* The cloud providers take the utmost care in imparting all security measures. Studies reveal that most security breaches occur on the client's side.
- *Software security breaches:* This is most dangerous, since the attackers can gain user credentials and can access even the confidential data. This can damage the management activities of the entire cloud environment.
- *Security policy failure:* Misinterpretation or low estimation of the need of cloud security practices may lead to weak security policies. This creates more vulnerable points to hack the cloud environment.

9.3.5 Failure Modes Due to Human Errors

Human operational faults are often the most underestimated category of failure mode in any type of system. Developing a skill set is the only way to mitigate this. The operational faults may be categorized as follows:

- *Failure due to misoperation:* This happens because of accidental activities due to erroneous human operation. The degree of damage can be estimated by understanding the level at which the activity has happened.
- *Failure due to misconfiguration:* Misconfigured software is a threat to itself as well as the entire cluster of datacenters. This can shut down the entire cloud services in no time.

9.3.6 Failure Modes Due to Environmental Causes

These are God-controlled causes that can cause devastation on the cloud infrastructure. They cannot be controlled, but efficient recovery actions can mitigate their impact. The most frequent environmental failure modes include:

- *Natural calamities and disasters:* Natural forces like heavy wind, cyclones, flood, thunder and lightning can cause service disruption. Also, power outages, fire accidents and riots can cause heavy damage to the entire infrastructure.
- *Failure in cooling systems:* The physical data servers and their supporting components will be in active mode 24/7. This heats up the entire setup. An improper or malfunctioning cooling system (heating, ventilation and air conditioning) can cause server shut down, hindering availability of the system

9.4 Cloud Reliability Prediction

Modeling cloud reliability is a long process that starts at the developer's environment and ends its journey at the client's site. The cloud services must ensure that they meet the reliability requirements and objectives agreed on by the client. A major part of reliability testing is conducted during the development ,phase. Many dependent and independent modes of reliability tests are done to the product/service. The failure data, which is very scarce, offer important insights into the developers to fine-tune their service and its delivery. These data are supplied to one of the cloud reliability prediction models to test whether the developed product adheres to the reliability objectives before deployment at the customer's site. If the objectives are not met, then many more testing schemes will be devised and changes will be done. Once the product is put into use in a smaller scale at the customer's site, it will undergo reliability testing protocols specific to the customer's operating condition. This assessment data will be useful in upgrading the product to higher levels. The sequence of steps is illustrated in Figure 9.3.

The assessment data collected at the end of the first cycle provide insights into the following fields:

1. Reliability of cloud service
2. Testing time
3. Rate of growth of reliability
4. Deviations between predicted reliability and reliability at customer's site

9.4.1 Cloud Reliability Prediction Models

The cloud reliability prediction models depend on the reliability importance (RI), which is a probabilistic measure of a specific cloud element that can cause a failure. It is otherwise defined as the rate of change in reliability over a period of time as given in Eq. (9.4).

$$RI(t) = \frac{\partial R_s(t)}{\partial R_i(t)} \tag{9.4}$$

where $R_s(t)$ is the reliability of the cloud at time t and $R_i(t)$ is the element's reliability time at the same time t. Computing this term will have a great impact on reliability prediction. The prediction models are rooted in Eq. (9.4) to derive insights into relaibility prediction. A variety of models were deployed in reliability prediction of the cloud under the class of combinatorial models, state space models and hierarchial models.

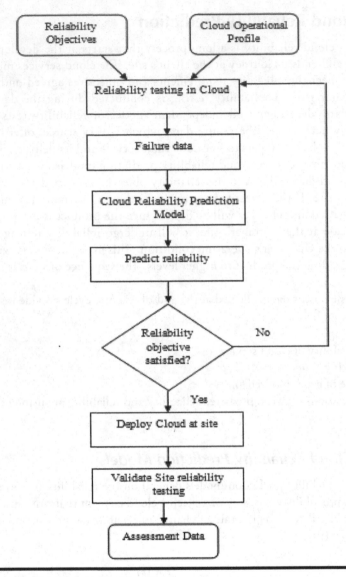

Figure 9.3 Reliability prediction steps.

9.4.1.1 Combinatorial Models

The combinatorial models are backed by mathematical equations as a representative notion for the problem under study. The popular combinatorial models in cloud relaibility prediction are the cloud-reliability block diagram (C-RBD), cloud-reliability graphs (C-RG) and cloud-associated fault tree (CAFT). All these models can be seen as extensions to classical approaches.

9.4.1.1.1 Cloud-Reliability Block Diagram (C-RBD)

C-RBD is a graphical representaion of the mathematical notion of the reliability element in cloud complex systems and subsystems in the cloud environment.

A sample C-RBD is shown in Figure 9.4. There are four templates of an RBD:

1. ***Series RBD:*** The entire system is said to be in safe reliable mode only if all the subsystems are reliable at the time of measuring the reliability.
2. ***Parallel RBD:*** This model returns the reliability of the subsystem, which has a maximum reliability measure.
3. ***Parallel-series RBD:*** This is a combination of the previous two models and is more appropriate for critical systems that have cascaded subsystems with reserved backup provisions. The subsystems are connected in series topology.
4. ***Series-parallel RBD:*** This is very similar to the previous one except the topology is parallel.

Every component is represented in C-RBD, such as the cloud server. Virtual machines (VMs) will have a specific rate of failure and failure distribution function augmented to them.

9.4.1.1.2 Cloud-Reliability Graphs (C-RG)

This is a systematic and graphical representation of cloud infrastructure as nodes and their interconnections as edges or arcs. Failure can be predicted in the absence of a channel between sources to sink the node of the represented environment. Each edge will be marked with failure probability, failure rates and so forth.

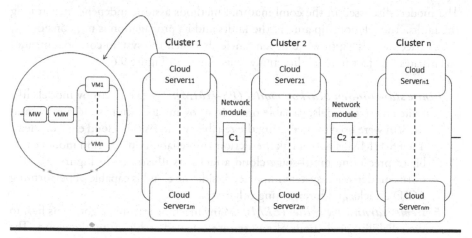

Figure 9.4   Cloud-reliability block diagram [6].

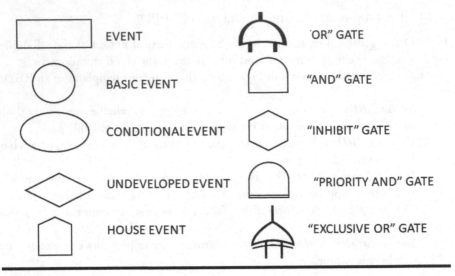

Figure 9.5 Symbols in the fault tree [7].

9.4.1.1.3 Cloud-Associated Fault Tree (CAFT)

This is a top-down approach suitable for both qualitative and quantitative assessments of reliability in cloud infrastructure. The tree becomes more granular at the leaves and it can clearly depict how the fault path propagated through the cloud environment. Some of the symbols used in fault tree construction are given in Figure 9.5.

9.4.1.2 State Space Models

The models discussed in the combinatorial methods assume independence among the faults. The relationship among the faults and its propagation is not considered. State space models capture the dependencies between the system components and culminates this fact in reliability analysis as shown in Figure 9.6.

> *Finite state hidden Markov model (FS-HMM):* Types of Markov models like finite context models, variable order Markov models, finite state models and so forth were used in predicting the reliability and risks in cloud environment. The FS-HMM is both a risk prediction and reliability prediction model capable of predicting multi-stage cloud attacks, as illustrated in Figure 9.7. The intrusion detection system imparted inside the cloud is capable of performing ACID attacks and forewarning other attacks.
>
> *Extreme learning machines (ELMs):* Many machine learning algorithms fit into the reliability predictions of any service-oriented architecture like cloud. The failure data collected from the reliability test results of the cloud computing

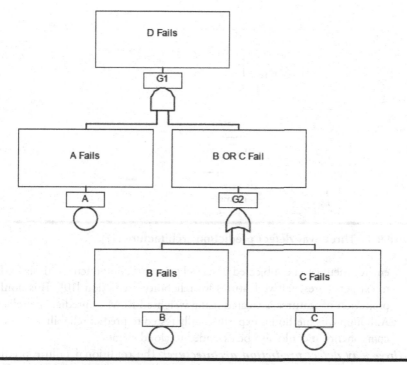

Figure 9.6   Sample fault tree [8].

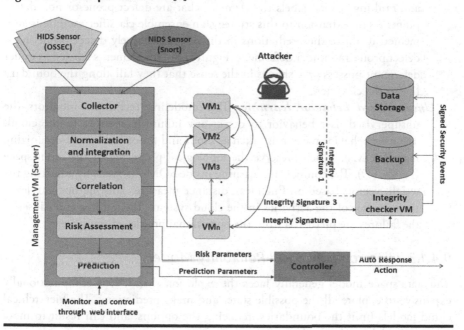

Figure 9.7   Finite state hidden Markov model [9].

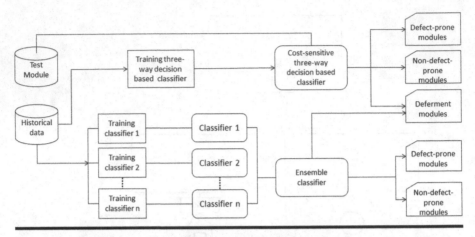

Figure 9.8 Three-way defect prediction architecture [11].

environment can be subjected to kernel principal component analysis (K-PCA) to extract representative features for reliability prediction [10]. This nonlinear projection of features is treated using weighted ELM to predict the reliability. Although this method is experimentally tested to predict reliability in software components, it could also be extended to cloud elements.

Three-way defect prediction architecture: The traditional failure prediction in software components is centered on a two-phased approach, classification and ranking, which labels the elements that are defect prone or non-defect prone. As an extension to this strategy, an ensemble classifier module is augmented to make the predictions in three labels, namely defect prone, non-defect prone and under deferment (Figure 9.8). The elements labeled as under deferment possess gray shades in the sense that they fall along the boundary line of the classifier.

Unsupervised behavior learning: This modeling technique monitors the unsupervised user behavior to detect any failure happening in the cloud. The user behavior pattern is taken as input and processed by self-organizing maps (SOMs), which preserve the topological properties of the input space (Figure 9.9). The competitive learning inside SOMs happens by adjusting the weight vectors based on Euclidean distance measure. This method can learn the behavior of the activities in the cloud system. The failures and causes of the failures are predicted from the operational profiles of the system.

9.4.1.3 Hierarchical Cloud Reliability Models

The state space model generally faces the explosion threat. It is computationally expensive to explore all the possible states and make predictions. The hierarchical cloud models limit the boundaries, reducing the options, and can result in more realistic modeling of complex systems.

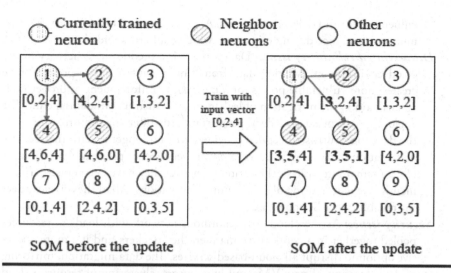

Figure 9.9   Training phase in self-organizing maps (SOMs) [12].

Stochastic Petri nets: The generalized stochastic Petri net (GSPN) tool is an economical option for the prediction of reliability of cloud environments. It accumulates faster transitions at any node under study in a time domain so that fault predictions occur at a faster rate. This is a hierarchical model best suited for large complex systems.

9.5 Challenges in Reliability Prediction in Cloud

Reliability prediction is a crucial phase in the architectural design of cloud development and deployment. The challenges combated by cloud architectures in implementing reliability prediction are discussed in this section.

Reliability issue in virtualization: The notion of virtualization integrates a number of VMs to act as a single entity. The individual servers may have different processing capabilities and other bottlenecks. This issue is prevalent among other hardware that is virtualized. This hinders the reliability prediction, since the performance and management planning cannot achieve their expected result due to the heterogeneous functionality of the hardware components. Also, this leads to problems in load balancing. The resources with low processing power will be overutilized and some will be underutilized. This will contribute to deterioration in the overall performance as promised by the service-level agreements (SLAs). Sprawling is a creation of VMs by combining more physical servers than is actually necessary [13]. This increases the chances for migration of services between VMs, causing security vulnerabilities and delayed responses. Also, the hypervisors will ensure maximum performance during migration, which could be avoided.

Data-related reliability issues: Data leakage is a predominant activity in the cloud environment. Moving data from single-point to multi-point storage creates more vulnerable points for *data leakage.* Enforcement of proper policies will aid in the mitigation of leakage of critical and confidential data. The deployed encryption and decryption standards offer maximum security to the data, but untrusted service providers can no longer ensure the security preservation of data. *Remanance of data* is yet another problem where images of data remain in a physical location even after they have been erased. This is mainly due to mirroring of data at multiple locations. All of these issues affect the reliability prediction strategy.

Security issues: As the cloud is an enormous network with loads of resources pooled together in a cooperative manner, the attackers find it a more attractive option to disrupt all cloud-based services. The data migration, mirroring of data, creation of new VMs and hypervisors, clustering of resources, load balancing, communication overhead, security concerns, intruders into logical and physical systems, poor access control policies and so forth are some of the serious security issues. They directly affect the reliability prediction success percentage. These unforeseen actions will lure attackers to the entire cloud setup.

9.6 Risks

Risk can be termed as an *event that adversely impacts the cloud environment.* The chief sources of risks are process, technology, people and hardware and software resources. Risks and issues have to be dealt with distinctively. Issues can be anticipated, whereas risks are unanticipated. Answers to the following questions are vital to mitigate the impact of risks in the cloud:

1. What will happen to the cloud environment?
2. When is risk likely to occur?
3. What is the probability that the risk may happen?
4. What is the ultimate outcome?
5. What are the symptoms that forewarn the occurrence of risks?

9.6.1 Cloud Characters or Risks

The characteristics of the cloud are on-demand service, broad network access, resource pooling, measured service and elasticity. All of them have their character-specific risks induced inside the cloud platform.

On-demand service: The cloud customers can scale up their demands from the cloud in terms of resources. This also scales up the reliability and availability latency in the cloud, thus it is unable to meet the SLA requirements.

Broad network access: Cloud computing spawns across a variety of networking platforms like wired, wireless, Internet, intranet and so forth. Connecting to these heterogeneous networks with security and quality assurance is highly challenging. The cloud service providers promise high quality of service (QoS) with lower latency, which in the real world becomes impossible because of the cross-networking paradigms.

Resource pooling: Enhanced resource utilization leads to risks like virtualization risks, jitter and latency due to resource contention, disruption of service due to migration and so forth.

Measured service: The pay-only-for-what-you-use model introduced the following risks: data accuracy and completeness and time stamps for the pricing model.

Rapid elasticity: Expansion and contraction of cloud services leads to service impact, reliability latency, availability latency of expansion and compression.

9.6.2 Cloud-Specific Risks

Resource and service sharing in the cloud faces the following unique risks:

- *Contention risks due to resource sharing:* Maximizing the resources leads to an overcommitted environment. This in turn increases the latency, thus degrading the QoS.
- *Failure containment:* As the cloud is a collaborative environment, the failure at one point may cascade and cause a series of failures.
- *Increased recovery latency:* Sharing of hardware resources increases the failure and recovery latency, since failure in one single component can lead to multiple failures, thus increasing recovery time.
- *No single-point failure hardware:* The availability of services and resources must be distributed. This causes scattering of data, causing equal risks at every point the data are mirrored.
- *Inefficiency due to high availability:* As more and more resources are pooled inside the cloud environment, the contention and communication overhead increases drastically. To maintain a trade-off between availability and resources pooling, the virtualization hardware must:
  a. Detect faults and failures on par with the native resource
  b. Work with agreeable failure and recovery latency
  c. Implement failure containment strategies
- *Policy considerations:* As the resources are pooled and scaled, special policies will have to be drafted to avoid pitfalls. The expectations and support extended from policies will have to be updated as when resources are shrunk and expanded.

- *Multi-tenant usage scenario:* Multiple independent instances will be spawning in the cloud platform serving different applications. Failure containment, service latency, reliability latency and availability latency are great causes of concerns.
- *Capacity risks:* When the capacity of the cloud is scaled up, additional online resources may cause elasticity problems. The multi-tenancy also contributes to the elasticity risks. This can enhance the capacity loss with latencies.

9.7 Risks Outlined by Cloud Service Providers

The schematic view of the risks expected by the cloud service providers during the development and deployment of cloud infrastructure is given in Figure 9.10. The categories are as follows:

- *Organizational risks:* The main tasks include planning of resources and changing management activities.
- *Technological risks:* The risks are imparted by technologies during development, portability and migration, infrastructure capability, compatibility and interoperating standards.
- *Data security:* Data security is involved in identity access management, multi-tenant architecture, backup and mirroring, data residues, data loss, leakages, distribution of data, privacy and security issues, encryption and decryption standards, access control, data segregation and so forth.
- *Physical security:* This includes issues with the data location, server location, physical security measures, networking components and so forth.

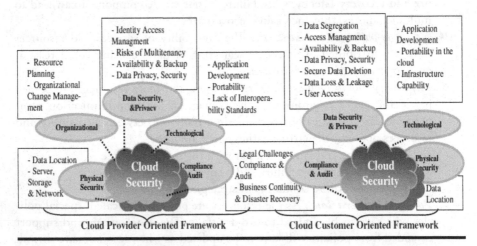

Figure 9.10   Granular view of cloud risk classes [13].

■ *Compliance and audit:* The compliance policies vary across geographical regions so they include ethical and legal issues, law and enforcement orders, auditing policies, business continuity and disaster planning.

9.8 Generic Risk Management

Risk management focuses on assessing the vulnerable locations in the cloud eco-system, which are more prone to threats. This must become a part of every phase of the software development life cycle (SDLC) model of cloud development. The security objectives of the cloud must be developed beforehand and must be a part of the SLAs. Patching the security flaws in the model is very inefficient and incurs more costs. A more generic framework for risk management in cloud architectures is given in Figure 9.11 and include the following phases:

Risk assessment: Analyze and understand the cloud platform to isolate the locale of the threats and vulnerabilities. The so-called elements must be categorized based on their impact on the normal functioning of the system. Also, refine the non-functional requirements of the cloud based on the vulnerabilities and threats. An important task in this phase is to decide on the baseline security controls to be imposed on the cloud and provision for continuous monitoring of the controls. The detailed security plan must be recorded for future references.

Risk control: This phase is responsible for monitoring and looking for any abnormal events happening in the cloud. The effectiveness of control measures and the impact of threats in the cloud have to be documented. Periodic reports of the cloud security status have to be maintained and reviewed.

Risk treatment: This phase assesses the security controls and their effectiveness. The approved operations or recovery measures will be decided and implemented to mitigate the effect of the threat.

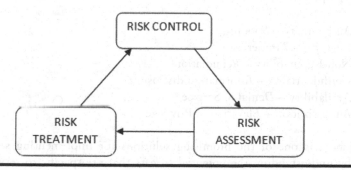

Figure 9.11   Generic risk management.

9.8.1 Cloud Security and Threat Models

The U.S. Federal Information Processing Standards (FIPS) is a widely accepted security model intended to ensure confidentiality, availability, integrity accountability and availability in cloud architecture. Any intended or unintended act in the service models should not cause modification denial of access or uncover data. The security objectives (SOs) in FIPS center on implementing measures to combat the above risks.

The Federal Information Security Management Act (FISMA) is a compliance act agreed on by all U.S. agencies. The responsibilities expected from the agencies include:

- Inventory maintenance of information systems
- Classify information and systems based on their risk levels
- Frame a proper system security plan
- Implement security controls
- Periodically conduct risk assessments
- Gets certified and accredited from a third-party audit
- Continuous surveillance and logging

All the cloud service providers must adhere to these principles to ensure integrity, availability and confidentiality.

A comprehensive threat model is shown in Figure 9.12. The model evolves among four phases. The first phase is analogous to identity and access management. The main tasks of this phase are to classify the assets and delegate the roles along with monitoring the resource usage for pricing. The second phase focuses on building trust metrics to guard the cloud platform. The third phase isolates the potential threats and the measures to combat these threats. The last phase is to rank the vulnerabilities to prioritize the tasks.

The STRIDE model is used more often among industries to include safety parameters inside the architecture. The term STRIDE strives to preserve the following properties:

- Authenticity – *S*poofing
- Integrity – *T*ampering
- Non-Reputability – *R*epudiation
- Confidentiality – *I*nformation disclosure
- Availability – *D*enial of Service
- Authorization – *E*levation of Privilege

This model is one of the promising solutions for implementing security measures by understanding the potential threats that are specific to service-oriented architectures.

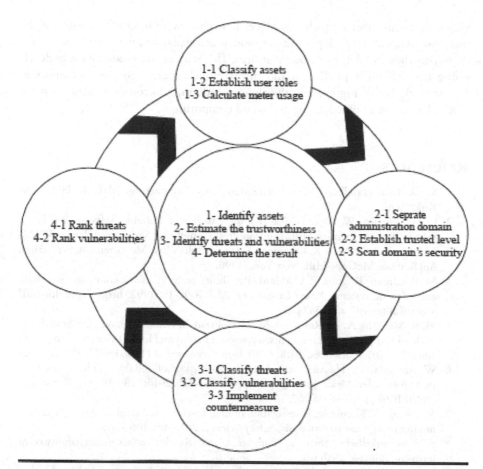

Figure 9.12 Comprehensive trust model for cloud.

The attack defense tree (ADT) threat model lists all of the potential intrusions possible inside a cloud platform along with its signatures and attack profiles [14]. This strategy considers the trade-off between the attack costs and defense costs before implementing the countermeasure for the attack or threat [15]. The knowledge obtained through the ADT will be helpful in reiterating the attack profile and signature to update the changes.

9.9 Conclusion

This chapter revolves around the reliability prediction in cloud computing platforms. The cloud-specific reliability assessment strategies and reliability prediction models are briefly discussed. The various sources of risks and threats emanating through the risk are dealt with elaborately. Cloud computing commits a greater vision to its customers, which introduces new challenges to combat. Some of the most popular industry-adopted threat models are explained, with ample scope for deploying those models in a cloud platform. This is an open research issue in developing new reliability prediction and threat models specific to cloud computing. As the world is shifting more to the cloud paradigm, it becomes evident for more researchers to focus on edge, fog and cloud computing.

References

1. M. R. Lyu, Handbook of Software Reliability Engineering, McGraw-Hill, New York, 1996.
2. L. H. Putnam, W. Myers, Measures for Excellence: Reliable Software on Time, Within Budget, Prentice-Hill, Yourdon Press Computing Series, New Jersey, 1992.
3. J. D. Musa, A. Iannino, K. Okumoto, Software Reliability: Measurement, Prediction, Application, McGraw-Hill, New York, 1990.
4. M. Friedman, P. Tran, P. Goddard, Reliability techniques for combined hardware and software systems, Rome Laboratory, RL-TR-92-15, 1992. https://apps.dtic.mil/dtic/tr/fulltext/u2/a256347.pdf.
5. M. R. Mesbahi, A. M. Rahmani, M. Hosseinzadeh, Reliability and high availability in cloud computing environments: a reference roadmap, Human Centric Computing and Information Sciences, 2018, 8: 20. https://doi.org/10.1186/s13673-018-0143-8.
6. W. Ahmeda, O. Hasana, S. Tahar, Formalization of reliability block diagrams in higher-order logic, Journal of Applied Logic, 2016, 18: 19–41. https://doi.org/10.1016/j.jal.2016.05.007.
7. M. Zhang, V. Kecojevic, Investigation of haul truck-related fatal accidents in surface mining using fault tree analysis, Safety Science, 2014, 65: 106–117.
8. Fred Schenkelberg, Intro to fault tree analysis. https://accendoreliability.com/intro-to-fault-tree-analysis/.
9. H. A. Kholidy, A. Erradi, S. Abdelwahed, A. Azab, A finite state hidden Markov model for predicting multistage attacks in cloud systems, IEEE 12th International Conference on Dependable, Autonomic and Secure Computing, 2014, DOI 10.1109/DASC.2014.12.
10. Z. Xu, J. Liu, X. Luo, Z. Yang, Y. Zhang, P. Yuan, Y. Tang, T. Zhang, Software defect prediction based on kernel PCA and weighted extreme learning machine, Information and Software Technology, 2019, 106: 182–200.
11. W. Z. Huang, Q. Li, Three-way decisions based software defect prediction, Knowledge-Based Systems, 2016, 91: 263–274.
12. D. J. Dean, H. Nguyen, X. Gu, UBL: unsupervised behavior learning for predicting performance anomalies in virtualized cloud systems, ACM, 2012, 191–200.
13. P. Saripalli, B. Walters, QUIRC: a quantitative impact and risk assessment framework for cloud security, IEEE 3rd International Conference on Cloud Computing, 2010.
14. P. Wang, W.-H. Lin, P.-T. Kuo, H.-T. Lin, T. C. Wang, Threat risk analysis for cloud security based on attack-defense trees, 8th International Conference on Computing Technology and Information Management (NCM and ICNIT), 2012, 106–111.
15. A. Amini, N. Jamil, A. R. Ahmad and M. R. Zaba, Threat modeling approaches for securing cloud computing, Journal of Applied Sciences, 2015, 15: 953–967.

Chapter 10

Experimental Analysis and Performance Enhancement of Security in Cloud Databases

T. Sasikala
Sathyabama Institute of Science and Technology

R. Ramya
SRM Institute of Science and Technology

Contents

10.1 Introduction

Due to the extensive resources of cloud providers, several experts consider security in the cloud environment to be more robust than in a domestic environment. RightScale [1], a well-known cloud industry guide with 997 information technology (IT) professionals, took a survey in 2018 regarding the challenges in adopting the cloud. Figure 10.1 shows that, according to the survey, security in the cloud is the foremost issue for 77% of users, and this seems to be a major challenge even today.

The report in Figure 10.2 shows that optimization of existing cloud use is the major initiative for cloud computing. Although security has been on the list for a long time, it still is a major challenge. A feasible solution for both security and optimization of the cloud has been attempted in this chapter. Since data in a cloud

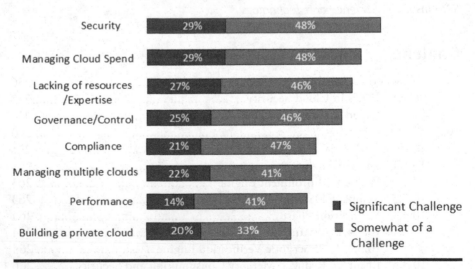

Figure 10.1   Cloud challenges report.

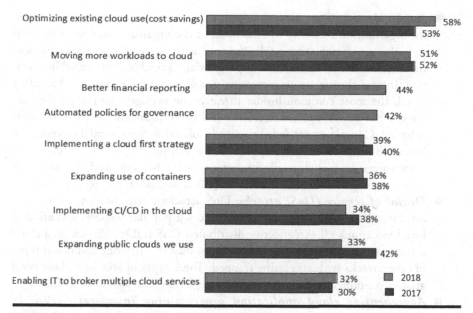

Figure 10.2   Cloud initiatives report.

environment could be exposed to an illegitimate person, the field of data security has expanded.

10.1.1 Issues in Cloud Security

Security issues arise in cloud computing as the cloud consumer data and the software used both exist in the premises of the cloud provider. This is a major threat from the user's perspective, and other threats are discussed below:

- **Data breaches:** A data breach can be defined as the intended or unintended leaking of secret data to illegitimate surroundings. In 2017, there were a number of data breaches; for instance, the Equifax breach that affected a minimum of 143 million users. Generally, breaches happen often in cloud data, damaging lives and their status, which take a huge amount of time to restore. A large number of organizations are tightening their existing security measures and re-evaluating their existing polices hoping to enhance the protection of the user data they store, even though there are regulations and laws to help in the event of a data breach.
- **Loss of data:** There is data loss in cloud servers. This may be caused by cyberattacks, which are malicious, or may be caused by non-malicious reasons including natural calamities such as earthquakes, floods and human errors, which may occur when an administrator from the cloud deletes files by mistake.

■ *Insider threats:* When a spiteful threat comes from within the organization to the organization's security by employees of the organization, contractors and so forth, it is known as an insider threat. The threat may be stealing confidential information or intellectual property or any valuable commercial information. Insider threats are an increasing problem and are persistent. According to [2], the most common insider threat is the negligent employee; they are responsible for 64% of the incidents and the rest are the result of criminal behavior. Complete knowledge about the following five essential categories of insider threat is considered important for a well-secured cloud data company. These categories include negligent responders, inadvertent insiders, insider collusion, persistent malicious insiders and discontented employees.

■ *Denial of service (DoS) attacks:* DoS attacks nearly occupy 14% of the total attacks in cloud environments. Yahoo, a popular website, was affected by a DoS attack [3]. An effective distributed DoS (DDoS) attack on a cloud service gives a virtual attacker the opportunity to carry out additional types of cyberattacks without getting trapped. These types of attacks include flood attacks, amplification attacks, resource depletion attacks and so forth.

■ *Apprehensive cloud application programming interfaces (APIs):* In cloud systems, APIs are the only facets outside of the reliable organizational frontier with a publicly accessible Internet Protocol (IP) address. Taking advantage of this gives virtual attackers a significant way into the cloud applications. This is considered to be a major problem. Cloud APIs represent a public front door for running applications.

10.1.2 Cloud Security Solutions

Cloud security solutions can be categorized into six categories as illustrated in Figure 10.3: data, availability, compliance, disaster recovery/business continuity planning, identity and access management (IAM) and governance. This chapter concentrates on data security and IAM. Some of the solutions provided in this area are as follows. In [4], Wang et al. have focused on the security of data storage in the cloud. They have ensured the accuracy of users' data in the cloud by proposing an efficient and supple distributed scheme with two outstanding features—the homomorphic token with distributed authentication of data, which is erasure coded. The proposed scheme achieves the inclusion of storage correctness and data error localization. It further supports safe and proficient vibrant operations on data blocks. Their security and performance analysis shows that the proposed scheme is highly efficient and resilient against complex failures.

Shen and Tong [5] discussed the protection mechanisms in the cloud computing environment. They have introduced a method to develop a protected computing setting for the cloud computing system by collaborating with a protected computing platform into the cloud computing system. In this scheme, few important

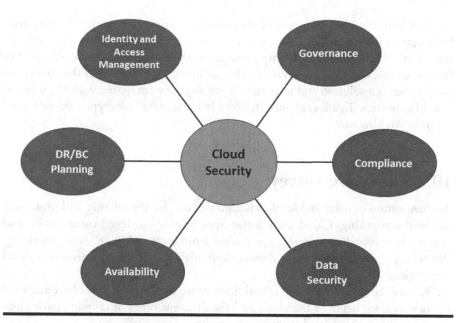

Figure 10.3   Types of cloud security.

protection services, which consist of authentication, confidentiality and integrity, are endowed within the cloud computing system.

Mobile security faces problems with limitations like input constraints and computational power. Chow et al. [6] described how cloud computing can deal with these issues. Their approach is based on a framework for maintaining authentication based on decision and behavior. By combining the two, a new authentication method for mobile technology was created. They manage trust through dynamic tuning and flexible policies. Even though cloud computing is efficient and promising, there are many challenges for data security since there is no vicinity in the data for the cloud user. To ensure the security of the data, Kalpana and Singaraju [7] proposed a method by implementing the Rivest-Shamir-Adleman (RSA) algorithm. RuWei et al. [8] have introduced an extirpation-based key derivation algorithm (EKDA) to manage the protection and confidentiality issues in cloud storage. The method they proposed combines lazy revocation and encryptions methods. Their experimental analysis shows that the proposed method could reduce the problems significantly and improve the access of data efficiently.

A biometrics system is another solution for providing security in the cloud. Biometrics-based security offers a better security based on the premise that there is involvement of that particular individual only. Since identity management and access control serve as the frontlines of cloud security, authentications in public security-based systems use biometrics as their driving force instead of passwords or security tokens.

Although these are just some of the existing solutions, methods like biometrics have certain disadvantages like cost and accuracy and speed of distance similarity measures, which give the similarity between two user biometrics data. This performance accuracy has been analyzed in this chapter and it introduces the concept of biocryptics as a solution and its performance accuracy compared with the solution using biometrics. This is explained in detail in the section "Biocryptic-Based Cloud Security Architecture".

10.2 Literature Survey

Authentication of users and services is a major issue for the reliance and protection of cloud computing. Cloud users suffer from heavily burdened computation and communication when systems, applications, products (SAP) in data processing, the Secure Sockets Layer (SSL) Authentication Protocol, is implemented in cloud computing.

Khan et al. [9] attempted to take this issue into consideration and have analyzed various security issues in the cloud and the different types of cryptographic algorithms that can be adopted to improve security.

Gampala et al. [10] explored the data security issues in the cloud that hamper its growth. They have implemented elliptic curve cryptography and digital signature to provide a better way of handling the security issue in cloud data. The survey about the various security issues in cloud computing is discussed by Ali et al. [11]. The survey also presents the current solutions to encounter these security issues. Further, it discusses the vulnerabilities in mobile computing in terms of security. Finally, research directions are discussed in the field of cloud computing. Popescu et al. [12] have solved the problem of suitable authentication at the Security Access Point level of cloud computing by a strong hybrid user authentication solution based on an image combined with text. No new hardware is required for this approach. This authentication approach is used without additional hardware. This test image-based solution receives its completion by the X.509 certificates. Load balancing serves as one of the major challenges in cloud computing, i.e., no resource is over-utilized or underutilized. Equal distribution of workloads has been taken into consideration in the work by Dasgupta et al. [13]. Thus, a novel method, which uses a load balancing strategy-based genetic algorithm (GA), has been proposed. Striving to balance equally, this work is done in the Cloud Analyst simulator. Results show that the proposed method works better and outperforms the existing methods.

Angadi and Gour [14] have proposed a new method for an offline signature recognition system. The system they introduced functioned in the stages of initial pre-processing, which consists of gray scale conversion, second binarization, third thinning and finally boundary box fitting, to build signatures ready for the feature extraction stage. A total of 59 global and local wavelet-based energy features were extracted and used to differentiate the different signatures.

Wang et al. [15] introduced a method for keeping the binary biometric representation safe. The security threat for a fingerprint template that hampers its performance is improved by the technique introduced by the authors.

Si et al. [16] have proposed a novel dense fingerprint registration algorithm, which has a composite initial registration followed by a dual-resolution block-based registration. This registration consists of energy function construction, local search and global optimization.

In a local search, a group of transformations of every input image block was found using image correlation with respect to the corresponding reference image block. In global optimization, a region-growing style algorithm was proposed to minimize the energy function. Experimental results show that the proposed algorithm produced more precise registration results and enhanced the matching performance by the fusion of minutiae matching and image correlation.

A technique based on text clustering is the right method to deal with the enormous quantity of text documents. Text documents include features that do not have proper information, which reduces the performance of the text clustering technique. Feature selection is an unsupervised technique that was used to improve the performance of the underlying algorithm.

Abualigah and Khader [17] have proposed the particle swarm optimization algorithm to resolve the feature selection problem, namely *feature selection* method using the *particle swarm optimization algorithm in text clustering* (FSPSOTC). This feature selection technique uses the *k*-mean text clustering technique to obtain more accurate clusters. Experiments were done using four text data sets with different characteristics. The results obtained showed that the proposed method (FSPSOTC) enhanced the performance of the existing text clustering technique.

Tome et al. [18] presented an experimental study of the uses of soft biometric values as additional information based on the explanation of human bodily features to advance challenging recognition of persons at a distance. Additionally, they have analyzed the available soft biometric information in various scenarios of different distances between the camera and the person. They have proved experimentally based on the results that the use of soft biometric traits is able to enhance the recognition of face-based adaptive fusion rules. Biometric technology provides a new level of security to various applications. Yet, if the biometric template stored is compromised, data loss is inevitable. Since a user's biometrics are irreplaceable and irrevocable, the loss of such data is a permanent loss of the user's identity.

10.3 Biocryptic-Based Cloud Security Architecture

In cloud databases, a user stores his data through a cloud service provider in the cloud servers, which are running in a synchronized, cooperated and distributed manner. Due to increasingly high outsourcing of data into the cloud, privacy of data in the cloud servers becomes a huge concern, and there is a need to shield the user data from illegal access in the cloud. The authors used biometrics as an authentication mechanism to allow users to access cloud data. To further improve the security of the sensitive data in the cloud, this chapter has introduced the concept of biocryptics and made an effort to explore the problems in a similarity search, which occurs while measuring the relevance between the stored template and the new template while enrolling. A biocrypto system takes an original template as input and gives an encrypted template as output; hence, a biocrypto system is said to have a high level of security. Applying such a biocrypto system in cloud environments could take care of the current existing security threats. Since deploying applications in the cloud successfully depends on the security, adopting biocryptics in cloud environments will provide the organizations with the benefits of reliability, cost-effectiveness and scalability.

The proposed architecture diagram is depicted in Figure 10.4. This novel methodology tries to enhance the security framework by authenticating the data extracted from the fingerprint image and tries to reduce the memory consumption utilized by biometric images by using biocryptics. Proposed cloud database security architecture consists of a feature analyzer; biometric enrollment engine, namely the key generator; template database; biocryptic verification engine and a matcher.

Initially during the enrollment phase, the user's biometric data, the fingerprint, is feature analyzed and is crypto transformed into a key. The sensors, biometric enrollment engine and the keys play a major role in the enrollment phase.

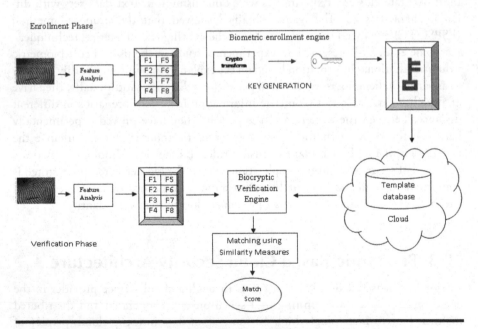

Figure 10.4   Proposed biocryptic-based cloud security architecture.

10.3.1 Feature Analyzer

In order to include all the key information essential for uniquely identifying an individual, the feature analyzer processes the image from the sensor and extracts the features that can be used to recognize the individual. The distinctive features of the fingerprint help with automatic recognition.

10.3.2 Biometric Enrollment Engine

This part of the proposed cloud security architecture involves crypto transformation of the stored template of the minutiae. This is illustrated in Figure 10.5 where the fingerprint minutiae are crypto transformed to generate keys of length 128 bits. This field of cryptography has been used to convert the minutiae template into a key. When the detected minutiae points for a particular fingerprint have been enrolled, a hash value for it is calculated using the message digest algorithm 5 with the given position (x, y), the angle and the type of each minutiae point. That is, every minutiae observed in the biometric fingerprint BK_i is described as given in Eq. (10.1)

$$m_i = (x_i, y_i, t_i) \qquad (10.1)$$

where x_i and y_i are the minutiae point and t_i is the kind of minutiae point that may be an ending of a ridge or a ridge bifurcation.

The hash value or key generated is of length 128 bits, which represents the set of minutiae points. During the enrollment phase the hash value/key for the entire template is stored so that it can be referenced during matching.

10.3.3 Template Database

When a fingerprint image is initially enrolled into a system, the template of the fingerprint, the essential minutiae, is generally related to a particular individual. This template is stored in any kind of database as a template for reference. The fingerprint templates obtained during subsequent acquisitions can be compared with

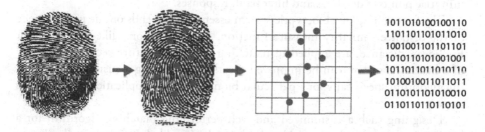

Figure 10.5   Feature extraction and key generation.

the template of reference, and the individual is identified by the similarity of the templates. Before this when there were manual systems, they used filing cabinets with cards that had fingerprints.

Today with the current technology, even though there are different types of distributed databases, templates are stored in a central database, which is a server connected to a network. The database chosen affects the provisions for the fingerprint template. The cloud database is considered here for storing the templates.

10.3.4 Verification Phase

During the verification phase, the newly generated key is checked with the key stored in the database. Every time a user needs to be authenticated this phase comes into effect. This phase includes the feature analyzer as in the enrollment phase and has the biometric verification engine.

10.3.4.1 Feature Analyzer

The feature analyzer of the verification phase involves the basic minutiae extraction process, which is composed of enhancement, binarization and thinning as is done in the enrollment phase.

10.3.4.2 Biocryptic Verification Engine

The key saved is matched with the encrypted fresh data that are to be authenticated in the biocryptic verification engine, with the help of similarity distance measures. Then, based on the matching, the particular user is authenticated. As a result, the secured data stored in the cloud is enhanced by storing biocryptic keys generated from biometric samples, reducing the cloud storage memory consumption. This solution has been proposed for handling fingerprint biometric data. The biocrytpic verification engine has the matcher in which the process of matching involves the comparison of two fingerprint templates and making a decision whether or not they belong to the same individual. Since the templates used are an output from feature extraction, the matcher must work on the extracted data, which can be minutiae points, ridge lines and filter bank responses.

The functioning of a biocryptic system essentially depends on the performance of the distance similarity measure function. Some functions, like Hamming or Euclidean distance, are applied to matching biometric feature vectors. Accuracy of a biometric system can be improved greatly by scheming a customized matching algorithm specifically for a particular biometric-based application that involves fingerprints.

Designing such a customized and well-performing matching algorithm for a biocryptic system needs to consider the noise that is added during the collection of data, good domain knowledge about the features and the efficiency of the proposed algorithm on cloud databases. Hence, the proposed biocryptic verification helps to compare and give the performance analysis of the matching algorithms.

The output of a matcher is generally a score that indicates the similarity between the templates and determines whether the individual can be accepted or rejected. Depending on the Minkowski distance, the matching process among two different processes takes place. In the case of Manhattan distance $\lambda = 1$, it can be only used for the L_1-norm. In the event of a Euclidean algorithm $\lambda = 2$, it is appropriate for the L_2-norm. Nevertheless, these two techniques have a specific limitation in distance matrix.

The Minkowski distance is used as variables on magnitude relation scales with an associated entire zero value. Even a pair of outliers with high-value bias disrespect the likeness given by one or two variables with a lower boundary. From the objective function, Eq. (10.2) is given as

$$d^{MKD}(i, j) = \sqrt[\lambda]{\sum_{k=0}^{n-1} |y_i - y_j|^{\lambda}} \tag{10.2}$$

In Eq. (10.3) d^{MKD} is the Minkowski distance between the real object i and fake object j, n is the absolute number of nodes in the system and λ is the order of the Minkowski metric. Even if it is defined for any $\lambda > 0$, it is rarely used for values further than 1, 2 and ∞. The Minkowski metric transformed for $\lambda = \infty$ is given in Eq. (10.3).

$$d^{MKD}(i, j) = \lim_{\lambda \to \infty} \left[\sqrt[\lambda]{\sum_{k=0}^{n-1} |y_i - y_j|^{\lambda}} \right] = \max|y_i - y_j| \tag{10.3}$$

The Minkowski metric of the order ∞ returns the space alongside that axis on which the two objects show the greatest entire difference. An algorithmic flow of the proposed biometric recognition in cloud computing is given in Table 10.1.

Table 10.1   Pseudo Code for the Proposed Methodology

Step 1: Generate the initial sensed Biometrics
Step 2: Evaluate the Minutiae feature Extraction (m_i) where $m_i = (x_i, y_i, t_i)$
Step 3: Generate Merkle Hash Tree
Step 4: Generate the keys
Step 5: Generate the MD5 hash function $k_g = MD5(m \| key)$
Step 6: Repeat this process for until generating new hashes
Step 7: Store the generated keys in the cloud
Step 8: For each trait check with the Minkowski distance calculate the value $d^{MKD}(i, j)$
Step 9: Identify the predicted individual
Step 10: End

Given a fingerprint matcher, its accuracy and speed performance in a realistic setting are evaluated to measure the system performance. During authentication, the biometric of the user is captured again and minutiae data are extracted to form the test template that is matched against the already stored template in the database. If the matching score is less than the threshold, then that person is rejected; otherwise, the person is accepted.

10.3.5 Ensuring Reduced Memory Consumption and Security

The major contribution of the proposed work of reducing the memory consumption and enhancing security of the cloud data is promised by introducing a Merkle hash tree authentication along with the Minkowski distance measure. This new method could provide improved security validation as it helps to avoid more memory consumption by using biocryptics. This work is well suited for the applications in which there is a need for huge biometric data storage.

Proposed security biocryptic cloud architecture ensures better performance by increased speed of access because of the use of biocryptics and by using the right similarity distance measure for comparing the keys. Choosing the right similarity measure has given better results in identifying the right individual rather than choosing random similarity measures.

The architecture can provide better performance in various domains. For example, in the area of health care it can help to reduce the burden of health care fraud by identifying the wrong individuals faster. It also ensures proper utilization of money spent on maintaining a patient's database by using biocrytics. Another example in the area of finance, by linking customers' biometric identities to their credit reports, the proposed method can identity fraud in credit and loan applications, which lose a huge amount of money every year.

10.4 Performance Analysis of Distance Methods Using Biometric Data

The proposed method has been carried out using MATLAB with the National Institute of Standards and Technology (NIST) Special Database 4 (NIST4) [19]. This is a fingerprint database that is made available for public use. The fingerprint image sizes are 388×374 pixels with a firmness of 96×96 dots per inch (dpi). The cloud.seasensesoftwares.com/916407 was the cloud that was used for this work.

10.4.1 Selection of Similarity Distance Methods

To measure how close sample data resemble a template data, a fresh sample has to be taken. A characteristic based on statistics of the data distribution is taken into account by a good similarity measure function. Some of the well-established measures are, Euclidean distance [20, 21], Mahalanobis distance [22, 23], Manhattan distance, Minkowski distance, Jaccard coefficient and Canberra distance.

10.4.1.1 Hamming Distance

The distance calculated between two strings that are of equal length by Hamming distance is the number of places for which the corresponding symbols are different. The Hamming distance between x and y can be given as dH(x, y), that is, the number of places where x and y are different. For example, for the strings 1011101 and 1001001, which are of equal length, when calculated the Hamming distance it gives the value 2. The third and fifth positions are different so they are given as dH(1011101,1001001) = 2.

The Hamming distance [24] can be given as the number of bits that are to be changed to turn one string into other. Rarely, the number of characters may be used instead of the number of bits.

10.4.1.2 Jaccard Coefficient

The Jaccard coefficient [25], which is sometimes referred to as the Tanimoto coefficient, measures similarity as the intersection divided by the union of the objects. The Jaccard coefficient for text compares the sum weight of shared terms with the sum weight of terms that are present in either of the two documents but are not the shared terms. The formal definition in Eq. (10.4) is

$$SIM_J(\vec{t}_a, \vec{t}_b) = \frac{\vec{t}_a . \vec{t}_b}{\left|\vec{t}_a\right|^2 + \left|\vec{t}_b\right|^2 - \vec{t}_a . \vec{t}_b} \tag{10.4}$$

The Jaccard coefficient is a distance similarity measure that has values between 0 and 1. When $\vec{t}_a = \vec{t}_b$ then it is 1, and when they are disjoint the value is 0, i.e., 1 means two objects are the same and 0 means the objects are totally different.

10.4.1.3 Canberra Distance

The Canberra distance [26] is defined as follows. It is quite similar to the Manhattan distance, but the absolute difference between the variables of the two objects is divided by the sum of the absolute variable values before summation. The generalized equation in Eq. (10.5) is given in the form:

$$d^{CAD}(i, j) = \sum_{k=0}^{n-1} \frac{\left|y_{i,k} - y_{j,k}\right|}{\left|y_{i,k}\right| + \left|y_{j,k}\right|} \tag{10.5}$$

10.5 Analysis over Biometric Data

The performance analyses of various similarity distance methods are done initially with biometric data and then with biocryptic data. Both data show interesting results based on metrics such as accuracy, F-Score and recall.

The experiment done in MATLAB starts with the performance analysis on biometric data. It has the login module where one is for the administrator and the other is for the user. Initially, by logging in as an administrator the image database is created and stored in the cloud. Now, once the database is created, the user logs in by giving a username and password. Once entered as the user, the user can select an image. Once the user chooses a sample image to be compared, a particular image chosen is as illustrated in Figure 10.6.

The comparison between the selected biometric images of the user with the images database stored in the cloud is done as previously explained. The comparison is done based on many distance similarity methods, such as Hamming, weighted Hamming, Euclidean, weighted Euclidean, Manhattan and Mahalanobis.

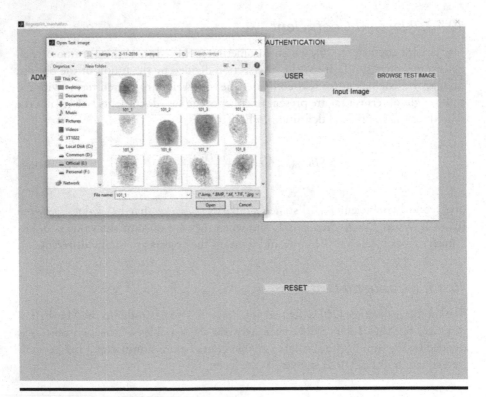

Figure 10.6   Selecting a biometric image.

The false match rate (FMR) and false non-match rate (FNMR) quantify the errors in this verification system. The false-positive identification rate (FPIR) and false-negative identification rate (FNIR) are used as the error metrics in this identification system.

10.5.1 Improved Performance of the Manhattan Method

Based on the performance metrics, the following analysis has been done. Table 10.2 lists the results for five biometric samples. According to the results, the Manhattan distance shows comparatively good results with other methods in all the samples taken into consideration.

The greater the distance the less is the similarity. The database we used had the maximum of dissimilar biometric fingerprint samples. Instead of identifying the other biometric samples as not the same, the widely used methods like Hamming, Euclidean and weighted Euclidean show that they are similar in most cases. In the majority of the samples, Manhattan does not hold false acceptance rate (FAR) and it outperforms the other similarity distance measures, as illustrated in Figure 10.7.

The results show that for biometric images in the cloud database, the Manhattan comparison distance similarity measure gives the most accurate result compared with the other distance similarity measures, which may sometimes accept a wrong individual as the right one. This seldom happens in a Manhattan distance similarity measure. Also, the widely and most commonly used Hamming distance

Table 10.2 Comparison of Distance Measure Functions with Biometric Sample Dataset

	Biometric Sample 1	Biometric Sample 2	Biometric Sample 3	Biometric Sample 4	Biometric Sample 5
Manhattan	22502	9416	25884	13144	16770
Hamming	2.540039e + 02	2.552930e + 02	2.540273e + 02	2.554453e + 02	2.554258e + 02
Euclidean	1.115745e + 04	2.882039e + 03	8.293131e + 03	3.260512e + 03	5.708954e + 03
Weighted Euclidean	7.889508e + 03	2.037909e + 03	5.864129e + 03	2.305530e + 03	4.036840e + 03
Mahalanobis	1.411291e + 02	3.769138e + 01	1.189785e + 02	4.544620e + 01	7.778393e + 01

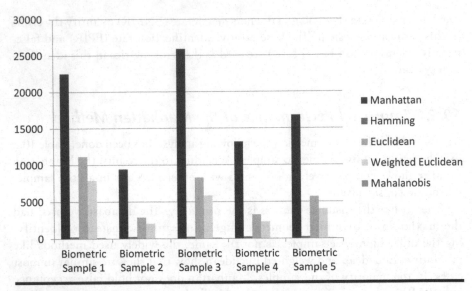

Figure 10.7 Comparison chart of similarity distance measures showing the out-performance of Manhattan distance.

performs poorly compared with Manhattan distance, enabling better solutions for comparing biometric images in cloud databases.

10.6 Performance Analysis of Distance Methods Using Biocryptic Data

Here the generated keys from biometric information are saved as biocryptic data in the cloud. The comparison between the keys is done, and the analysis of methods is discussed below.

The methodology proposed is tested with other similarity distance measures, namely Hamming, Euclidean, weighted Euclidean, Canberra, Bray-Curtis, Akritean, weighted Hamming, Mahalanobis and Manhattan. The metrics considered for evaluation of performance are FPIR, FNMR, FNIR, FMR, accuracy, F-Score and recall, where it has been shown how the proposed method outperforms the other methods. In the experiment, the proposed method has been analyzed with similarity distance methods. About 150 images whose encrypted images were stored were considered for the experiment. The results are listed in Table 10.3. Based on the results, the Minkowski method gives surprising results compared with widely known methods like Hamming and Euclidean

Table 10.3   Comparison of Performance Using Input Fingerprint Images

Various Distances	*FPIR*	*FMR*	*FNIR*	*FNMR*	*Recall*	*Accuracy (%)*	*F-Score*
Minkowski	0.1	0.1	0.5	0.1	0.95	97.25	0.94
Canberra	0.375	0.4	0.385	0.273	0.72	82.25	0.71
Bray-Curtis	0.2	0.5	1	0.2	0.1	60.01	0.1
Hamming	0.1	0.5	1	0.3	0.4	60.2	0.4
Manhattan	0.6	0.2	0	0.5	0.5	40.34	0.49
Euclidean	1	1	0.2	1	0.2	20.1	0.2
Mahalanobis	1	0.1	0.1	0.5	0.5	40.39	0.49
Weighted Hamming	0.4	0.5	1	0.1	0.2	25.8	0.2
Akritean	0.2	0.5	1	0.2	0.25	60.4	0.25
Weighted Euclidean	1	1	0.1	1	0.3	30.21	0.3

distance methods. When fewer images were considered, accuracy was better in Minkowski compared to others.

10.6.1 Outperformance of Manhattan Distance

The F-score, recall and accuracy had higher values compared with other methods, especially Canberra, which was very close when fewer inputs were considered. While calculating the F-Score, the Mahalanobis distance method also performs similar to the Canberra method. Canberra is able to give near value to Minkowski, but Minkowski, with its unbeatable performance in all means of accuracy, recall and F-Score, has proved that it can be best applied and is best suited for biocryptic data in cloud settings.

The performance metrics of FMR, FPIR, FNIR and FNMR were all considered and used for the distance methods. The results show that the FMR value was considerably low in the Minkowski method compared with other methods that have a little more FMR similarly with other metrics. In the overall analysis illustrated in Figure 10.8, it can be concluded that Minkowski is best suited for a cloud database with biocryptics.

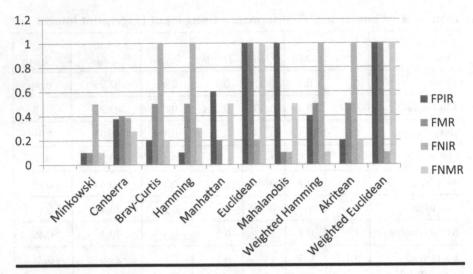

Figure 10.8 Comparison of FPIR, FMR, FNIR and FNMR.

10.7 Conclusion and Future Work

Biocryptics works around the vital principle of protection and privacy of data. Data that are most prone to attack are stored biometric templates. Hence, when such data are stored in the cloud database, it becomes mandatory to have a highly secured biometric-based mechanism to protect the data. The proposed methodology mainly achieves authentication to ensure the biometric identity and stores only the biocryptic data, assuring less memory consumption; that is, keys are stored instead of images. Since cloud databases are insecure, they require more effective methods to accomplish mutual authentication; hence, a highly secured biocryptic-based mechanism should be used. To achieve this, an efficient Minkowski distance-based Merkle hash tree authentication has been proposed.

Next, considering the comparison between biometric/biocryptic data, various distance similarity methods are available. Selecting the right method plays a crucial role in achieving better security. Although various similarity distance measure functions are available, the proposed method has proved Manhattan distance identified more individuals correctly compared with other methods in the case of biometric data, and the Minkowski distance provides better results than the other methods in the case of biocryptic data. These methods have been compared based on parameters such as accuracy, recall, F-Score, FMR, FNMR, FPIR and FNIR. Thus, the Minkowski method proves to be a more suitable one to store and retrieve biocryptic data from cloud environments. Future enhancements include the following:

- This work uses the cloud environment where it can be extended to retrieve data in Big Data environments and in further examples.
- The size of the key, which is stored in the database, can be increased for the next level of security.
- The experiment has been carried out using MATLAB, but it can be done using other tools in the future.

References

1. RightScale 2018 State of the Cloud Report Uncovers Cloud Adoption Trends. (2018), https://www.globenewswire.com/news-release/2018/02/13/1339982/0/en/RightScale-2018-State-of-the-Cloud-Report-Uncovers-Cloud-Adoption-Trends.html#:~:text=%20Key%20highlights%20from%20the%20RightScale%202018%20State,cloud%20costs%20is%20top%20initiative%3A%20Optimizing...%20More%20.
2. Ponemon Institute. (2013), Moving Beyond Passwords: Consumer Attitudes on Online Authentication, a Study of US, UK and German Consumers, https://www.ponemon.org/local/upload/file/NokNokWP_FINAL_3.pdf. (Retrieved: April 2013).
3. Deshmukh, R. V. and Devadkar, K. K. (2015), "Understanding DDoS attack and its effect in cloud environment," Procedia Computer Science, Vol. 49, pp. 202–210.
4. Wang, C., Wang, Q., Ren, K. and Lou, W. (2009), "Ensuring data storage security in cloud computing," In 2009 17th International Workshop on Quality of Service, IEEE, pp. 1–9.
5. Shen, Z. and Tong, Q. (2010), "The security of cloud computing system enabled by trusted computing technology," In 2010 2nd International Conference on Signal Processing Systems, IEEE, Vol. 2, pp. 2–11.
6. Chow, R., Jakobsson, M., Masuoka, R., Molina, J., Niu, Y., Shi, E. and Song, Z. (2010), "Authentication in the clouds: a framework and its application to mobile users," In Proceedings of the 2010 ACM workshop on Cloud computing security workshop, ACM, pp. 1–6.
7. Kalpana, P. and Singaraju, S. (2012), "Data security in cloud computing using RSA algorithm," International Journal of Research in Computer and Communication Technology, Vol. 1, No. 4, pp. 143–146.
8. RuWei, H., XiaoLin, G., Si, Y. and Wei, Z. (2011), "Study of privacy-preserving framework for cloud storage," Computer Science and Information Systems, Vol. 8, No. 3, pp. 801–819.
9. Khan, S. S. and Tuteja, R. R. (2015), "Security in cloud computing using cryptographic algorithms," International Journal of Innovative Research in Computer and Communication Engineering, Vol. 3, No. 1, pp. 148–155.
10. Gampala, V., Inuganti, S. and Muppidi, S. (2012), "Data security in cloud computing with elliptic curve cryptography," International Journal of Soft Computing and Engineering (IJSCE), Vol. 2, No. 3, pp. 138–141.

11. Ali, M., Khan, S. U. and Vasilakos, A. V. (2015), "Security in cloud computing: opportunities and challenges," Information Sciences, Vol. 305, pp. 357–383.

12. Popescu, D. E. and Lonea, A. M. (2013), "Hybrid text-image based authentication for cloud services," International Journal of Computers Communications and Control, Vol. 8, No. 2, pp. 263–274.

13. Dasgupta, K., Mandal, B., Dutta, P., Mandal, J. K. and Dam, S. (2013), "A genetic algorithm (GA) based load balancing strategy for cloud computing," Procedia Technology, Vol. 10, pp. 340–347.

14. Angadi, S. A. and Gour, S. (2014), "Euclidean distance based offline signature recognition system using global and local wavelet features," In 2014 Fifth International Conference on Signal and Image Processing (ICSIP), IEEE, pp. 87–91.

15. Wang, S., Deng, G. and Hu, J. (2017), "A partial Hadamard transform approach to the design of cancelable fingerprint templates containing binary biometric representations," Pattern Recognition, Vol. 61, pp. 447–458.

16. Si, X., Feng, J., Yuan, B. and Zhou, J. (2017), "Dense registration of fingerprints," Pattern Recognition, Vol. 63, pp. 87–101.

17. Abualigah, L. M. and Khader, A. T. (2017), "Unsupervised text feature selection technique based on hybrid particle swarm optimization algorithm with genetic operators for the text clustering," The Journal of Supercomputing, Vol. 73, No. 11, pp. 4773–4795.

18. Tome, P., Fierrez, J., Vera-Rodriguez, R. and Nixon, M. S. (2014), "Soft biometrics and their application in person recognition at a distance," IEEE Transactions on Information Forensics and Security, Vol. 9, No. 3, pp. 464–475.

19. Watson, C. I. and Wilson, C. L. (1992), "NIST special database 4, fingerprint database," U.S. National Institute of Standards and Technology, March 15.

20. Sturn, A. (2000), "Cluster analysis for large scale gene expression studies," Pattern Recognition, Vol. 3, No. 8, pp. 84–96.

21. Yampolskiy, R. V. and Govindaraju, V. (2006), "Similarity measure functions for strategy-based biometrics," In International Conference on Signal Processing (ICSP 2006), Vienna, Austria.

22. McLachlan, G. J. (1999), "Mahalanobis distance," Resonance, Vol. 4, No. 6, pp. 20–26.

23. Xiang, S., Nie, F. and Zhang, C. (2008), "Learning a Mahalanobis distance metric for data clustering and classification," Pattern Recognition, Vol. 41, No. 12, pp. 3600–3612.

24. Vimal, A., Valluri, S. R. and Karlapalem, K. (2008), "An experiment with distance measures for clustering," In Proceedings of the 14th International Conference on Management of Data, pp. 241–244.

25. Huang, A. (2008), "Similarity measures for text document clustering," In Proceedings of the 6th New Zealand Computer Science Research Student Conference (NZCSRSC2008), Vol. 4, pp. 9–56.

26. Androutsos, D., Plataniotiss, K. N. and Venetsanopoulos, A. N. (1998), "Distance measures for color image retrieval," In Proceedings of the 1998 International Conference on Image Processing, ICIP98, Vol. 2, pp. 770–774.

Chapter 11

Cloud Execution Model to Attain Quality for Non-Functional Testing

D. Sudaroli Vijayakumar and D. Monica Sneha

PES University

Contents

11.1 Introduction

One of the crucial components of the software development process is testing. Testing is not merely a process of executing code to criticize its failures, it is the parameter that provides confidence to stakeholders about the quality of the product. Testing validates the correctness and completeness of the product. Since this phase of the software development process ensures quality, it should also be carried out with utmost care and concern. Traditionally, testing is carried out through the software testing life cycle model (STLC), which includes various stages of the testing process similar to the software development life cycle. The STLC commences with defining the test specifications, planning, execution, defect tracking and management, report and final testing. The way testing is performed depends on the chosen development model. Even with a good feedback system, many conventional models fail to provide quality and agility. Irrespective of the model chosen, conventional approaches fail to meet the deadline. The testing phase eventually starts at the end of the release phase, where there is no room to test, fix and release the product at the right time. This puts a great deal of pressure on finding a better testing strategy that can balance all these factors.

Thus, the demand for a development model that can start testing activity parallel to the development phase grew. Agile methodologies and DevOps adoption satisfied this requirement, and the feedback system became efficient. Agile methodology is quite impressive because it has considerably reduced the cost for testing and fixing bugs. Because the agile process efficiency is good compared with other conventional approaches, organizations turned their focus toward optimizing this process to see a considerable reduction in terms of cost and maintenance.

Customer satisfaction is centered on agile methodology. Satisfying the customer does not necessarily mean checking whether the requirements mentioned in the specification are met. Delivering a good quality product both in terms of the functional and non-functional specifications is mandatory to satisfy the customer for a longer duration. Functional testing can be verified better in conventional approaches; however, to test the product's non-functional features organizations need to make a considerable investment in terms of hardware and supporting software. Even if organizations invest, achieving 100% quality for non-functional testing is still a nightmare. The better optimal solution to satisfy this requirement is the adoption of cloud-based testing. Some of the apparent benefits of cloud-based testing are as follows:

- Testing the product like customers in the environment is the primary requirement to ensure good performance. In conventional testing, this may incur a number of costs, and the setup, once made, if found unsuitable, requires complete reinstallation of the setup. This can be performed very easily in cloud-based testing.
- If the organization works specifically on a data-intensive application, investing in high-end servers and maintaining it, the company has to bear additional expenses. Also, these servers may not be usable for all the projects that are being handled by them. These additional costs can be considerably reduced by cloud-based testing as it provides a renting option.
- The major form of non-functional testing is when the performance and load of an application can be tested very easily using cloud testing. With this type of testing, the team can make different configurations as necessary.
- Scaling up and down the resources is a major attraction of cloud-based testing.

Thus, continuous feedback system methodologies like agile combined with the cloud can make major differences in the way the testing process is carried out. This combinational testing, if it promises quality, can serve as a better optimization strategy for organizations to carry out the testing process seamlessly. The remainder of this chapter focuses on the aspect of attaining quality in cloud-based testing. The discussion starts with the quality parameters in testing both in terms of functional and non-functional testing. The next section briefly addresses the parameters that are necessary if the testing is performed in the cloud. A more in-depth discussion regarding the parameters that fail to provide value in terms of quality is provided later. Last, the focus is to depict the feasibility of cloud-based testing and the supporting frameworks and tools that can make cloud-based testing an option for the users.

11.2 Quality Achievement in Conventional Testing Methodologies

Quality in software is hypothetical; yet, one can acutely feel its absence. The term quality takes various forms and definitions, but the simplest definition of software quality is that the product behaves as it is supposed to behave. To identify the functionalities, the product is generally measured with various parameters more generally referred to as quality parameters, which are directly proportional to the requirement specifications.

11.2.1 *Categories of Requirement Specifications*

In the process of software development, the first and foremost step is defining the requirements clearly without any ambiguity. These requirement specifications define the product both in functional and non-functional perspectives.

11.2.1.1 *Functional Testing*

This type of testing is performed based on the functional requirement specification that represents the mapping of the input to output. Functional testing works in conjunction with the functional requirement. Functional testing validates whether the designed application behaves as defined in the requirements document by supplying the necessary input and validating the corresponding output. In functional testing, some of the points that are validated include checking for main functions, usability both in terms of success and failure conditions.

This functional testing is performed in various stages as depicted in Figure 11.1.

In the process of testing the functionality of a product, the developer validates the entire code by examining the functions and determines whether the procedures are returning the right values. This is referred to as unit testing that does not demand skilled testers to perform it.

The next level in this hierarchy is to build verification testing that ensures the completeness of the build. At this stage, complete unit testing is performed and a product suitable for testing is provided to the tester. The transition from a development environment to a testing environment for the product happens at this stage. Immediately after smoke testing, sanity testing is carried out. It briefly verifies that the major functionalities of the application are consistent enough to carry out the testing process further.

Regression testing is also performed to ensure that any newly added features do not conflict with other features. Once this phase is successfully completed, the entire functionalities are verified accurately to make the product satisfactory for the customer. Once the testers are confident, the product developed is complete and usability testing is performed in a controlled environment. The customer is also a

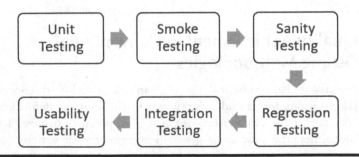

Figure 11.1   Levels of functional testing.

part of this testing process, and the satisfaction level of the customer decides if any improvements are necessary. These stages of functional testing aim to achieve correctness and completeness from a user's perspective. Thus, the quality parameter in functional testing is conformance to the requirements specifications. Conformance is measured in terms of the degree of completeness and correctness. The qualitative factor for completeness varies with stages. In unit testing, completeness is measured by the number of lines of code executed.

At the other stages, completeness is measured by the way the product behaves. Completeness is directly correlated to the correctness; thus, the completeness in other stages is measured via correctness. In conventional approaches, the functional testing process does not require sophisticated tools for performing automation and demand for newer technologies. The need to migrate to cloud-based testing to test functionality is very limited because there are fewer quality parameters. There are also proven shreds of evidence that claim that the entire functionality testing process cannot be automated except to rely on automation tools for the generation of test cases.

11.2.1.2 Non-Functional Testing

One of the most important aspects to ensure good quality, efficiency and performance of a product is to test it under unfavorable conditions. This area of testing demands a huge number of quality parameters, even if it is being tested for correctness and completeness. Non-functional testing sometimes is not viewed as a separate entity of testing as it ensures the correctness and completeness of functional testing by measuring the parameters in non-functional parameters. The simplest example that can differentiate these two is the way functional and non-functional testing is performed for a simple login button. The functionality of a login button is to ensure that the logging happens successfully, and that can be answered only if after logging in it goes to the next page within a specified period. This specified period is the performance of the application, which is a non-functional requirement. Thus, to ensure correctness and completeness, we rely on non-functional testing. Through non-functional testing, the product is tested for its flexibility, usability, security, response, performance and so forth. The types of non-functional testing are depicted in Figure 11.2.

> *Performance:* Non-functional testing is carried out to measure the performance of the product. The performance efficiency of the product is measured in terms of scalability, customer satisfaction and response time. Various testing strategies used to measure the performance are through load, stress and response time. The higher the value of load and stress, the better the product is and the lower the response time.
>
> *Reliability:* Reliability is the desire to understand product behavior under an unfavorable condition in terms of stability, downtime and integrity. Exposure of the product to different environmental conditions with unfavorable configurations is essential to understanding its reliability.

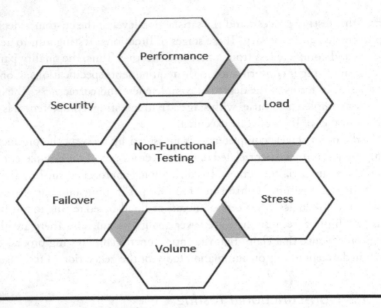

Figure 11.2 Non-functional testing.

Security: One of the crucial non-functional measurements is security. To test for this, the product is validated for its confidentiality, integrity and availability. These three primary goals of security identification enable one to understand the architectural weaknesses in the product.

Usability: This process aims to understand how users feel when the product is exposed to them.

Maintainability: To test maintainability, the flexibility of the software product is measured with the coding practices so that the transfer from one development team to another goes seamlessly.

This overview of conventional testing methodologies possesses certain restrictions that stop the testing of non-functional requirements.

■ Performance testing requires high-end computing power that may become unworkable for small- to medium-sized organizations.
■ Every non-functional test requires specialized tool support, which may vary from test to test. This may be unaffordable for small- to medium-sized organizations.
■ To measure reliability, the product should be exposed to different environments that are absurd.
■ Expert-level experience is required to build suitable test cases for non-functional testing.

There is some clear evidence that non-functional requirements are not accurate when using conventional testing methodologies. It is very interesting to note that most of the parameters that stop organizations from meeting high-quality requirements are due to the inadequacy of resources. Thus, the solution to all these issues with conventional testing methodologies is cloud-based testing.

11.3 Cloud-based Testing – Is It Feasible in Terms of Quality?

The need for the right resources, the right environment, the right tools and the right guidance are the reasons that conventional testing methodologies fail. Because of this, businesses naturally migrated over to the cloud to enjoy its benefits. Cloud-based testing was originally initiated to provide adequate resources for testers and eventually broadened to achieve agility and performance. Cloud-based testing aims to leverage performance, and in turn the application is expected to be tested for scalability, accessibility, reliability and security. Due to the technology trend, cloud computing has now become an indispensable attribute and has changed the way companies are handling business, providing services and so forth. With its numerous benefits, organizations are migrating to a cloud-based environment for maintenance and services. Complete migration to the cloud can provide fruitful results when the right methodology is adopted for the process.

11.3.1 Overview of Cloud Computing and the Migration Process

Cloud computing [1] is nothing but providing essential resources and services over the Internet at a low cost with good quality. Thus, the umbrella term *information technology* (IT) can be provided as a service to the users [2]. Organizations attempting to fully utilize the power of cloud computing are slowly migrating to cloud-based computing and storage environments. The process of migration is depicted in Figure 11.3. Depending on the type of infrastructure required, organizations

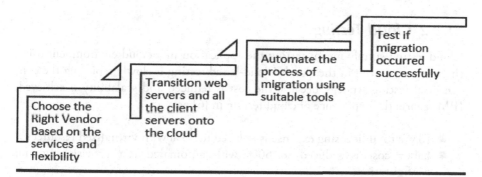

Figure 11.3   Cloud migration process.

choose a suitable vendor. With a suitable vendor, the selection of deployment models is an essential step.

11.3.1.1 Deployment Models

■ *Public cloud:* This is the most known and used form of deployment model that is owned and operated by cloud service providers. Anyone adopting a public cloud does not incur any infrastructure cost. The resources are shared, and the connection to the public cloud is generally through the Internet or private wide area network (WAN).

■ *Private cloud:* The entire cloud is owned and operated by a single organization. Public cloud providers also offer private clouds.

■ *Community cloud:* Technically, the community cloud is slightly different from the public cloud in terms of the people who can access it. Generally, this type of cloud is built by a single organization that rents the setup to people with similar interests.

■ *Hybrid cloud:* As the name signifies, this represents a mix of deployment models. Generally, hybrid models are preferred by organizations to secure sensitive data in the private cloud. The common tasks can be carried out in the public cloud.

There are pros and cons for each deployment model. Depending on the type of data, the organization chooses a particular type of deployment model. With the right deployment models, organizations can hire the required resources in the form of services mentioned, such as infrastructure as a service (IaaS), product as a service (PaaS), software as a service (SaaS) and testing as a service (TaaS) [3]. SaaS provides the user interface as a service. This does not require stand-alone installations of the application. The application is made available to the user through the Internet. PaaS makes various platforms available, which in turn allows users to create applications using the cloud platform [4, 5]. IaaS allows organizations to use different hardware configurations.

11.3.2 Cloud Testing

Cloud testing simply means testing the application in a cloud environment using the resources found in the cloud. Cloud-based testing is slowly replacing the conventional testing strategy because the cost is reduced and scalability is achieved. IBM reports the experience of cloud testing in [6] as

■ IBM's total licensing expense is reduced to 75% with virtualized resources.
■ Labor cost is reduced to 50% with automated test provisioning and configuration.
■ Product quality is incremented to 30%.

Cloud-based testing can take various forms:

Testing in a cloud: The cloud infrastructure is used to perform the software testing process.
Testing of the cloud: Under this, testing can take various forms:
- Testing the platform itself if the testing is done for the cloud provider.
- Testing at the infrastructure level.
- Testing the software that has been created to deploy it in the cloud.
- Migrating the test process to the cloud.

Testing viewed as a mere process of execution would not be the right strategy if one wants to achieve good testing results in the cloud. Cloud testing is not an execution environment; rather, it requires a great deal of management, planning and varying roles and responsibilities. Before the decision is made to use cloud-based testing, the organization needs to find out if this strategy is applicable to them by performing a strengths, weaknesses, opportunities and threats (SWOT) analysis. If SWOT analysis provides satisfactory results in terms of cost reduction or similar factors, then an organization can decide to use the migration strategy. The well-established test process is something essential if one decides to use cloud-based testing. If an organization is concentrating on manual testing, then cloud-based testing would not be the ideal choice. Another reason for companies to migrate to the cloud is technological advancements. Big Data processing-based tests are quite easy to handle in the cloud environment; however, it demands the testers to be exposed to technological advancements. Most organizations advance fast, compete effectively, shorten provisioning time and transform the way testing is performed. Irrespective of numerous benefits, testing inside a cloud environment demands to validate the application for cloud-specific quality parameters, which can be termed as *benchmark parameters,* for cloud testing:

- **Elasticity:** This is the speed the cloud environment can scale up or down the computing resources, hardware, software and so forth, according to the changing demand of the tested application.
- **Response time:** The time interval between the request for resources and the response for the request.
- **Agility:** This is the ability of the cloud environment to understand the demands of the tested application.
- **Scalability:** This is the ability of the cloud environment to automatically scale up the resources and to provide better response times.
- **Variability:** Real-time support for increased response time, throughput, and variability.

All of the abovementioned quality parameters in the cloud aim to improve the performance of cloud testing. To answer the query – Is cloud testing feasible in terms of quality? – the very important quality parameters related to non-functional testing must be dealt with in a detailed manner. Achieving quality in cloud testing remains challenging, and it demands an understanding of the quality challenges in the cloud and a suitable approach to overcome these challenges.

11.4 Quality Achievement in the Cloud – Use Case Approach

Significant due dates and less capital consumption requiring quick accessibility of testing in the cloud environment is the arrangement for this use case. Such undertakings depend on the cloud to carry out their total testing exercises. This requests 100% quality from the cloud merchant. Does cloud-based testing truly give certified quality testing? Let us attempt to answer this query with an approach that appears to show that accomplishing this performance is not conceivable with conventional testing techniques.

The key to identifying software performance happened through a specific test model that directed the entire load test implementation to the cloud. As performance is also a major concern under quality check, let us discuss a suitable performance test model using the web application. The performance model tests the application under low, medium and heavy loads. The load categories are identified by the relationship between concurrent users and optimal users. The maximum system load can never be verified under conventional methodology due to restrictions in terms of cost and resources. The way we identify the performance depends on the indicators, which impact reliability and the overall system performance. Applications tested in the cloud that become certified for quality parameters, especially for performance, availability, throughput and utilization, need to be verified. The performance test model should consider these indicators. Web-based applications have grown dramatically recently as there is a dramatic increment in digitization. It is not like the earlier days when the least amount of significance was given to testing web applications for non-functional features.

Now, most of the activities are performed at clicks by the users and it becomes unavoidable to serve the customers with the right information at the right time. So, organizations need to test the web application for quality parameters to retain customers. The web application that needs to be tested should be deployed in an environment in which the exact mimic of real user behavior is available. This is one of the most fundamental points in performance testing. If one wants to ensure reliability in performance tests, it becomes nearly impossible if the key test scenarios and load distribution are not exposed to real user behavior. The way to make the performance test reliable is through careful planning of the workload.

11.4.1 Reliable Performance Test Models

The performance test model is reliable only if the application is tested under a similar production model. If a company needs to model an efficient reliable performance model, it must have ample knowledge about the application under test (AUT). The performance of an application must be tested under major business transactions that will contribute directly or indirectly to performance. Some of the sample AUT performance scenarios that will help testers in recognizing the common business transactions might be a part of the web application.

11.4.1.1 Load Testing

Performing load testing for a web application can be carried out through a sequence of steps (as depicted in Figure 11.4) that aim to give meaningful scenarios and a performance model as well as the associated target load, metrics, execution and analysis of the test results [6].

The entire process of load testing needs to be executed with proper planning and the right use of adequate resources to attain meaningful results. Every set of activities, resources and efforts cannot be explained in detail here as it varies depending on the AUT. Briefly, a set of actions the users generally do on a web application is identified that would greatly help. Instead of the tester spending more time identifying the set of actions for every application, this set of actions can serve as a guideline for all similar load testing for web applications. Of course, the tester needs to identify any new scenario that needs to be a part of the load test cases. As we are aware, load testing is one of the time-consuming processes and is practically infeasible, even under conventional testing, to test every user action under load. The 80-20 Pareto principle objective should be an ideal one even under cloud testing. Even under a cloud, 80% of the performance issues should be identified with 20% of the test scenarios. It is up to the tester's knowledge to identify which 20% of tests should be a part of load test scenarios. If this is not carefully identified by the performance testing team, it would incur high cost and time.

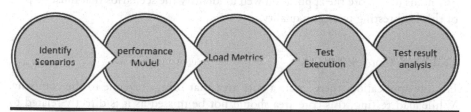

Figure 11.4 Load testing process in cloud.

11.4.1.1.1 Load Test Scenarios

Selecting the right test scenario is very important when properly utilizing the cloud environment as well as the right quality within a specified period. The list of load test scenarios will help the performance testers choose the right set of load set scenarios for the AUT.

Consider the Indian railway framework, which has numerous branches territorially and is a very complex distributed organization that creates around 1,20,000 tickets each day. Each ticket following period is 45 days, and it is anticipated to store the ticket online for about a year. Typically, using a few numbers to test this in the cloud could be a better choice than embracing routine techniques. Generally, around 160 GB of information is created daily, and each look result is obtained by performing a 1-TB information look that has the least esteem. Copies of the information ought to be considered more than once.

If an analyzer anticipates testing this case using a conventional strategy, it would be illogical to test this for efficiency, scalability and reliability. For such cases, a cloud bed would be supportive. This case is an illustration of a type of performance testing called load testing. Load testing is performed in a cloud environment to ensure predominant performance. Is it conceivable to test predominant performance in the cloud? Yes, better performance is conceivable by using certain strategies. This case can work by using several techniques that would make the complete testing process in the cloud more profitable.

11.4.1.1.2 Never Missed Scenarios

Consider that this use case lets us identify the user interaction scenarios. From a users' point of view, for the specific case we have considered, the booking process as well as the ticket availability details should be available with less response time. The point that we need to consider is that the user aims for better performance at places that they commonly use. If an application is not load tested under this scenario, then this would contribute directly to customer loss. For an e-commerce application, the product catalogue display must be load tested. How can one identify the most used scenarios for the AUT? These types of scenarios can be identified with web server log files, testing the application with beta testers. Aided with these data, one needs to explore the application well to identify the scenarios that must be part of this load testing to ensure quality.

11.4.1.1.3 Core Scenarios

For any application, there exists a core area that brings revenue to the company. While load testing, this core area should not be missed as it is directly related to company growth. In our use case, the core scenario is booking tickets. These tests can be identified by understanding the marketing material for the given application.

11.4.1.1.4 Asset-Intensive Scenario

The AUT resource consumption is subjective. While performing load testing, one needs to identify the scenarios that would consume more resources. This is again a crucial point of testing that if missed would have a serious effect on the system performance. Generally, whenever the application uses the database for serving the requests it would consume more resources. This can be identified by the tester with interaction from the developer and their own experience.

11.4.1.1.5 Technology Scenarios

One of the scenarios that might not be worth considering under the 80-20 principle is the technology-specific scenario. This is often missed because it does not need to be considered for every application. Depending on the AUT, if such a scenario is found it is mandatory to include that as a part of the cloud testing.

11.4.1.1.6 Festive Scenarios

Most users start using the railway reservation system during holiday times. If this is not tested for load, it would affect the production environment during those periods. While deciding on the load testing scenarios, festive scenarios need to be considered important. This again can be decided by the web server log files and experience.

11.4.1.1.7 Agreement Scenarios

This might not be a critical load testing scenario to satisfy user needs. But from the companies' perspective, these documents hold a great deal of significance and they that must be tested before going into production.

The selection approaches for these scenarios again depend on the AUT, and the performance testing team should consider their experiences when selecting the test scenarios for cloud-based performance testing. These scenarios will help to come up with a better performance strategy model to achieve reliability in cloud testing.

11.4.2 System Model for Successful Implementation of Load Testing in the Cloud

Achieving quality parameters for non-functional testing in the cloud is subjective. Certain applications using TaaS to test the deployed application in the cloud might yield a better outcome in terms of measuring its performance. The system model adopted for successful implementation of load testing in the cloud is presented in Figure 11.5.

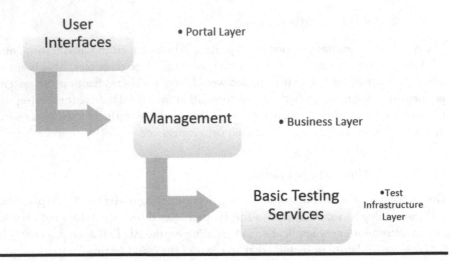

Figure 11.5   System model for load testing in the cloud.

The previously mentioned system model is depicted in [7] and [8]. As depicted in Figure 11.5, the portal layer serves as a way for the users to register for that software and gain access to run and monitor the tests. The business layer serves as a combination of many functionalities wherein the user's scripts are recorded. The management and control policy for the tenants is well maintained using the business layer in the form of a script recording that can help testers simulate the real workload. If one needs to identify the available resources for running a specific test, they should be identified. This is again taken care of by the business layer by scheduling and test control. Simulating the resources is done through the virtual machine (VM), and the resource manager keeps track of all the VMs and performs the process of resource allocation, which is again taken care of at the business layer.

Another important responsibility of the business layer is a test center that identifies the performance of the test data in terms of throughput and response time. The test infrastructure layer provides the essential testing services that are needed for performing load testing. The IaaS layer is simply the VMs that are essential for hosting the software and load test it. Most of the load testing–supported cloud environment typically involves the user creating the required test with proper configuration information, such as the duration of the test and the number of workloads. This request created by the user is submitted as a testing service to admission control and the schedular in the business layer. The schedular, by identifying the available resources, decides to accept or reject the test. If the schedular schedules the test to run in the environment, then the test center will get to know the details of the VMs that need to simulate the workload to the system under test. The performance analyzer then identifies the performance of the system under test. With such a well-defined system model to carry out load testing in the cloud, one would opt for cloud-based testing as it ensures the verification of the quality parameter of the load testing.

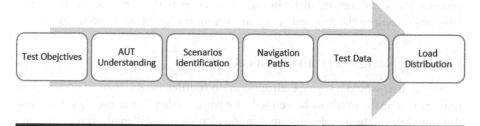

Figure 11.6 Activities of performance testing model.

11.4.2.1 Tasks of a Performance Model

Performance testing is not an easy activity as it requires proper strategy as well as the right execution. The listed tasks, if followed, in the creation of a performance model would assist one to build a better performance model. The activities of a performance model are depicted in Figure 11.6.

11.4.2.1.1 Defining Objectives

Performance, if not measured accurately with appropriate indicators, would be a complete failure. In our case, how much time should the application take to return a search result? How many concurrent users are allowed per transaction? What is the maximum transaction limit the application can handle? What should the maximum resource requirement be for the successful execution of the application?

The answers to the abovementioned points form the test objective. This generally in terms of performance testing is mentioned with terminologies such as response time, throughput, resource utilization and maximum user load. These objectives, if clearly defined, would ideally focus the work of the performance tester to create a better performance.

11.4.2.1.2 Understanding

Irrespective of the type of testing, if a tester aims to do fruitful testing he or she should understand the application as a developer, tester and end user. Performance testing is now deviating from this point, which also demands a clear understanding of the AUT in the form of the different types of users using this application. The tester also needs to understand if the business scenario for each of the users is different or similar.

11.4.2.1.3 Key Scenarios Identification

As discussed in section "Load Test Scenarios", which load scenario is essential to ensure quality? The selection of key scenarios can be all of the various categories mentioned in that section or a reduced selection set. This purely depends on the knowledge and experience that a tester has that will add value to the testing process. Based on that, one should identify the appropriate scenarios from this group of the scenarios.

11.4.2.1.4 Navigation Path Identification

How each user would navigate each application is different. As a part of performance testing, this again needs to be verified to ensure quality. Each user is unique and the way they might be using the application also may be different, so it is an infeasible option to test each user's navigation path. This again requires careful planning to determine which would be a suitable choice for navigation path testing. A performance test selection model ensuring reliability would expect to test such tests as well. Below are some guidelines that would assist the tester to produce a suitable test set:

- Understanding the user manuals that possess the sequential steps about how the application is going to be used.
- Beta testers/exposing the application to various users would also help one to identify the different explorations.
- Log files come in handy to track the usage of the users.
- Sincerely, as a user, exploring all the possible ways to use the application.

11.4.2.1.5 Unique Test Data

The instructions we have seen so far paved the way to simulate the application test in the cloud; however, this is not enough. Accurate simulation is possible with a unique set of test data, and some general questions asked by testers would end with this type of data. Some of the example test data are mentioned in Table 11.1. The time a user spends on a specific path, what type of test data should be used for a specific path and situations where multiple navigation paths are tested are also included in the table.

If multiple navigation paths are involved, identifying a suitable test is more complex for the tester. Some points that could act as guidelines are:

- Avoidance of the same test data for multiple navigation paths.
- Database status needs to be checked periodically to avoid overload.
- Inclusion of invalid test data to mimic the real-world environment.

Table 11.1   Unique Test Data for Multiple Paths for the Use Case

Scenario	Action	Input Data	Output Data	Think Time
Browsing available tickets with existing user account	Login	Username Password		2–3 seconds
	Browse	User type	Category	60 seconds

11.4.2.1.6 Load Distribution

Once the scenarios, paths and test data are identified, figuring out their distribution is the next task. It is quite common that some paths are used more, whereas others are not used as often. Considering the festive scenarios, the number of users booking the tickets would be higher, requiring consistent maintenance by the administrators. This may not be the case during the other period. So, identifying the relative distribution of scenarios needs to be considered for the performance test execution model. The various points discussed, such as beta testers, tester experience and logs, would contribute to identify the load distribution scenarios. It would be worthwhile to consider a use case that shows cloud-based testing is not the right choice for this scenario. Consider an account management system that scans around 4000 invoices and direct these invoices to the appropriate approval. This system has been deployed in the cloud and tested for the load. It freezes often enough so that a delay is associated with each approval, affecting the overall performance of the system. This system is designed with multiple servers ranging from web and database types. Suppose the objective is to identify the cause of the deficiency in the quality parameter. It then is almost impossible to reproduce the bug because there is no pattern to the system failures. This kind of use case does show that denoting all quality parameters of non-functional testing can be met. Although organizations enjoy the benefits of scalability, flexibility and low-cost testing from the cloud, the reasonableness in using cloud testing depends on the utilization case.

11.4.3 Steps to Adopt for Better Performance Results in the Cloud

- Cost is a major concern when we decide to migrate the environment to the cloud [9]. The load might end up incurring high costs if everything is migrated in a single phase. Instead, if the problems at various phases are isolated, this can help the organization to achieve better performance at a low cost. The strategy must be adopted before complete migration to follow incremental load testing in the cloud.
- Any organization that tries to adopt cloud-based load testing would unquestionably think about the security breaches [10]. Performing an encrypted communication between the load generator and controller would reduce the hazard level to a minimum. The most feasible way to perform this is through a one-time password check.
- The adaptability of holding multiple cloud providers can be advantageous in the cloud because testing loads under multiple locations can yield sensible results. It is beneficial for the tester to conduct practical large-scale tests.
- The utmost care must be taken to collect logs whenever performance degradation prevails. Options must be made possible to keep track of every possible type of information on the infrastructure. The Infrastructure might include database servers, web servers and so forth.

If carefully made, cloud-based stack testing is not distinctive from conventional testing except that proper planning is essential to satisfy the non-functional quality parameters.

11.4.4 Difficulties That Hinder Testing in the Cloud

- The point of concern in cloud-based load testing is the debuggability mode accessibility. This mode may not be possible in a cloud environment because it causes testers to ideally think about migration to the cloud.
- Because the cloud is a multi-tenant area, data theft is a concern and can only be avoided with appropriate arranging and steady carefulness [11].
- Service outage and upgrade notifications from cloud providers come over a short period of time, causing hindrance to manual validation.
- Upgrading the environment at times leads to newer framework adoption that sounds distressing for certain people as they are quite comfortable with the older framework. This causes delays in delivery as this would take more time for a tester to understand the framework and take action appropriately.
- Live upgrades impact the current connected SaaS users.

These are some of the challenges that apply generally to cloud-based testing. These will have an impact on performance testing.

11.5 Cloud-Based Tools to Support Testing

As discussed previously, performance testing requires proper planning, and assistance from tools would enhance the testing experience in the cloud. In terms of resources, this requires a scalable distributed environment [10, 11]. The following tools might be useful to carry out performance testing in the cloud:

- A web-based simulation environment that simulates the physical computing resources.
- To concatenate performance test tools, simulated interfaces are essential.
- Integration in the cloud would require the assistance of application programming interface (API)-based frameworks.
- Cloud-based non-functional testing solutions at different levels are more tools of interest.
- A cloud-based tracking solution is also required for auxiliary software testing.

Since this chapter is focused on non-functional testing, let us see some of the popular performance testing tools.

11.5.1 SOASTA Cloud Test

This tool is one of the top cloud-based test tools used to simulate thousands of virtual users for testing web applications [12]. Irrespective of the adopted deployment, the worker node can even be distributed to handle both private and public clouds. SOASTA performance test planning is like the performance test execution model in that it includes proper planning followed by configuration and execution.

SOASTA is powered with a repository that includes test scenario recordings and unique data. This repository helps to do the test execution faster. It also includes three distributed services for creation, execution and result from analytics. Another feature of SOASTA is the analytics dashboard, which can handle the results of the distributed load tests. This tool is found to be beneficial for small- to medium-sized businesses.

11.5.2 LoadStorm

LoadStorm achieves the perfection of load testing with no scripting language assistance. The traffic using this tool is realistic, and detailed reporting is also possible [13]. Using LoadStorm without any restriction on the number of behavior emulations can be performed. If the application demands testing with different user profiles with different test data, this tool allows one to perform this task very easily by incorporating the comma-separated values (CSV) data into the virtual users. This enables testing of different scenarios with as many navigation paths possible. Another helpful feature from this tool is its validation tool, which allows one to perform debugging to a certain extent.

LoadStorm acts as a stress testing tool as well. The amount of load that this tool can provide is significantly beyond imagination. Both the very low and very high load stress testing for an application can be performed using LoadStorm. This tool also has an important feature that handles the breakdown of a component. The interface of the LoadStorm is very simple with real-time performance graphs for performance indicators.

11.5.3 AppPerfect

The worst part of the business is that we create it and then we destroy it. This could happen when an application demand grows exponentially, erasing the benefits of the application. AppPerfect serves as a fully automated load, stress and performance test tool. This is an open source tool that takes care of design configuration and hardware restriction issues. The test recorder is Hypertext Transfer Protocol (HTTP) and Hypertext Transfer Protocol Secure (HTTPS) with unlimited user support. The recording in AppPerfect is like recording a browser activity. The host monitoring is generally down with built-in support. It provides almost all the capabilities that come with paid software. Nearly every support necessary to perform major non-functional testing is available in AppPerfect [14].

11.5.4 Cloud Sleuth

This is the preferred choice for organizations that need a tracing solution. This is particularly helpful in collecting logs. Because this provides an option for tracing the distributed data models, it is a premium choice with larger companies. Cloud Sleuth is used through an ID that is similar to the HTTP request and response.

The top choice of tools exclusively meant to perform non-functional testing is discussed. However, there are specific category tools like Watir, which can perform the application testing in Ruby.

Choices for vulnerability, network and automation tools in the cloud are unlimited. A few tools that are most suitable for cloud security testing include Wireshark and Nessus. Cloud test, AppPerfect and LoadStorm are ideal choices for load and performance testing.

11.6 Cloud-Based Automation Frameworks for Testing

Test automation frameworks hold a significant place in cloud testing. Building an automation framework in the cloud would benefit the testers by simplifying the work. Automation frameworks automatically create and execute test cases. Test automation frameworks consist of a set of processes, tools and protocols. Most of the organizations today are moving to agile and DevOps where continuous testing is essential with faster outcomes. Agile and DevOps demand the automation framework to be a part of the cloud testing as this reduces the maintenance cost and the efficiency is better. Organizations that are growing and need to balance out the resources and cost would opt for automation frameworks.

Successful achievement of quality application with reasonable cost is defined as the test execution and accuracy is good but the return of investment is better. If an organization holds a cloud-based automation framework, then the advantages are limitless including real-time communication. Testers are equipped to gain access from anywhere and perform the tests. Automation under the conventional environment is slightly different from the cloud automation framework. Generally, the cloud automation framework comprises infrastructure, deployment and self-healing automation. As the name denotes, infrastructure automation is making the necessary resources available in the cloud so that the test can be replicated. Deployment automation denotes the process deployment so that manual effort is reduced. Self-healing is automatically coming out from error.

11.6.1 Selenium Automation Framework

Selenium is open source, compatible with most browsers and an easy cloud-based automation framework. This framework is not language specific and provides parallel execution of tests.

Most of the web applications are deployed in the cloud and tested. Selenium can be used with cloud services for testing web applications across multiple platforms. It can also be used as an automation framework, which is simple and Excel based. The user has the flexibility to choose the specific test case that needs to be executed. Excel support scripting enables users to create test cases more quickly.

11.7 Conclusion

As we are enjoying the privileges of digitization, performance is significant to every user. Organizations are more concerned about testing the application for non-functional components aided by advanced technologies for the cloud. Performance achievement of a product or application is vital in this extremely competitive world. For every concept, ten similar applications exist, and the user opts for an application that provides better performance. Stakeholders are striving very hard to achieve excellent performance for their application in production. This demands a huge investment for cloud-based non-functional testing to achieve quality, which requires a complete simulation of the real production environment in the cloud. The proposed reliable performance test model is crafted to address each aspect of the application if tested under production. However, this requires a great deal of planning that includes the consistent interaction of the stakeholders, marketing teams and other teams in the organization. Thus, practically such types of pre-planned production environments in the cloud are a concern, especially to start-up companies. The execution model would pass the quality check and can be termed as reliable; however, practically this remains unresolved in the cloud. Mature organizations might get better results with such types of performance models. Non-functional testing achieving 100% quality check in the cloud is purely dependent on the AUT and the tester's performance plan to address all the quality parameters.

References

1. V. Priyadharshini and A. Malathi, "Survey on software testing techniques in cloud computing," arXiv.org, vol. cs.SE, no. 8, pp. 2572–2575, 2014.
2. V. Katherine and K. Alagarsamy, "Conventional software testing vs. cloud testing," Int. J. Sci., vol. 3, no. 9, pp. 1–5, 2012.
3. https://clds.sdsc.edu/sites/clds.sdsc.edu/files/.
4. B. Rimal, E. Choi, and I. Lumb, "A taxonomy and survey of cloud computing systems," In: 2009 5th International Joint Conference on INC, IMS and IDC, IEEE, pp. 44–51, 2009.
5. P. Harikrishna and A. Amuthan, "A survey of testing as a service in cloud computing," In: 2016 International Conference on InComputer Communication and Informatics (ICCCI), pp. 1–5, 2016.

6. R. Malhotra and P. Jain, "Testing techniques and its challenges in a cloud computing environment," SIJ Trans. Comput. Sci. Eng. App., vol. 1, no. 3, July-August 2013.
7. OW2, Bench4Q, 2012. [Online]. Available: https://svnlegacy.ow2.org.
8. Trustie, Bench4Q, 2012.
9. H. Kim, et al., "IoT-TaaS: Towards a prospective IoT testing framework," IEEE Access, vol. 6, pp. 15480–15493, 2018.
10. H. Pei, B. Yin, and M. Xie, "Dynamic random testing strategy for test case optimization in cloud environment," In: IEEE International Symposium on Software Reliability Engineering Workshops (ISSREW), IEEE, pp. 148–149, 2018.
11. W. Wang, N. Tian, S. Huang, S. He, A. Srivastava, M. L. Soffa, and L. Pollock, "Testing cloud applications under cloud-uncertainty performance effects," In: IEEE 11th International Conference on Software Testing, Verification and Validation (ICST), IEEE, pp. 81–92, 2018.
12. SOASTA. PDCA12-70 datasheet. [Online]. Available: http://www.SOASTA.com/.
13. LoadStorm, Benefits of a load testing tool. [Online]. Available: https://loadstorm.com/load-testing-tool/.
14. AppPerfect, Performance testing. [Online]. Available: http://www.appperfect.com/services/performance-and-functional-testing/performance-testing.php.

Further Readings

J. Hurwitz, M. Kaufman, and R. Bloor, Cloud Computing for Dummies. New York: Wiley Publishing, Inc, 2010.
H. Li, X. Li, H. Wang, J. Zhang, and Z. Jiang, "Research on cloud performance testing model," In: IEEE 19th International Symposium on High Assurance Systems Engineering (HASE), IEEE, pp. 179–183, 2019.
C. Guo, S. Zhu, T. Wang, and H. Wang, "FET: Hybrid cloud-based mobile bank application testing," In: Proceedings of the IEEE International Conference on Software Quality, Reliability and Security Companion (QRS-C). IEEE, pp. 21–26, 2018.
M. Ficco, R. Pietrantuono, and S. Russo, "Hybrid simulation and test of vessel traffic systems on the cloud," IEEE Access, vol. 6, pp. 47273–47287, August 2018.

Chapter 12

Fault Tolerance Algorithms for Distributed Computing

Beaulah Soundarabai
CHRIST (Deemed to be University)

Pethuru Raj
Reliance Jio Platforms Ltd.

Contents

12.1 Introduction

12.1.1 Distributed Systems

A distributed system is a collection of independent computing devices that work together to create and present a single system image or a single coherent system view to its users. It has two important aspects: the first is the connection of independent devices into a network, and the second is collaboration of all the nodes to create the single system view, which is the heart of the distributed system. The beauty of distributed systems is that the nodes can be any device ranging from a simple sensor device to high-performing mainframe machines. The design objectives of distributed systems are to share the system's hardware and software resources with an easy access, which should hide the details of resource distribution to achieve transparency. The system should be able to accommodate new nodes by having scalability [1].

12.1.2 Dimensions of Distributed System Scalability

Scalability is one of the important goals of a distributed system, as there is always room to include new devices. Scalability can be measured in three dimensions:

- *Size scalability:* More resources can easily be added without affecting the system performance. In fact, due to the addition of resources, the system's performance is expected to go high, as there is better load sharing with an increased availability.
- *Location scalability:* Users and the resources can be present anywhere across the globe, but the delays due to communication will be hardly noticed.
- *Administrative scalability:* The system is scalable over multiple but independent administrative domains. This describes the policies that resolve conflicting permissions for the resource utilization and security restrictions.

12.1.3 High-Performance Distributed Systems

Cluster and grid computing models are the most important high-performance computing designs in distributed systems. In cluster computing, the underlying hardware has similar types of workstations, which are connected closely to solve a single large problem. The connection is established by high-speed local area networks (LANs).

In grid computing, there are many subsystems over the network with each subsystem administered by different governing agencies. There is heterogeneity with respect to software, hardware and deployment of the network. When this grid computing system outsources its infrastructure such as hardware, software and storage as a service for various application users, it is called cloud computing.

12.1.4 Load Balancing Services

Load balancing services are a very simple pattern incorporating the replication. These services have a number of scalable servers, and these servers are replicated to be identical to each other to support the traffic and to balance the load [2]. These load balancers primarily use round robin (RR) algorithms or a tracked session. Horizontally scalable replica servers are equipped to handle many users in parallel. As the services grow, they are replicated to support the high availability and for fault tolerance.

12.1.4.1 Load Balancers' Readiness

Creating replicas of stateless servers alone does not initiate the tasks of start the load balancers completely. There should be a readiness probe to be built and ready to be deployed that decides when the replica of the application restarted. This probe message is used to identify when the system is ready to start its service. Most applications require a time unit to be initialized to start servicing. This process may include establishing the database connectivity, downloading and serving metadata files over the network and loading the necessary plug-ins. During this initialization period, the replicas are getting ready but are not yet ready for servicing, so the readiness probe, before allocating the services to these servers, is inevitable.

12.1.4.2 Session Tracking Service

Many implementations of stateless load balancer models route the requests to all the replicas from all requesting users. This seems like it ensures the even distribution of load, but it might not increase the throughput. There can be a requirement for the requests from a particular user that needs to be serviced by the same server. For instance, the cache memory is full of that user's data and, if all his requests are sent to the same server, it will end up having cache hits more times than if it is transferred to other machines. Hence, there should be a session tracking service to send all of the requests of a single user that are mapped to the same instance of the replica, whenever possible. This service can be performed with the help of hashing the Internet Protocol (IP) addresses of both the source and the destination.

If the IP addresses are constant, the implementation is very simple. But with external IP addresses, due to network address translation (NAT), this IP-based session tracking does not work well. External IP addresses are tracked via cookies or with application-level tracking. When the services increase or decrease, the number of replicas will also scale up or down accordingly. In such a condition, consistent hashing functions are used to reduce the impact of such scaling issues [3]. This session tracking service will make the replicated services of stateless servers work to their fullest potential in achieving scalability, availability and reliability through redundancy.

12.2 Sharded Services

In the previous section, we saw the replicas that were completely homogeneous in nature and capable of processing each request. Sharded services are a little different from the replicated services, as each instance of the shared services are not capable of processing the whole request, only a part of it alone. The root of the load balancer distributes the subset of the request to the respective shard for action. These sharded services are used in stateful services alone, whereas the replicated services can be used in stateless services in general. When the request size is too huge and cannot be handled by a single server, shards do the service together. Figure 12.1 depicts the comparison of shared and sharded services.

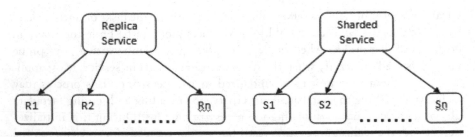

Figure 12.1   Overview of shared service and sharded service.

12.2.1 Caching in Sharded Services

The cache memory of shared services is built between the frontend and the requests of users. As caching is directly connected to the optimization of performance, in a shared cache there can be too many cache misses if the particular shard has failed and this situation continues until the restoration of the shard instance [2]. In shared service, a specific request is only mapped to the same shard; it would lead to transient fault and the system should recalculate the data whenever there is a cache miss due to failure. Even then, there would be a delay noticed in terms of performance, due to this calculation, which is more tolerable in the presence of a fault.

12.2.2 Cache Replicas of Shards

When the entire system is dependent on the cache memory of shards, it is not acceptable to lose the entire data from the cache shards due to its failure; at the same time, there would be another cache shard that would scale up to hold the load at that moment. Both of these actions have their own limitations, and these issues can be well handled when we replicate the shard service.

This avoids the single server issues of bottleneck situation and single source of failure. So, instead of having a single shard to handle a particular subtask, there will be replicas available to balance the load when all replicas are alive and to overwork to mask the failure of one or a number of replica failures. Designing such a shared shard would be complex as the cache of each particular shard copy should be synchronized to maintain the consistency of the data.

12.3 Distributed Ownership Election

In a centralized system, there is only one copy of any application that establishes the ownership, and this owner process can take care of critical section issues and can ensure the mutual exclusion of a particular shard. But the restriction is that scalability is limited due to the restriction of replication and reliability, which is an important setback whenever the ownership process fails and unavailability persists until the owner process is down. To attain reliability and scalability, distribution of the requests among the replicas of distributed services is essential. When the ownership is necessary among the replica handling, we come across the distributed ownership election. The most important but complicated task is to establish a distributed ownership among the distributed system services.

The easiest implementation of such ownership is to have a single replica of the service over the distributed system. As there is only one replica, the owner implicitly without the overhead of establishing an election. However, we do not get the full advantage of distributed systems and we still experience the problems faced in centralized systems.

If there are more instances of a service in the system, only one of the instances is the owner for any moment and that instance is known as the master or owner; hence, it is called ownership election or master election. This election is definitely an overhead, and it happens whenever a failure of the owner is experienced. There are distributed consensus algorithms that are automatically invoked when there is a need for an election.

12.3.1 Concurrent Data Manipulation

With the assistance of owner process and locking mechanisms in place, two instances to hold the lock for a concise period of time are possible. This may happen due to the faster and slower clocks in the machines, which these instances rely on. The processor might free up the replica before allowing the next hold, whereas the previous lock could have had a timeout and some other instance could own the lock. To avoid such an unwanted action, a robust system should be built. There should be a function in place to double check the availability of the lock before allocating the next instance to acquire the lock, such as the following function:

```
Boolean Function (lock x) islocked(){
Return x.locked AND x.locktime+0.5 * x.ttl >now()
}
```

where ttl is the time to live. Once it expires, the key is set back to the unlocked state. With this function, if executed before any lock assignment, the probability of two instances acquiring the lock simultaneously is protected.

12.4 Centralized, Decentralized and Distributed Systems

The importance of understanding the centralized, decentralized and distributed systems is significant for organizations as this is the gist of any advancement in the fields of core networking, web-oriented services, financial companies and many more. Each of these systems has their own potential and limitations based on their functioning. Few are secure, efficient or stable based on their underlying design. Organizations can choose the best system based on their application requirements.

One might require services of a system that is very small with a few computing devices in the interconnection with a few users or clients, or one can require a very strong and powerful system that spans between continents. The major challenges in both systems are the security, cost, scalability and fault tolerance. The best example of a distributed system is the World Wide Web (WWW), which is the largest network in the world. It brings heterogeneous systems from the vast geographical regions together.

In the centralized system, the various user terminals are connected to a centralized server or a network owner. This centralized server is the only hub for all the data and software resources. It is very easy to develop, and a quick installation is also possible. It is strong as it has a powerful gigantic processor and is consistent because it is the only instance of data resources. The main limitation of this system arises when this single server crashes. The availability and the reliability of any powerful system is its major disadvantage. Since all users are dependent on a single server, there would be delays creating the bottleneck situation to the server. Security is yet another issue as all the user data are available with the owner store.

In the decentralized systems, there is no single server responsible for the entire storage and processing. There are many owners or servers in the system trying to tolerate the faults. When a few servers are down, the other servers work together to mask the faulty servers by providing the availability to users.

Resources will continue to be available until the last server instance is alive, and the faulty servers can be repaired while the system is still functioning reliably. However, the security threat remains the same as it exists in the centralized system. Because there are multiple copies of the resources across the network, the maintenance of the replicated resources is a time-consuming and tedious activity. If the replication maintenance does not work well, the performance of the entire system is of no use due to inconsistency.

A distributed system is analogous to a decentralized system, but it does not have a centralized server and avoids the problem of decentralization. The software and hardware resources are shared between the users of the system, with a goal to reduce the cost of the individual resource and to improve performance. The uptime of the system is improved as the independent faults and failures do not bring the whole system down. It also has better transparency and security. Resource sharing is highly achieved in a distributed system with extreme scalability and powerful fault-tolerant algorithms. The major research issue of distributed systems is the betterment of the fault-tolerant and synchronization algorithms. The cost of maintenance is also very expensive in a distributed system, which is a big overhead, but it cannot achieve reliability without it.

12.5 Decentralized Algorithms

The characteristics of any distributed algorithms are as follows [4]:

- No machine has all of the information about the overall system state.
- Every machine is decision-based on the locally available information.
- One machine's failure does not bring down a task or the whole system.
- There is no global clock for the entire system.

These four characteristics describe the nature of any decentralized algorithm that runs on a distributed system. The non-availability of the global information and global clock does not have any impact on the algorithm, and it would still run consistently, which may delay a bit and lower the performance if there is a failure of some of the systems. To make any decision, these algorithms rely on the local information alone. The local processes are expected to be synchronized with each other by sharing their status and the course of action with each of the local groups. Synchronization across the system definitely requires a global clock across the machines.

Even when the clock times are synchronized to a common time, they will start to drift away due to a fast or slow clock. There should be a continuous monitoring of the time, and at every time interval the time needs to be corrected to jointly work to accomplish the tasks of the distributed system. The synchronization can be internal or external. The external synchronization requires an external clock for reference with which the processes synchronize their times. Some processes have their time synchronized among themselves and do not require a global clock reference, which is known as internal synchronization. The relative ordering of events is more than enough because maintaining the exact physical time for those processes requires only a logical clock synchronization. Real-time critical applications such as a flood alert system, an aircraft control system and so forth require physical clock synchronization and these processes are synchronized internally and externally [5].

12.6 Fault Tolerance

Fault is inevitable in any of the computer systems, and fault tolerance is one of the highly researched subjects in the technological world. Fault tolerance in a distributed system describes how a process or a machine responds to an unexpected fault of hardware or software. The two components of fault tolerance are detection of fault and recovery from the fault. Both components work hand in hand to achieve the objective of masking the fault. It is a very challenging task to keep the system alive and reliable when there is a fault. The common fault tolerance mechanisms are replication, resend, activity logs and checkpoints. Checkpoint is the most used simple fault-tolerant model of distributed systems. It saves the state of the system at every time interval regularly on a stable storage. If a crash is experienced, the system uses this state to restore the services from the very last checkpoint instead of redoing the entire task [6]. The message log is another model that handles failure, and it is cheaper than the checkpoint model. There are pessimistic, optimistic, optimal and causal approaches on the logging protocol. All four models of the protocol aim for recovery to the state, which is at on par with the other processes. A distributed system has influenced the users of the system to be dependent on it. This dependability is very closely related to and is directly proportionate to fault tolerance. If there is no user or a process depending on the system, the system fault is not going to bother anyone, but if there are lots of internal processes and many users depending on the system functioning, even a simple fault needs to be masked and addressed quickly. Dependability is a compound of the following features [7]:

- Availability
- Safety
- Reliability
- Maintenance and recoverability

Availability: It refers to the property of a system that is operating with high probability. The system is always available to its users with respect to both hardware and software resources and services, regardless of whether a fault exists or not. The mostly desirable system is one that works at any given point of time [8].

Safety: This is the assurance of no catastrophic effects for the resources and no unauthorized usage of resources permitted. When a system fails temporarily, there should be a high degree of safety to be maintained for the resources. For instance, even if there is a very small fault for a fraction of time in an aircraft navigation system or in a nuclear power plant, it would not only affect the system variants but the effect would be disastrous. Fault tolerance along with high safety is very important here [8]. When we witness such disastrous events, we understand that it is very hard to build such safety systems.

Maintenance and recoverability: Finding and recovery from the failure of the system is instant and automatic, even without the knowledge of the user. It discusses how a failed system can be repaired easily. High degree of availability is the result of a highly maintained system.

Reliability: Resources and services of the system are always trusted and even in the presence of failure, the system will continue to exist.

When there is a failure in a centralized system, it would be a single source failure, so it is a complete failure. The main advantage in the distributed system is that it experiences only partial failure when one or many of its servers fail. The probability of all the servers going down for the whole system is very low. The distributed system handles this partial failure in a way that it can recover from the failures automatically and by maintaining the consistency and performance.

12.6.1 Three Metrics of Fault Tolerance

The following are three metrics that are closely related to fault tolerance and are used to measure the time of failure and repair:

- *Mean time to failure:* Refers to the time of average until the fault of a component.

- **Mean time to repair:** Refers to the time of average needed for repairing the fault of a component.
- **Mean time in between failures:** It is the total time of mean time of failure and mean time to repair.

A distributed system fails if it is designed to offer a number of services to its user but cannot provide one or more services in completeness. Error is a state of the system that leads to failure. In computer network transmission, if the receiver does not receive all the packets that are sent or receives a few damaged packets, we say that the packet is with error. To resolve this error, error checksum or retransmission of the packets are required. A bug in the program may lead to the entire program crashing, leading to program failure. Dependable systems are expected to control the error or the faults. There should be individual attention given to remove, prevent, forecast and tolerate the faults. The most important one is the fault tolerance, as it expects the error of the fault and it exists continuously to its user services while trying to remove the fault quickly.

12.6.2 Classification of Faults

Faults are classified as transient, intermittent and permanent. Transient faults happen once or twice and disappear later. If the same operation is performed again, the fault is not seen. It may happen when plugging the hardware devices in, when there is interference over the transmitters of the microwave and so forth. Intermittent faults happen and then go away. Later, the same fault may be experienced again. When service engineers check such issues, the fault would be removed. A permanent fault is the one that exists continuously until the problem is addressed. Bugs in the software, disk head crashing and a burnt chip are examples of such faults. Failures are classified into many schemes in the distributed system, which are discussed in the following section:

- **Crash failure:** Before a crash failure happens, the system works perfectly; when a crash failure happens, the server or the component goes silent and suddenly halts.
- **Omission failure:** When a server does not respond to requests, it is called an omission failure. Omission failure has two subcategories, namely send omission and receive omission. When the send buffer overflows and the server does not receive the packets faster, a send omission occurs. In this case, the sender needs to resend the packet to the server with the help of timer and acknowledgment messages. When a server does not respond only to the incoming messages, it is a receive omission. Send omission describes the failure in sending out the messages.
- **Response failure:** When a server responds incorrectly, it is known as response failure. The server's deviation from the right flow of control is known as state transition failure.

- *Timing failure:* This failure happens when the sending or receiving does not happen within the physical time interval. When a server responds very late to a request, there is already a performance failure error, which occurs as the delayed response is denied response for critical applications.
- *Byzantine failure:* The most serious of all failures is the Byzantine failure. It is also known as the arbitrary failure. These failures do not fail silently; the components continue to exist even when the system is malfunctioning [9]. The server produces the results that are never supposed to be produced, and it cannot be understood as a wrong output. Silent failures deal with the Byzantine failures without any harm to the system variants.

An asynchronous system has no prior information about the speed of execution, rate of message delivery time and so forth. Here no process, say x, can come to a conclusion that a process, say y, has crashed, just because x did not observe any action from y. There can be a real crash, or the message alone is lost or the message is still on the way and might not reach the process in the near future. The synchronous system has a bounded message delivery time and execution speed. Here, unlike the asynchronous system, process x can conclude that process y has surely crashed due to its non-response within the stipulated time. There is no pure synchronous system existing in the world. This does not mean that all distributed systems are asynchronous; rather, they are partially synchronous. As in most cases, a distributed system behaves as a synchronous system; sometimes, there will not be a bounding time and timeouts to predict the actions, hence, it behaves asynchronously.

12.7 Byzantine Fault Tolerance

In distributed networks, Byzantine fault tolerance (BFT) enables the system to come to an agreement even when some of the available nodes in the network fail silently or they respond with erroneous information. A collective decision is the solution followed by this model to nullify the effects of faulty nodes. It is derived from the very famous Byzantine generals problem, where a few generals became traitors to destroy their own countries. BFT is the model for state machine replication in asynchronous systems like the internetwork by Lamport and Schneider [10]. The model maintains the liveness and safety properties of $\lfloor (n-1)/3 \rfloor$, where n represents the number of faulty replicas, to ensure linearizability. This means that, for the fault tolerance among n replicas, there can be at most $\lfloor (n-1)/3 \rfloor$ faulty terminals allowed. If there is a requirement of improved fault tolerance, then we need to increase the number of replicas. Linearizability guarantees the correctness of the process, when an object is dealt by many processes in parallel; in turn it ensures the safety property. It also ensures a trusted reply to all its clients. The service may be delayed if there is a denial of service attack, until the existence of the attack. Byzantine node failure can malfunction in any of the following ways:

- Failure to give resultant information.
- Gives resultant information that is misleading.
- Gives resultant information of incorrect value deliberately.
- Gives resultant information of different incorrect values to different nodes of the system.

12.7.1 Consensus Problem

The consensus problem [10] is a famous and familiar problem in distributed computing and serves as a base for many algorithms. The problem states that in an execution, all the processes that are not faulty should produce the same output. A simple solution is having all the processes output the value zero. Each process is to have a local input value and to output the same when every other process also has the same input value. In chain arguments, a chain or sequence of executions needs to be constructed in such a way that every pair of consecutive executions is indistinguishable to both or at least to one of the two processes. If, in each of these executions, all the processes have the same result as the other process in the pair, then the proof follows that the entire chain of all executions has the same result. The consensus problem has two properties that need to be satisfied by the output values:

- *Agreement property:* All the output values are the same.
- *Validity:* Every output value is one from the input values.

This consensus problem is applicable to both an asynchronous and synchronous system in which the process can be faulty.

12.7.2 Impossibility of a Consensus Problem with Byzantine Failure

In a synchronous message exchanging model, let us assume that the network is fully connected and every process can communicate with each other's processes directly. Let us also assume that the system is prone to Byzantine failures. We consider the consensus problem on this synchronous system with f Byzantine processes. These Byzantine processes behave incorrectly with wrong messages, or they might send the right message with a long delay, or the messages might not be sent at all. There are two theorems:

Theorem 1: It is impossible for the three processes to have a consensus if one among them is an arbitrary process.

Theorem 2: It is impossible for the $n \leftarrow 3f$ processes to have a consensus, where n is the total number of processes and f is the Byzantine faulty processes.

The proofs for the two theorems are given by Fischer et al.[11].

12.7.3 Practical BFT

The practical BFT (pBFT) works in four subtasks:

1. The client sends a service request to the leader or primary process.
2. The leader node sends this received request to all secondary backup processes by a broadcast message.
3. All the nodes, including the primary and secondary nodes, carry out the requested service task and reply back to the client.
4. The service request is considered successful when the client receives $f+1$ replies, where f is the maximum number of nodes that are faulty.

All the nodes of the system are divided into three groups: client, backup and master. Master and backup nodes are the replications. The pBFT algorithm has three phases, pre-prepare, prepare and commit. The system does the broadcast three times for each operation, which is a complete waste of network utilization. The number of nodes needs to be fixed here, so there is no room for scalability in this model. The result is valid only if the replies from at least $f+1$ nodes are the same. As we expect, faulty systems are also present in the system. The fault can be on the primary node itself. There are a number of variations proposed for this pBFT algorithm. In the verifiable BFT (vBFT) model, the result is decided based on the voting of the available system. There are only two phases in vBFT, prepare and commit. It reduces the number of broadcasts, which results in less network bandwidth utilization. Also, it can work with more faulty nodes compared with pBFT.

12.7.4 Proactive and Reactive Fault Tolerance Techniques

Reactive technique is applied to reduce the force of fault by creating multiple copies of the resources, and retry is another model used to keep doing the task again and again until it is successful. In the checkpoint model, the system saves the state of it at every time interval with a checkpoint name. When a failure is encountered, it simply goes back to the last checkpoint to resume instead of starting fresh from the beginning. This concept is commonly used in a distributed transaction system to enhance the system performance [12]. Reactive models use load balancing, pre-emptive migration and self-healing techniques during fault tolerance.

12.7.4.1 System Properties

There are two desired properties of the distributed system's consistency, namely liveliness and safety. Both properties are essential for the correctness requirements of the system. These are distinct properties and often get confused with each other.

- **Liveliness:** It guarantees that the system will continue to exist in spite of concurrent execution of various processes. It states that "surely there will be something good happening". In real life, we can give an example as, due to the strong legal system in place in our constituency, we can say that the murderer will be punished in due course, which is something good. Also, in distributed systems, the successful completion of a process, fault detection and fault recovery are part of the liveliness property. This liveliness property cannot be violated by the distributed system, whereas the safety property can be violated for a short span of time.
- **Safety:** The safety property states that "something that is a bad thing does not happen". When the system receives a fault or a termination, this property is violated; if violation occurs, it is always a finite processing. In real life, in spite of a perfect legal system, we cannot ensure that the innocent citizen will never be punished, but when it happens it is really bad and the punishment should not be prolonged.

In a distributed system, we do not expect the rollback of transactions or cascade abort in the distributed transaction, we do not desire the processes to become orphans without any parent process, we do not except two different processes inside a critical region section and so on. In general, time-bounded liveliness cannot be guaranteed, whereas time-bounded liveliness is guaranteed because surely something good will happen in a short span of time. With the help of a global snapshot algorithm [12], distributed systems transit from one global state to another.

12.8 SWIM Protocol

SWIM stands for Scalable Weakly-consistent Infection-style process group Membership protocol. This protocol maintains the membership details of the system among the processes. The locally created and maintained membership list of the local group is provided to each process. The membership list consists of the presently available non-faulty processes.

Thus, the main objective of this SWIM protocol is to provide each process with the list of non-faulty processes, called a "membership list". This list is very important for all the processes to communicate with each other for coordinated activities. The protocol has two important activities:

- *Identifying the available process:* This task involves the methodology of how to identify that a process is alive or failed. Finding the faulty processes is the main goal of this task.
- *Dissemination of the membership list:* The second task is as important as the first one;it sends the notification of the present membership list to other processes.

The protocol is expected to work with correctness and should be fast enough to detect the failure and circulate the list; it also should accommodate the newly joining nodes, making it scalable.

The efficiency of the SWIM protocol is determined by the following metrics:

- *Accuracy or correctness:* How many processes are marked as faulty when they are not;i.e., what is the rate of false positives?
- *Completeness:* This describes whether the algorithm could identify all the failure processes.
- *Network load:* This describes the amount of network utilization for one round of successful execution.
- *Failure detection speed:* This describes the average time interval between the time the process becomes faulty and the time at which it is found in the process group.

Any user or client prefers the SWIM protocol to be fully complete with percent accuracy, i.e., to be able to identify each error correctly with no false detections or no false positives. According to the impossibility result [11], full completeness and accuracy can never be guaranteed in an asynchronous system. The SWIM protocol tries to reduce the rate of false positives by giving away the accuracy for completeness. It has the following two components:

1. *SWIM failure detector:* The protocol's failure detector module has an integer S and a time T to detect the faulty processes. After every time period, T, a process, Ma, chooses any one process at random from the membership list, Mb. Within the time period if it does not receive the acknowledgment message from Mb, then Ma chooses another S process at random to ping Mb. All the processes from the S list will in turn ping Mb on behalf of Ma. If they receive acknowledgment from Mb, they notify Ma of the same. If process Mb has failed, no processes in the chosen S list will receive acknowledgment, thus Ma concludes that Mb is faulty and updates this information with the disseminator component. SWIM uses different processes to reach Mb, with which it can avoid network congestion, on the path between Ma and Mb.

   Suspicion method: Whenever process Mb is healthy but slows down due to a heavy load or network partition, it is falsely marked as faulty by the protocol. To avoid this, there is a subprotocol proposed called the suspicion subprotocol. The suspicion module, on receiving a message that *Mb* is not responding, does not mark *Mb* as faulty; instead, it marks it as a suspect and sends this information to the other nodes. When any process finds *Mb* responding to it, it will ping all processes with the alive message of *Mb*.

2. ***Disseminator:*** The SWIM disseminator component receives all the failure updates from the processes of the group, and it makes a multicast about the failure of this processes' *Mb*. The members of the group remove the process *Mb* from their local membership list. As the SWIM protocol is scalable, it accommodates newly joined processes. There can be a chance for a process to leave the group. Before leaving the group, those processes message this disseminator about the leaving information. The disseminator does the multicasting of processes that have left the group as well as processes that have newly joined. All the processes do the necessary update on their local membership whenever they receive a message from the disseminator. There are improved versions of disseminators proposed with infection style message passing as an epidemic or a gossip spread among a population, where the packet loss is proved minimal.

12.9 Gossip and Epidemic Protocols

In a huge distributed system, it is very difficult to know the state of the whole system due to the large number of scalable nodes. There is always a requirement for communicating with other nodes for different reasons. There are many algorithmic approaches and articulations to derive the state of the local group processes. There is no best solution to this problem due to network issues. In a distributed cloud service, there is no possibility of multicasting or even storing the graphical representation of a complex network [13]. Distributed systems use a gossip protocol. The name of this protocol is derived from spreading the messages through human gossip and epidemic spreading of a virus. Epidemic theory says that starting with a single infection, the time taken to infect the entire population takes a logarithm of the total population size. Based on this epidemic theory, gossip protocol performs the task in $\log(N)$ steps, where N is the total number of processes of the network. The key aspect of this protocol is the repeated probabilistic information exchange between two peers.

In probabilistic mode, the nodes choose the peers in a non-deterministic way from a pool of potential peers of the overall participating nodes. Here, there is a high probability of repetition, so the protocol might lead to a never-ending process. Gossip protocols work in a situation where there is a high degree of failure dynamism and there is a need for high scalability of the system. Information dissemination is the most natural application of gossip protocols. The information can be in the form of a simple message, or the updates that have to be enforced on the replicas of a database, livestreaming audio or video packets. Whatever the task, the underlying concept of the gossip protocol is that one or a few nodes initially have the piece of information, and they should cooperate to diffuse the data pieces to those that do not have them.

12.9.1 Gossip Protocol Methodology

A process in the group chooses another peer process at random to exchange the information. The data communication happens between the two peer processes. Each process goes through the previous two steps and processes the data it receives. The four steps are repeated at every time interval by all the processes in the network to disseminate the information. The process of the network group is classified into any one of the three following categories:

- **Susceptible (S):** The processes of this category do not know anything about the information.
- **Infective (I):** The processes of this category know the information and are busy spreading it.
- **Removed (R):** The processes in this category know the information, but they do not spread the information any more.

The infective process tries to spread the information at regular intervals to a peer process at random in the network. The susceptible process does not know about the message that is being spread. If the peer process, while receiving the information, is susceptible, then it will become infected and start to spread the received information to other nodes. A node goes to a removed category if there is no need to spread the information as all its neighbors have already received the information.

This protocol works the same way as spreading rumors among human beings. Person x first receives the rumor and tells it to person y. Person y, in turn, tells z, and parallelly person x is still spreading the rumor with yet another new person. This continues until every person's known friendship group receives the rumor. The strategy relies heavily on the selection of the best peer process with which to share the information. Mathematical models prove that the selection model converges in a few rounds and can spread the information to the entire network in $O(\log(N))$ steps, where N is the total number of processes.

Gossip protocols are not commonly used for message communication but are used for database replication, maintaining the group member list, failure detectors and for aggregations. Blockchain technology uses gossip protocols. This protocol is very simple, as it has a few lines of code and is completely symmetric; that is, all the processes execute this same identical code. Also, gossip protocols work in any network topology, if they are sufficiently connected, with enough bandwidth.

12.9.2 Limitation of Gossip Protocols

The overall idea of the gossip protocol is a small but periodic message exchange over the complete network, which limits the data communication capacity. New events of the important message exchanges slow down due to the aggregate network bandwidth utilization by the protocol. Often, this type of disseminating protocol becomes prey to vulnerable attacks and data corruption, unless the data that are sent are self-verifiable.

12.10 Fault Tolerance Models

Fault tolerance models [4] are commonly classified into hardware and software fault tolerance categories. Hardware fault tolerance provides secondary hardware devices like memory, disk drives and multiple power supplies. Failure due to hardware components and ensuring availability of backup hardware components is the focus of this model. The redundant components do not wait for the fault to occur to start the services, but they always work along with the main replica to increase the availability, throughput and load balancing.

Static and dynamic software procedures operate on software fault tolerance categories to mask the software faults and errors [14]. Along with these two major categories, there is also a third one. System fault tolerance works with checkpoints and error detection mechanisms in the stored applications. When a fault is found, this system fault tolerance invokes the correction method.

12.10.1 Assessment of Fault Tolerance

To assess the fault tolerance capability of each node of the system, an algorithm is proposed by Bhardwaj and Goundar [15]. Initially this fault tolerance factor is always fixed to the value 1, flexibility for adaptability to N, where $N > 1$. The algorithm measures the minimum and the maximum fault tolerance from the configuration of the node itself. Research has also focused on analyzing fault tolerance results on cloud environments to check the following metrics:

1. ***Throughput:*** This is the number of jobs executed and completed in a unit time, which is expected to be high.
2. ***Response time:*** This is the total amount of time taken to respond to a request of a service.
3. ***Scalability:*** When a new node connected, it should not affect the system's performance and capacity.
4. ***Availability:*** This is reliability and uptime of a system to its user applications.
5. ***Performance:*** This is the total amount of jobs accomplished successfully by a system.

12.11 File Replication and Maintenance

In a large-scale distributed system, the clients of the system demand high reliability with respect to the availability of critical resources. To achieve this availability, the resources are replicated a number of times and are placed in different servers to ensure the fault tolerance with respect to availability, even if some servers with the copy are down.

Advantages of data replication in a distributed system are as follows:

- **High availability:** The system keeps on giving the copy of the file, even if some servers are not functioning.
- **Read scalability:** Many read queries can be given access together instead of as a mutual exclusion model because it is not going to update the file, with which high throughput can be achieved.
- **Low latency:** Since there are many copies, the file can be kept closer to the user geographically to serve the resources, which minimizes the latency. Netflix streaming and content delivery networks are examples of such service.

The system overcomes network issues because it continues to function even in the presence of network failures.

With these advantages comes the biggest concern of consistency of replicated components of the resource, which has been extensively researched. Whenever the resource is updated, all of its replicas are also expected to be updated simultaneously to ensure its consistency. There are many updated policies proposed; two important policies among them are write invalidate and write update. It is impossible to enforce all the copies of a particular resource to be consistent, i.e., to have the same content at any point of time. It is not possible due to the network imperfections. Even with this issue, it is still possible to get the right content of a resource with the policies on the replication maintenance model.

Leaderless, single leader and multi-leader are popular data replication approaches. Leader data replication performs the copying in synchronous or asynchronous mode.

12.11.1 Synchronous and Asynchronous Replication

In synchronous mode, when a *write* request is given to a leader, it sends the *write* request to all its subordinates to perform and waits for each to acknowledge it. After receiving all the acknowledgments, it notifies the client with a *successful write* message. In asynchronous mode, the leader does not wait for all of the acknowledgments after sending the *write* request. There may be consistency issues in this mode as there is no follow-up of acknowledgments. Synchronous mode replication ensures data consistency all the time with the latest version of the data, and all the read requests are assured with consistent results; they do not need to go for a roll-back operation due to inconsistency.

The leader replication happens in three ways:

1. ***Statement-based replication:*** The leader keeps the log of every write operation in the form of an insert or update or delete query and forwards the log to its subordinates to perform the same operations. There can be inconsistency if the order of operations changes, which is possible in asynchronous systems.
2. ***Write ahead log:*** Each query is written into a log file called *append only log*, even before it gets executed on the leader's node. That is why this leader replication is called the write ahead log. This log file is used by the subordinates to replicate the data file. Oracle and PostgreSQL use this type of data replication. This log is tightly coupled with a storage engine and it contains the minute details of disk block and bytes information about the data writes [16].
3. ***Row-based replication:*** The writes are expressed in the level of row-wise records, hence the name, row-based replication. A delete contains data to identify the rows to be deleted, an update contains the new values as well as the data to identify the row to update the new value and an insert of the new data contains all the new values of each column. If a transaction contains multiple row writes or update or delete queries, then all the participating rows are added in the log. The Binlog of MySQL uses this row-based replication model.

The conventional approach for maintaining the consistency on replication maintains a master replica and enforces that if any change is made in any of the other replicas, the master replica needs to be informed instantly. Vardhan and Kushwaha [17] have proposed another approach to update the master replica. Instead of updating the master replica, the replica with the latest version becomes the master replica; henceforth, all the replicas are notified of this, and the new master replica becomes the owner of the resource.

12.12 Conclusion

Distributed systems are bound to fail frequently due to various internal and external reasons and causes. There are several ways prescribed by information technology (IT) experts and computer scientists to overcome this problem. Designing, developing and deploying fault-tolerant systems is the way forward. There are many techniques and tips expounded by IT pioneers and pundits to achieve fault tolerance.

However, implementing fault tolerance is not an easy task as distributed systems are increasingly composed out of disparate and distributed systems. There are more possibilities for any distributed system to fail. This chapter has discussed distributed systems and their performance metrics. It also discussed the types of fault tolerances, various metrics related to fault tolerance and the consensus problem. The capacity planning and management aspects of a system to ceaselessly function in the presence of simple and even complex faults such as Byzantine faults are also described with respect to SWIM and gossip protocols.

References

1. M.Van Steen and A. S. Tanenbaum, "A brief introduction to distributed systems," *Computing*, vol. 98, pp. 967–1009, 2016. https://doi.org/10.1007/s00607-016-0508-7.
2. B. Burns, Designing Distributed Systems: Patterns and Paradigms for Scalable, Reliable Services. O'Reilly Media, Newton, MA, 2018.
3. Cosmos Gaming Hub. Fault Tolerance in a Distributed System Forming a Blockchain, 2018. https://medium.com/cosmosgaminghub/fault-tolerance-1800d3093657.
4. A. S Tanenbaum, Distributed Operating Systems. Prentice-Hall, Englewood Cliffs, NJ, 1995.
5. A. Sampath and C.Tripti, Synchronization in Distributed Systems. In: Meghanathan N., Nagamalai D., Chaki N. (eds), Advances in Computing and Information Technology. Advances in Intelligent Systems and Computing, vol. 176. Springer, Berlin, 2012. https://doi.org/10.1007/978-3-642-31513-8_43.
6. J. Hursey, J. M. Squyres, T. I. Mattox, and A. Lumsdaine, "The design and implementation of checkpoint/restart process fault tolerance for open MPI," IEEE International Parallel and Distributed Processing Symposium, pp. 1–8, 2007. DOI:10.1109/IPDPS.2007.370605.
7. H. Kopetz and P. Veríssimo, Real Time and Dependability Concepts. In: Distributed Systems, Second Edition, 1993.
8. A. Ledmi, S. MounineHemam, and H. Bendjenna, "Fault Tolerance in Distributed Systems: A Survey," 3rd International Conference on Pattern Analysis and Intelligent Systems (PAIS), 2018.
9. A.S. Tanenbaum and M. Van Steen, Distributed Systems: Principles and Paradigms. Prentice-Hall, Englewood Cliffs, NJ, 2007.
10. H. Attiya and F. Ellen, Impossibility Results for Distributed Computing, Synthesis Lectures on Distributed Computing Theory. Morgan & Claypool Publishers, 2014.
11. M. J. Fischer, N. A. Lynch, and M. Merritt, "Easy impossibility proofs for distributed consensus problems," *Distributed Computing*, vol. 1, no. 1, pp. 26–39, 1986.
12. A. D. Kshemkalyani, "Fast and message-efficient global snapshot algorithms for large-scale distributed systems," *IEEE Transactions on Parallel and Distributed Systems*, vol. 21, no. 9, pp. 1281–1289, Sept. 2010. DOI:10.1109/TPDS.2010.24.
13. H. Wang and K. Guo, "Byzantine Fault Tolerant Algorithm based on Vote," 2019 International Conference on Cyber-Enabled Distributed Computing and Knowledge Discovery (CyberC), 2019.
14. C. Storm, Fault Tolerance in Distributed Computing, Specification and Analytical Evaluation of Heterogeneous Dynamic Quorum-Based Data Replication Schemes. Vieweg Teubner Verlag, 2012, pp. 13–79. https://doi.org/10.1007/978-3-8348-2381-6_2.

15. A. Bhardwaj and S. Goundar, "Efficient fault tolerance on cloud environments – A survey," *International Journal of Computers and Applications*, 2018.
16. S. Verma, Data Replication in Distributed Systems, 2019.https://medium.com/@sandeep4.verma/data-replication-in-distributed-systems-part-1-13f52410faa3.
17. M. Vardhan and D. S. Kushwaha, "File replication and consistency maintenance mechanism in a trusted distributed environment," *CSIT*, vol. 1, pp. 29–49, 2013. https://doi.org/10.107/s40012-012-0002-0.

Index

Printed in the United States
by Baker & Taylor Publisher Services

Printed in the United States
by Baker & Taylor Publisher Services